# Comparative and International Education

## 2nd edition

*An Introduction to Theory, Method, and Practice*

**David Phillips and Michele Schweisfurth**

BLOOMSBURY ACADEMIC

LONDON · NEW YORK · OXFORD · NEW DELHI · SYDNEY

BLOOMSBURY ACADEMIC
Bloomsbury Publishing Plc
50 Bedford Square, London, WC1B 3DP, UK
1385 Broadway, New York, NY 10018, USA
29 Earlsfort Terrace, DUblin 2, Ireland

BLOOMSBURY, BLOOMSBURY ACADEMIC and the Diana logo are
trademarks of Bloomsbury Publishing Plc

First edition published 2007
Second edition published 2014
Reprinted 2004, 2015, 2016 (twice), 2017, 2018, 2019, 2020 (twice), 2021

A catalogue record for this book is available from the British Library.

ISBN: HB: 978-1-4411-2242-1
PB: 978-1-4411-7648-6
ePDF: 978-1-4411-0721-3
ePub: 978-1-4411-7454-3

Phillips, David, 1944 December 15-
Comparative and international education : an introduction to theory, method, and
practice / David Phillips and Michele Schweisfurth. – Second edition.
pages cm
Summary: "Comprehensive introduction to comparative and international education"–
Provided by publisher.
Includes bibliographical references and index.
ISBN 978-1-4411-2242-1 (hardback) – ISBN 978-1-4411-7648-6 (paperback) –
ISBN 978-1-4411-0721-3 (epdf) 1. Comparative education. 2. International education.
3. Education–Cross-cultural studies. I. Schweisfurth, Michele, 1962- II. Title.
LB43.P54 2014
370.9–dc23
2013036188

Typeset by Fakenham Prepress Solutions, Fakenham, Norfolk NR21 8NN
Printed and bound in Great Britain

To find out more about our authors and books visit
www.bloomsbury.com and sign up for our newsletters.

# Comparative and International Education

# Contents

*To Val, and to Martin*

# Acknowledgements

In writing this book we have benefited from the advice of many people, especially our colleagues in Oxford and Birmingham and our graduate students.

We are particularly grateful to Professor Lynn Davies and Dr Muham mad Nazir in Birmingham for reading drafts, and to Professor Clive Harber and Dr Chris Williams for helpful discussion on content. In Oxford, the late Jason Nicholls and Kimberly Ochs read various versions of the text and made many useful suggestions, as did members of the MSc course in Comparative and International Education during 2005–6.

Our special thanks go to Professor Erwin H. Epstein of Loyola University, Chicago, for a most helpful critique of the draft text.

We are obliged to Professor Mark Bray for permission to include Figure 4 in Chapter I and to Elsevier for allowing us to reproduce the diagram from *Society, Schools, and Progress in Eastern Europe* by Nigel Grant (1969).

For very helpful comments on early drafts on the second edition, we would particulary like to thank Jeremy Rappleye and Robert Arnove.

# Foreword to the First Edition

On visits to universities and at professional conferences, I occasionally ask graduate students in comparative education to describe our field. I am troubled to find that their definitions, besides not resembling my own, are usually vague, hesitant, often meandering, and even arbitrary, and their knowledge of the field falls sadly short. When I probe further, I find their views are gleaned from a poorly defined array of courses, uninformed by the commonly accepted meanings conveyed by authoritative texts. Most surprisingly – but a major reason for this condition – is that not infrequently these students have never had an introductory course, or, if they have had such a course, it usually lacked content about comparative education as a field of study, as if comparative education had no origin and no corporate or cumulative body of literature.

Now, that is quite different from what one finds in other fields. For example, in sociology – a field in which I have had considerable experience, having taught sociology courses for many years and published in some of its journals – graduate students know what they are about. Ask sociology majors what sociology is, and, without giving identical definitions, they will tell you that it is the systematic study of human society and social activity. Unlike comparative education students and practitioners, sociologists have a secure and stable understanding of their field's nature. They know who its founders are and where it was founded, as well as the origins of its major journals, the leading contemporary figures, and major epistemological approaches. They have a sense of their field's boundaries. This greater common understanding is forged by a well-established initiation process in the form of graduate training.

By contrast, comparativists have a much looser affinity of interests and lack norms for inducting people into the field. I have the impression that almost the only common identifier is affiliation with one of the professional national or regional comparative education societies. Those are splendid organizations, but affiliation and participation alone, in my view, are hardly enough to sustain coherence. Indeed, securing a firm future for comparative education must begin with a movement to agree on reasonably common norms about our field's nature and boundaries, and with having a sense of a palpable history. Such a movement should require establishing commonly accepted standards for preparing comparativists.

But, then, exactly where is such a movement to begin? I contend it should be with authoritative texts authored by scholars who truly know the field, who have long labored in its vineyards, and who have demonstrated through years of outstanding scholarship that they merit the trust to convey knowledge most needed by future generations of comparativists. I believe the present volume, authored by individuals who are among the most accomplished scholars of comparative education, is such a text.

Most volumes that serve as course textbooks in comparative education are compilations of readings. However valuable the individual readings may be, these compilations are unable to furnish the coherence and historical and epistemological breadth needed by novices to grasp the scale and richness of comparative education. The present text provides students of comparative education with the grounding they need to perform confidently as comparativists.

But this textbook does more than simply offer a proper introduction to the field. In several areas, this volume goes further than any other material available to explain the inner workings of comparative and international education. In particular, the description and elaboration of international education activity found here is unequaled anywhere in the literature. The treatment of the relationship between national development and education is multifaceted and refreshing. And, the authors' own pre-eminent expertise on the essential topics of educational transfer and citizenship education show through in a way that few if any other works can match. Those who gain a command of this book's contents need never apologize for not knowing the historical roots, the epistemological platforms, and the essential boundaries of our field.

Erwin H. Epstein
Chicago, Illinois, USA

# Foreword to the Second Edition

Now it is more difficult to remain local than to become international. For students and teachers alike, globalization continues to open innumerable possibilities to experience the world – overseas travel, international degrees, cosmopolitan cyber communities, transnational institutions, global rankings, employment abroad, and – often seated right beside us – 'foreign' classmates and colleagues. Never before in human history have so many individuals, over such a short span of time, ventured beyond the comfortable familiarities of the local.

As such, a new sort of person is rapidly taking shape: one continually crossing borders; conversant in contrast, yet conscious of continuity; comfortable with constant comparison. We are unmistakably witnessing the emergence of international man (and woman, of course!), rooted in a new comparative way of life: the ceaseless negotiation between local past and global future. Individual journeys out of the domestic both reflect and are reflected in our collective global future. It is little wonder then that education systems are being rapidly transformed worldwide, even while such changes only propel us faster and further towards such formations.

Against this wider backdrop, it is easy to understand why more people are finding their way into the field of comparative and international education and why this exceptionally well-done introductory text is so important. Almost daily we come across work on education that appears international, but – upon closer inspection – has simply reframed the local in global terms: in impassioned pleas, for example, to 'surpass Shanghai' that only deepen pre-existing policy preferences or in appeals to implement 'global best practice' that reflect local predilections of a privileged few. This 'local' work is produced by those who have felt the unmistakable pull of our global age, but who lack the knowledge of theory, training in methods, and experience with practice to move beyond the confines (and consequences) of a limited worldview. Such a move requires experience, then reflection, but most of all a systematic intellectual introduction: initiation into a more rigorous contemplation of the comparative way of life. This text accomplishes just that.

One important way it does so is by situating itself right on the threshold of past and future. Refreshingly rich in history, the text reminds us that while the scale of the comparative way of life is unprecedented, it is not new. Long before terms such as globalization and transnational became part of our everyday vocabulary, there were those intrepid few who were already deeply immersed in the comparative way of life, names like Sadler, Kandel, Hans, Bereday, and Eckstein among many others. The academic field of comparative education emerged, in large part, out of their roots and routes: experiences of continually crossing borders, constant comparison, and their resulting meditations on theory and method. They were the first instances of international man. What is most surprising is just how many of the insights they left behind for us are still relevant today. In arranging to meet these forebears (Chapter 2), this volume shows that we are not alone in our questions; introduces us to guides from the past who point the way forward towards the enduring lessons of comparative life.

Yet, unlike many introductory texts that seek to ensure continuity with the past, this volume also pushes us to go beyond history. It recognizes that the world has changed dramatically, perhaps fundamentally. Unlike earlier generations, international man can today no longer rely on the comfortable confines of nation-state borders, nor rest on the certainties of national citizenship. The authors thus light the way forward for us: offering analytical models that do not rely on national boundaries (Chapter 1), spotlighting the study of educational transfer processes across nations (Chapter 3), contemplating the meaning of global citizenship (Chapter 4), and repeatedly challenging us to consider the developed and developing world simultaneously. All along the way, they help us wade through the veritable alphabet soup of new terminology – IEA, TIMSS, OECD, EFA, UNESCO, BAICE, WCCES, CIES, IMF, UNDP, MDG, PTR, SAQMEC, for example – so that we have enough energy left to forge our own path forward. They also lead us deep into the intricacies of large-scale studies of pupil attainment such as PISA that now so dominate discussions of the future of education globally (Chapter 8). The importance of the issues they raise will soon become apparent when, upon hearing that you study educational internationally, people inevitably ask: So who has the world's best education system?

Indeed, the text is dotted with points whose significance is not immediately clear. Why does it matter whether the field is a discipline or has 'disciplinary-like' features? What difference does it make if one chooses to emphasize universal or context-specific findings? Why is theory important when we are faced with a range of pressing, concrete educational problems?

Aren't these merely academic debates that have little to do with education in the real world? I vividly remember having similar doubts when the comparative way of life led me into the field several years ago. Yet, rather quickly, lived experience revealed the importance of having confronted such enduring questions early on. In debates with those from the 'disciplines', discussions with classmates, designing original studies, collecting data in the field – 'doing' comparative and international education quickly reveals that such questions are not merely 'academic' but confront all of us – sometimes explicitly, but often implicitly – at nearly every interaction with the outside world. In this way, such questions actually point to issues that lie at the very heart of the comparative way of life: how do we relate to those in the (still local) traditional disciplines as we give shape to a new global perspective? Does familiarity with one other country make one international or does it require something more expansive? Towards what ends should the comparative way of life serve?

All and all, this introductory text accomplishes more than its modest authors suggest it does. It therefore deserves to be read closely, but also as something more. Without a doubt, it succeeds in providing a comprehensive overview of the field, engaging with the key issues, past and present, and moving readers to a point where they can begin to formulate their own perspectives and projects – theoretically, methodologically, and practically. Having read it, readers can consider themselves 'initiated' into the field and are no longer in danger of falling unwittingly into the 'local' trap: simply reframing limited worldviews in global terms (and thereby limiting themselves). Engaged narrowly as a standard introduction to an academic field of study, readers will achieve all of this by working through this highly accessible, beautifully organized, and well-written text.

However, this work allows us to accomplish even more if we engage it in another way: by viewing it as a doorway leading deeper into the comparative way of life. One's personal journey and the academic (re)search need not remain separate. In fact, they never really are. What was true of the field's forebears remains true for us today: the best work always emerges from the confluence-cum-contemplation of the two together. Read in this way, this introductory text is also an invitation to engage in a more systematic contemplation of one's individually emerging comparative way of life. As its authors repeatedly pull back historically, then shoot us forward into the present, we are constantly encouraged to reflect on the legacy of our own local past and the probable direction of our global future. If we take the time to engage with the text in such a personal, self-reflective way, not only do we avoid becoming the provincial 'surpassing Shanghai' and 'best practices' sort of person, but we find ourselves already engaged in actively shaping international man, personally and collectively. How we live our individual comparative life of today undoubtedly shapes the face of our collective global future of tomorrow.

Jeremy Rappleye
Kyoto, Japan

# Preface to the Second Edition

When this book was first published in 2007 our intention was that it might prove useful as a basic introductory text for anyone interested in the study of education in comparative and international contexts. It has been gratifying to observe that it has been used in courses in many countries as a core textbook and that it has led to lively debate about the issues it addresses.

Comparative and international education are contested fields, and there is much disagreement about key aspects of what is entailed by this important area of educational inquiry. It has not been our intention to provide easy answers; rather we have been concerned to present cases and to stimulate discussion. This is what an introductory text should set out to do.

In revising the original text we have attempted to reflect changes in the field by bringing the discussion up to date and adding references to literature published in the interim period. In doing so, we have generally built on rather than replaced the original text, in order to sustain the sense of history that we believe is important in understanding the field. Given the growing importance of policy borrowing, both as an area of inquiry and a *de facto* reality, we have created a new chapter focusing on this topic.

In the process of revision, we have been struck by how much of what we wrote for the 2007 edition is truer than ever: there are more international schools; university internationalization has accelerated and become even more central to higher education agendas; the drive to the Millennium Development Goals has had successes but also last-minute panics and concern for the post-2015 world; and cross-national tests of achievement have become more and more central to government discourse and policy borrowing. And yet, despite all this, somehow, people remain anxious about the status of the field: an anxiety that seems ill founded under the circumstances.

David Phillips and Michele Schweisfurth

# Introduction

Research in 'comparative education' must provide new means of perfecting the science of education.

*Marc-Antoine Jullien*[1]

The study of education in increasingly globalized contexts inevitably draws us towards comparison. Instant access to complex and up-to-date information on most aspects of foreign systems of education makes the initial task of comparison more straightforward than it has ever been. The work in education of international organizations – principally the United Nations Educational, Scientific and Cultural Organization (UNESCO), the Organisation for Economic Cooperation and Development (OECD), the International Association for the Evaluation of Educational Achievement (IEA), and the World Bank – is widely disseminated and available both in print and online. Communication over distance has never been easier through a plethora of electronic means. International contact not only as a result of ease of travel but also as a consequence of political and economic agreement in various configurations further facilitates knowledge of 'elsewhere', of 'the other' – and increasingly 'elsewhere' is less foreign, 'the other' is more familiar, and individuals have identities which embrace them all. And comparison, an instinctive intellectual response to anything requiring analysis, is an activity that aids our opinion-forming and decision-making on an everyday basis. We are all comparativists now.

Systematic comparison is common in many fields of academic inquiry. The quotation from Marc-Antoine Jullien above, dating from 1816–17, follows on from a statement to the effect that researchers in *comparative anatomy* had advanced the study of anatomy.[2] And academic domains like comparative religion, or comparative literature, or comparative politics and government, are firmly established as legitimate and illuminating areas of serious research.[3] Comparative education, as we shall see, has a long history, with its origins in the early years of the nineteenth century as states in Europe and elsewhere were taking first steps towards the creation of national systems of education. Reference to what was happening elsewhere in terms of educational provision was a natural feature of the early policy debates. But it took some considerable time before those engaged in making comparisons began to systematize their activities, to think in terms of a theory of comparative education and its accompanying methods. While Marc-Antoine Jullien can be counted as one of the very earliest exponents of systematic international inquiry in education, and while significant investigators like Victor Cousin in France, Horace Mann in Massachusetts and Matthew Arnold in England did much to further educational comparison, it was not until the end of the nineteenth century, with the scholarly work of Michael Sadler[4] in England and William Torrey Harris[5] in the USA, that the methodical collection of comparable data began in earnest and that the problems involved in making comparisons in education started to be consciously addressed.

By the 1960s, it was common for universities and colleges to offer courses in comparative education as part of the initial training of teachers, and a body of work was established by prominent comparativists like Isaac Kandel, Nicholas Hans, Friedrich Schneider, Joseph Lauwerys, Edmund King, Brian Holmes, George Bereday, Harold Noah and Max Eckstein, and others in Europe, the USA, and elsewhere. The work of these significant figures in the modern history of comparative education can be read with profit today. They come from a wide variety of backgrounds and cover between them the various traditions that together have made comparative education such a rich field. While there is no agreed common ground methodologically in their writings – notably King and Holmes can be seen to differ fundamentally in their approaches – there is, nevertheless, as we shall argue, a sense in which each investigator has added incrementally to the body of previous investigators, so that a complex interweaving of methods becomes possible and arguably very desirable in a field of such multi- and inter-disciplinary variety. It is sadly a feature of some of the present theoretical writing in comparative education to ignore or to be dismissive of many of the earlier generation of comparativists who did so much to establish the subject as a field of academic inquiry – what Epstein and Carroll have described in a telling phrase as 'abusing ancestors'.[6] We shall attempt to show that while new and legitimate perspectives have developed, there is still much value in recalling the work of earlier scholars and a great deal to be learnt from it.

Despite or precisely because of its richness and variety, comparative education does not in our view constitute a discipline in the normal sense: we shall describe it in the discussion in Chapter 1 as a 'quasi-discipline', since it has many discipline-like features without demonstrating a unifying approach to its subject matter. This is not an inherent weakness of the subject: on the contrary, by bringing together so many disparate traditions in research and by drawing upon a wealth of theoretical approaches, comparative education stretches beyond the parameters of a single discipline and is the richer for it.

'We are all comparativists now'. As comparative inquiry has grown, academics in all of the contributing disciplines of education, and others in cognate fields, have become increasingly involved in comparison. The participation of sociologists, historians, economists, psychologists and other specialists, particularly when they are part of teams of investigators, has been welcome not only for the expertise they bring but also for their different perspectives on the many issues with which comparativists are concerned. Likewise, education generalists and practitioners have an important role to play in grounding comparisons in classroom realities.

So far, we have talked exclusively of comparative rather than international education. Definitions of what constitutes comparative education are problematic enough; the term 'international education' poses further problems. 'International education' in one limited sense can be about international schools and their work; in another sense it can be about the work of international organizations (UNESCO, the World Bank, etc.); in yet another it is often taken to include everything that has to do with education in developing countries. As one leading contributor to the field has put it:

> The term has such wide usage that almost any statement relating to international education offers ample opportunity for ambiguity in interpretation. It is often associated with the related concepts of global, intercultural, multinational and multicultural education, and shares a great deal of conceptual territory with dimensions of comparative education.[7]

This sharing of 'conceptual territory' justifies the term 'comparative and international education', but its widespread use creates more difficulties of interpretation, as we shall see in Chapter 1. What we have been concerned to do in this introductory study, however, is to argue for the essential interaction of the two component parts of the term. As we put it, comparative studies are usually (though not exclusively) international in nature, and international studies are implicitly comparative. The fields are interdependent, and a disservice is done to both if they are regarded as discrete and so separated for the purposes, for example, of the syllabuses of university courses. A comparativist should be aware of the full range of issues with which international education is concerned; a specialist in international education should be informed about the complexities of educational comparison and understand the role of comparative inquiry in generating and testing the theories widely in use.

We hope that the second edition of this book will continue to be of relevance to a number of audiences. Firstly, one of our purposes is to provide researchers specializing in other branches of educational studies with some basic information about comparative and international education and how it might be of relevance within their own specialist areas of educational research. Secondly, students of education may use it to see their own studies in a more global framework, and international students may find it helps them to contextualize their own perspectives in relation to what and how they are learning in the context in which they are studying. Thirdly, for learners and researchers new to the field of comparative and international education it can serve as an introductory overview from which to begin a more in-depth exploration. Readers may wish to focus on particular chapters of the book, depending on their areas of interest. Not everyone, for example, will be concerned with the development of comparative and international education as a field, or with the theories associated with the relationship between education and development. However, we have attempted to maintain a balanced overview of these 'twin fields', and would encourage newcomers to do the same, not least because of the inter-relationships between these twins to which we have alluded above. In an increasingly interconnected world, educationally and otherwise, no one is left untouched by these phenomena or the theories, methods, assumptions and practices that have underpinned them.

Inevitably, from time to time we focus on particular ways of looking at comparison which reflect positivist or other stances. We do so not because we advocate one approach over another but because it is important to cover the principal approaches that have characterized development in comparative inquiry. Where we believe that 'learning lessons' on the basis of the informed understanding of other systems is a fundamental purpose of comparative education, we see dangers in taking a law-making ('nomothetic') approach to the outcomes of comparative research and so would warn against any reading of the text that gives undue credence to such an approach.

As this is an introductory text, it goes without saying that it is exhaustive in neither breadth nor depth. We have also chosen to focus primarily, although not exclusively, on formal schooling, although informal and non-formal forms of education could be equally rich subjects for discussion. The critiques of formal schooling are many and its alternatives are diverse, but we would direct readers particularly interested in such specialist fields as adult education or home schooling to texts which focus on these areas, to complement the analysis here.

Given the subject matter and potential audience, despite being based in the UK we have tried to adopt as international a perspective as possible. We have, on the whole, not used extensive examples from specific countries, as these tend to date quickly. We hope that the book is relevant to an international readership, and we invite comparison of our perspectives with those elsewhere.

In what follows, we shall provide first a general survey of what it means to make comparisons in education, when we shall be concerned with definitions, with discussion of the nature of comparative investigation in education, with the uses and purposes of comparative inquiry, and with what comparativists do. We shall then, by way of an excursus, provide an outline account of how comparative education has developed as a field of academic activity.

Chapter 3 focuses on policy transfer, which some have argued is at the heart of comparative education, and which has shaped education internationally in increasingly profound ways. Examples of 'borrowers' and 'lenders' are explored and we present useful models for the analysis of the process of transfer.

In Chapter 4 we turn to international education, where we explore the many facets of this ambiguous term, from international schools through education for development. We consider questions of who might be considered an international educational researcher, and what skills are demanded.

Chapter 5 then continues our coverage of international education with a focus on issues of development. The relationship between schooling and development in its many forms is theorized and problematized.

Chapter 6 addresses questions of method in comparative education, concentrating on such fundamental issues as description, causation, explanation and prediction, together with problems of ethnocentricity, language, and research design and analysis; and we propose a new structure for comparative inquiry.

Chapter 7 develops the discussion of method, focusing on education and development and the research perspectives employed within it.

In Chapter 8 we examine the outcomes of comparative research, considering large-scale investigations of pupil attainment (such as PISA and TIMSS) and surveys monitoring progress towards education for all.

In Chapter 9 we provide illustrative examples of how international comparative studies have informed our understanding of key issues in education, namely education and political transition, education in post-conflict societies and small states, pedagogy, and citizenship education.

We conclude by taking a future-oriented perspective on the questions and challenges that comparative and international educationists face in this evolving field of inquiry.

# Notes

1. '[…] les recherches sur l'*éducation comparée* doivent fournir des moyens nouveaux pour perfectionner la science de l'éducation'. *Esquisse d'un Ouvrage sur l'Education Comparée*, pp. 173–4.
2. 'Les recherches sur l'*anatomie comparée* ont fait avancer la science de l'anatomie', ibid., p. 173.
3. We might also mention comparative philosophy, comparative linguistics, and comparative law.
4. Michael Sadler (1861–1943) was one of the most prominent educationists of his day. His important work in comparative education dates from his time as Director (1895–1903) of the Office of Special Inquiries and Reports of what became the Board of Education. See Phillips, 'Michael Sadler and Comparative Education'.
5. William Torrey Harris (1835–1909) was a philosopher and educator who was superintendent of schools in St Louis, Missouri and later US Commissioner of Education (1889–1906). His writings were prolific and included influential annual reports from St Louis and his editing of Appleton's 'International Education Series', which included studies of a vast range of educational topics with strong comparative and international coverage.
6. Epstein and Carroll, 'Abusing Ancestors: Historical functionalism and the postmodern deviation in comparative education'.
7. Thompson, 'International Education: Towards a shared understanding', p. 5.

# 1

# Making Comparisons

Comparative education covers a vast field which does not correspond to any strict normative definition.

*Debeauvais*[1]

Comparisons are, it is said, odious, particularly to the objects compared; nevertheless, the basis of all knowledge is comparison.

*Hughes*[2]

## The nature of comparative investigation in education

Even a cursory survey of writings in comparative and international education will reveal a preoccupation with defining the field. In contrast to many more established areas in educational inquiry, there seems to be a fundamental insecurity in terms of positioning the work that comparativists are engaged in, to the extent that they feel obliged to offer justifications for what they do and the methods they use. In this book, we aim to outline and develop some of these justifications while emphasizing the strengths and growing importance of the field, however difficult it may be to define its boundaries.

We are concerned in this study with what in the first instance appear to be two separate aspects of educational study and inquiry. Comparative and international education, by virtue of being associated in one phrase linked by 'and' are taken to be implicitly separate, and it is this perceived separateness that provides us with the starting point for an examination of what this important area of education covers. As we shall see, a comparative study is usually (though not exclusively) international in nature, and an international study is often comparative (though not necessarily or explicitly so.) In common usage in the UK and elsewhere, however, 'comparative' studies are frequently (and in our view absurdly) associated with the western indus-trialized world, while 'international' education tends (for us wrongly) to imply the study of education in all its forms in the developing world. These problems in usage have emerged largely as a result of the titles and focus of books and journals and from the nature of university courses.

Erwin Epstein has characterized 'comparative education' as referring to:

> a field of study that applies historical, philosophical, and social science theories and methods to international problems in education. Its equivalents in other fields of academic study are those dedicated to the transsocietal study of other social institutions, such as comparative government, comparative economics, and comparative religion. Comparative education is primarily an academic and interdisciplinary pursuit.[3]

Here the emphasis is on interdisciplinarity and the parallel is established with other long-standing and more recently introduced comparative fields (which do not seem, incidentally, to need as much defence in terms of what they are essentially about). In his description of 'international education' Epstein argues that it:

> fosters an international orientation in knowledge and attitudes and, among other initiatives, brings together students, teachers, and scholars from different nations to learn about and from each other. International education also includes the analysis and description of such activities. Many practi-tioners of international education are experts on international exchange and interaction. Their activities are partly based on a knowledge of comparative education.[4]

In Epstein's view – despite international education apparently being dependent on comparative expertise – comparative and international education are essentially complementary, allowing academics and practi-tioners in both fields to collaborate closely. And it is this interaction between the two fields that will be the focus of much of our present study.

Epstein's definition brings out an aspect of education that constitutes a field of its own, namely the investigation of education in international schools and in the context of efforts to educate for international under-standing. Here the role of the International Baccalaureate (IB), for example, is a focus of inquiry. George Walker, one-time director general of the IB, has suggested the questions that characterized the twentieth-century research challenge for international education in this kind of context:

- Can we describe the key concepts of international education that set it apart from other categories of education?
- Is 'international-mindedness' one such concept and, if so, what does it mean in practice?
- In what cultural environment does international education seem to grow the strongest roots?
- Which administrative structures give it the best support in schools?
- What pedagogic style is the most effective in achieving its goals?[5]

But for the most part 'international' education embraces areas of inquiry way beyond a focus on international schools and their activities, important as they are.

The British comparativist and historian of France W. D. Halls produced a useful explanatory schema which describes how he saw the relationship between the various activities that can be subsumed under both 'comparative' and 'international' education. He regards international education as a sub-set of a wide range of activity within comparative education, which in turn constitutes 'both a method and an object of study'. It is method inasmuch as comparativists have devised approaches to the analysis of educational phenomena in different countries and contexts; and it is an object of study insofar as it involves examining other countries and their education systems in much the same way as we might study French history (as Halls did) or the geography of Sweden.[6] Halls's schema is reproduced in Figure 1.

Halls sees the categories he lists as overlapping rather than being mutually exclusive, and he admits that there is 'clearly no agreement among comparative educationists as to the use of terms'. But the schema is still useful in helping us to understand the inter-relationships between the wide range of activities that together make up comparative and international education.

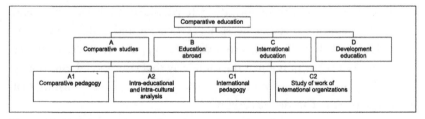

**Figure 1** Halls's typology of comparative education
(Source: Halls, *Comparative Education*, p. 23)

In this typology 'comparative pedagogy' is defined as 'the study of teaching and the classroom process in different countries'. (Though this would seem an obvious task for comparative research, it remains a clearly under-represented area.) 'Intra-educational and intra-cultural analysis' is seen as an investigation of education through various levels, with due attention to context (historical, social, cultural, etc.). 'Education abroad' is taken by Halls to mean 'the study of an educational system or systems other than one's own'.

'International pedagogy' is defined in terms of a wide range of possible investigation; it is the study of:

- teaching multinational, multicultural and multiracial groups
- education for international understanding
- peace education
- international population and ecology
- intra-cultural differences and their resolution, textbook development, the harmonization of curricula and international teaching norms.

Study of the work of international educational institutions covers policy issues such as the international recognition and acceptability of qualifications, educational exchange, and cultural agreements. (Now, it would include international surveys of educational attainment.)

Halls defines 'development education' as 'the production of plans to assist policymakers, particularly in 'new nations', the development of appropriate educational methods and techniques, and the training of personnel to implement programmes'. The typology does not, however, reflect the essential connectedness of 'comparative' and 'international' education as the starting point for a 'mapping' of the field.

We shall consider 'international education' in greater detail in Chapter 4. First, however, we must look more closely at what we mean by 'comparative education' as a field of inquiry. Does comparative education fulfil the essential requirement for a *discipline* to be 'a branch of learning or scholarly instruction' with its own discrete rules and methods? Or should comparative education rather be seen, as Epstein and Halls indicate, as a contributing field within the cross-disciplinary activity that constitutes 'education' as a subject, in much the same way that educational philosophy or sociology or psychology or history provide necessary support within that multifaceted area of academic activity?

António Nóvoa puts the arguments against comparative education as a coherent discipline very forcefully when he writes:

It is quite easy to line up the arguments against a field which has never succeeded in defining either a proper objective or even a method, which is mid-way between scientific research and political intervention, which is shot through by working practices which depend rather on a certain academic folklore than a systematic production of knowledge, which despite some notable exceptions is peopled by researchers of little prestige in the academic world; we could even go so far as to denounce the illusion of being able to build a discipline on a method, comparison, which is inherent in every scientific approach.

That is a fierce verdict. But Nóvoa continues in the same paragraph to put the arguments in favour of comparative education as a multi-disciplinary activity:

It is also very easy to praise a field which looks for explanations beyond national limits, which calls on multi-disciplinary approaches, which does not hesitate to come to terms with the inevitable links between educational research and educational action; the plea in favour could go so far as to assert that comparative education is the quintessence of the educational sciences, since it is situated at […] 'a higher epistemological level'.[7]

'A higher epistemological level' would situate comparative education in terms of the methods and validation of knowledge above investigative approaches which are more tied to the rules of any one of the contributing sub-disciplines of education.

A thorough analysis of comparative education as a field has been undertaken by Maria Manzon. She asks in particular: 'How can a field of study survive, develop, and perpetuate itself if its scholarly community are unclear, much less unanimous, about their field's identity, aims and contents?' And: 'Why is comparative education institutionalised as a distinct field when its intellectual distinctiveness seems to be blurred?'[8] And the first section of a magisterial two-volume study edited by Robert Cowen and Andreas Kazamias[9] contains ten articles which describe in detail the 'creation and re-creation' of the field.

In contrast to those who are concerned about the wide-ranging nature of the field, Rolland Paulston, who made a considerable contribution to the 'mapping' of comparative education, spoke of the liberating nature of involvement with a field that is not constrained by the dicta of any particular discipline:

Comparative education by definition is generic: it's a synthetic field. That's why I got into it in the first place. It offered me the most freedom … to create,

> to work with my ideas and with other people's ideas. [...] In almost any disciplinary field you get hammered into a disciplinary way of seeing [...] and that's it. [...] Most people, once they are hammered into a disciplinary mould, a way of seeing – be it Marxist or positivist or humanist, whatever, find it very difficult to change to [...] different – let alone tolerate other – views to the point where they can be recognised as legitimate competing views.[10]

In this interpretation, the strength of the subject lies in its *not* being a discipline in the accepted sense.

We once heard a student remark – not unsupportively – that the problem with the comparative and international course he was following was that it was about all aspects of education in every country of the world throughout all time. The field is potentially as immense as that. Comparativists cover a huge range of topics which demand expertise in many areas of academic inquiry. What brings them together in an identifiably coherent way is the common attempt at comparison, and comparison is a method used by various disciplines rather than an activity which can conceivably be described as a discipline in itself.

Patricia Broadfoot has argued that 'the comparative study of education is not a discipline: it is a context',[11] and it is perhaps her identification of the centrality of context that provides the clearest imperative for those in comparative education to develop understanding through a number of contributing disciplines (history, sociology, psychology, etc.) in their endeavours in comparative inquiry. Comparativists, operating as they do within a multidimensional subject, are essentially generalists, and among the many competences expected of them is a knowledge of and sympathy for the methods of such other kinds of inquiry. To them might be added the 'culturalist' approach advocated by Halls.[12] It is axiomatic to expect that comparativists will take into account the historical, cultural, social, economic, etc., contexts in which educational phenomena are observed, and that they must be sensitive to and knowledgeable about what these contributing areas of expertise can offer. We can only properly understand an educational phenomenon in terms of the contextual factors that have created and shaped it. Indeed, it is essential in comparative studies to insist on the centrality of context for degrees of explanatory power.

George Bereday, a polyglot international scholar with formal qualifications in history, sociology and education, argued strongly that comparativists should also have a sound knowledge of the language of any country used in their comparative investigations and that they should immerse themselves

in the culture. What is more, they should also have a common 'parent discipline': Bereday suggests 'political geography' or political science insofar as
it covers comparative government and international relations.[13] We agree
that the individual comparativist does indeed need a strong base in a
parent discipline but we argue that it is one of the strengths of comparative
scholarship and research that those engaged in developing the field have
roots in *diverse* disciplinary backgrounds. That, for example, Edmund King
was a classicist, Brian Holmes a physicist, George Bereday a historian by
origin, reinforced their common effort in the field. Our readers will wish
to know that one of us is a linguist and cultural historian by origin, and
the other uses perspectives of critical sociology and interactionism in her
work. While both of us are based at universities in the United Kingdom,
one has close knowledge and experience of education in Germany, while
the other, although from Canada originally, has taught and undertaken
research in a range of developing and transitional countries. Different disciplinary backgrounds and different degrees and types of experience provide
different perspectives and introduce different methodological approaches.
Indeed, the involvement in comparative educational investigation of those
who would not describe themselves as comparativists is to be welcomed
for the additional insights their participation brings, especially when teams
of researchers are engaged in collaborative inquiry. This is potentially the
greatest inherent strength of large-scale studies of the kind undertaken by
IEA or the OECD.

If we conclude that comparative education is not a discipline in the strict
sense of the word, it nevertheless has sufficient discipline-like qualities to
be described as a 'quasi-discipline' and as such plays an important role
in every field of inquiry in the many subjects that make up the study
of education, from investigations that are firmly rooted in disciplines
(psychology, sociology, social psychology, philosophy, history …) to studies
of a cross-disciplinary nature in such areas as assessment, special needs,
early childhood learning, home-school relations, accountability, etc.

The common aim to develop ways of making comparison is what links
the heterogeneous body of scholars and researchers engaged in comparative
education. And comparison, of course, is a fundamental aspect of intellectual inquiry. We use comparison in order to make judgements and reach
decisions (whether subjective or objective) as to whether something is, for
example, bigger or smaller, prettier or uglier, pleasant or unpleasant; and
to make moral, ethical, logical and other kinds of philosophical judgements about whether one set of conditions or one course of action is better,

preferable, more desirable, etc., than another. In this regard comparison is indispensable to our thought processes.[14] It should therefore be quite natural that we should use comparison as a basis for decision-making in a field like education where we must frequently make all kinds of judgements as to what course of action to take in particular circumstances and at particular times. Bryan Magee reminds us of Plato's view 'that good judgment consists equally in seeing the differences between things that are similar and the similarities between things that are different'.[15] We might, indeed, expect that all concerned with education should be involved in comparisons of one kind or another as they reach decisions about such matters as what to teach and how to teach, or how to manage, reform or evaluate an education system, or how to assess and examine performance.

What is more, the 'comparative method' is a cornerstone of classical sociological investigation. Durkheim describes it as follows:

> We have only one way of demonstrating that one phenomenon is the cause of another. This is to compare the cases where they are both simultaneously present or absent, so as to discover whether the variations they display in these different combinations of circumstances provide evidence that one depends upon the other. When the phenomena can be artificially produced at will by the observer, the method is that of experimentation proper. When, on the other hand, the production of facts is something beyond our power to command, and we can only bring them together as they have been spontaneously produced, the method used is one of indirect experimentation, or the comparative method.[16]

We have in comparative education the advantage of being able to examine situations which cannot be set up experimentally at home. 'Indirect experimentation' in Durkheim's sense is an expression which might profitably be used more frequently to describe what comparativists do as they explore the advantages and disadvantages of models observed in one context which could provide lessons for policy in another. An example of such 'indirect experimentation' would be the attention given to the 'reading recovery' methods developed in New Zealand and enthusiastically investigated and adopted by education authorities in the USA, Australia, the UK, and elsewhere.[17]

But many problems arise when we attempt to conceptualize how comparisons might be made and the purposes to which they might be put. In what follows we shall consider the purposes of comparative inquiry, analyse what comparatists do, and ponder the uses and abuses of comparative evidence. In Chapter 2 we shall discuss how the field has developed since its earliest days.

# The uses and purposes of comparative inquiry

Beyond the basic and essential level of data collection and analysis, we can identify a range of other purposes of comparative inquiry in education. There would probably be broad agreement that 'learning from the experience of others' would rank very highly. This might indeed be the single most important purpose we can identify to justify – in essentially practical terms – what comparativists do. The 'learning' involved might result in an effort to *improve* provision 'at home', but equally it might help us to *understand* more fully what it is that has helped to form the system of education of which we are a part. This is of course what Michael Sadler emphasized in a much-quoted speech delivered in Guildford in 1900 that has become one of the key texts in comparative education:

> The practical value of studying [...] the working of foreign systems of education is that it will result in our being better fitted to study and to understand our own.[18]

This is a deceptively obvious statement concealing the basic truth (rehearsed above) that it is through the act of comparing that we define our position on most issues that require the exercising of judgement. Sadler's point was developed by Joseph Lauwerys:

> Comparative education is not normative: it does not prescribe rules for the good conduct of schools and teaching. [...] It tries instead to understand what is done and why.[19]

As Bereday put it, 'to understand others and to understand ourselves is to have in hand the two ingredients of comparison'.[20]

Halls points out that 'many, if not most, comparative studies in education, like those in similar fields such as comparative law or criminology, are undertaken for *meliorist* purposes'.[21] And, indeed, notions of 'reforming', 'improving', 'doing better' are usually prominent in the many attempts that have been made at defending comparative endeavour.

Another commentator reports 'general agreement' on the following purposes of comparative education:

> (a) to promote knowledge; (b) to assist reform and development; (c) to improve knowledge about one's own educational system; and (d) to promote international goodwill.[22]

This is reminiscent of a checklist of aims which Brian Holmes felt in the 1970s was 'widely accepted':[23]

> comparative education should lead to a greater understanding of the processes of education; (2) it should promote interest in and information about particular national systems of education and be able to explain why they are as they are; (3) it should facilitate the practical reform and planned development of school systems; (4) it should promote desirable international attitudes among those who study it.

Farrell mentions firstly intrinsic interest, and secondly '[providing] ideas and approaches which may have relevance and usefulness in one's own country'.[24] Schneider cites better understanding of the countries compared, including the 'home' country, and recognition of their strengths and weaknesses; the extraction of paradigms, models, and methods for the solution of practical problems and the implementation of educational reform; and the breaking-down of prejudice and the establishment of international thinking in education.[25]

One succinct definition of the subject brings out the basic purposes of description and evaluation made possible through such contrast: 'The study of two or more national systems of education, as existing now and as historical developments, in order that differing approaches to similar problems may be described and evaluated'.[26] It is this attraction of difference that is so compelling in comparative studies and that has informed the work of comparativists from the early beginnings of their various endeavours.

Halls identifies three main aims of comparative education:

1  To provide an educational morphology, i.e. a global description and classification of the various forms of education (as undertaken by UNESCO and the OECD, etc.).
2  To determine the relationships and interactions between the different aspects or factors in education, and between education and society.
3  To distinguish the fundamental conditions of educational change and persistence and relate these to more ultimate philosophical laws.[27]

He believes that the establishment of truth in such studies cannot be reached by *logical* processes (despite the methodological tools of the social scientist) but by an *analogical* process, i.e. through 'a process of arguing from similarity in known respects to similarity in other respects'.[28]

In the light of the above, we might attempt a composite list of defences of comparative studies along the following lines:

The comparative study of education:

- shows what is possible by examining alternatives to provision 'at home'
- offers yardsticks by which to judge the performance of education systems
- describes what might be the consequences of certain courses of action, by looking at experience in various countries (i.e. in attempting to predict outcomes it can serve both to support and to warn against potential policy decisions)
- provides a body of descriptive and explanatory data which allows us to see various practices and procedures in a very wide context that helps to throw light upon them
- contributes to the development of an increasingly sophisticated theoretical framework in which to describe and analyse educational phenomena
- serves to provide authoritative objective data which can be used to put the less objective data of others (politicians and administrators, principally) who use comparisons for a variety of political and other reasons, to the test
- has an important supportive and instructional role to play in the development of any plans for educational reform, when there must be concern to examine experience elsewhere
- helps to foster cooperation and mutual understanding among nations by discussing cultural differences and similarities and offering explanations for them
- is of intrinsic intellectual interest as a scholarly activity, in much the same way as the comparative study of religion, or literature, or government, is.[29]

There is in these various attempts to define the purposes of the comparative investigation of education a particular focus on processes of learning and understanding and the benefits in terms of improvement that those processes might bring. The most obvious consequence of learning from and understanding what is happening 'elsewhere' in education is that we might be persuaded of the advantages to be gained from *copying* or *emulating* successful practice as it is manifest in other countries – what has become generally known as 'borrowing'.

If one of the principal aims of comparative inquiry in education is to identify good practice elsewhere, it follows that such good practice might be seen as potentially adoptable in (and adaptable to) the 'home' context. We might 'learn from' the foreign example and attempt reform that could benefit from its perceived advantages. Analysis of the transfer of ideas from one setting to another is a highly complex matter to which comparativists have devoted considerable attention. We shall examine policy transfer in detail in Chapter 3. But first we must consider ways in which comparative inquiry can be misused.

Harold Noah cites instances of misreporting of foreign practice – 'exaggerated and distorted reports' – and reminds us of the essential conditions for the taking-up of ideas gleaned from elsewhere:

> The authentic use of comparative study resides not in wholesale appropriation and propagation of foreign practices but in careful analysis of the conditions under which certain foreign practices deliver desirable results, followed by consideration of ways to adapt those practices to conditions found at home.[30]

This is a salutary pointer to the dangers inherent in a simplistic faith in 'borrowing'. The foreign example needs first to be understood within its proper context; only then can its adoption 'at home' be considered.

Noah mentions also misreporting (exaggeration, distortion) of information which, when unchecked, can result in a misplaced enthusiasm for foreign educational ideas and practices which might originally have been properly investigated and reported upon. The educational experiments (new teaching styles, reformed curricula, changed forms of assessment, etc.) which can follow such misreporting and misplaced enthusiasm might be very damaging.

One example of misreporting would be the way in which Prais and Wagner's important paper of 1985 on schooling standards in England and Germany has been used. Their interesting conclusion that 'attainments in mathematics by those in the lower half of the ability range in England appear to lag by the equivalent of about two years' schooling behind the corresponding section of pupils in Germany'[31] has been frequently misreported as a finding that *all* British pupils lag behind their German counterparts by two years of schooling. In 1990, a full-page insertion in *The Times Educational Supplement* showed three children sitting at desks, the middle boy being a head taller than the boy and girl on each side of him. The caption read 'If a British third-former [i.e. a pupil aged 13–14 years] went to Germany, he'd be in a different class'. And the accompanying text asserted (more generally still) that 'international tests show that, in mathematics, British teenagers lag behind German teenagers by the equivalent of two academic years'.[32]

The misinterpretation of results is another instance of abuse of comparative education cited by Noah. With more and more complex data available through studies such as those produced at regular intervals by IEA and the OECD's Programme for International Student Assessment (PISA) surveys, it is not uncommon for journalists and others to focus on an apparently significant 'result' and to use it in ways not supported by the evidence, which often takes expert knowledge to understand in its complexity.

Noah also mentions the dangers of ethnocentricity, of seeing things only through the observer's own perspective. To be aware of an inclination towards an ethnocentric view of the world is one of the earliest lessons that investigators and commentators must learn. But, again, it is too often the case that 'problems' are seen through a perspective informed by a perception of education from within a very particular set of circumstances. Noah argues that there is 'a spurious color of definiteness' to assumptions of generalizability to other contexts from the experiences of western industrialized nations.

# What comparativists do

An important set of problems relates to what comparativists do. We might reasonably assume that they are for the most part concerned to compare; but in reality much work done within comparative education is not overtly comparative in Neville Postlethwaite's sense of 'examining two or more educational entities by putting them side by side and looking for similarities or differences between or among them'.[33] Single country studies constitute a substantial element of 'comparative' inquiry, as an examination of papers in any particular issue of journals like *Comparative Education* or *Compare* or the *Comparative Education Review* will reveal.

Such studies, undertaken by scholars outside of the country they are investigating, are defended, however, in terms of their being implicitly comparative, since the authors are observing phenomena 'elsewhere' through 'foreign' eyes. And collection of the detailed information – interpreted for an audience outside of the country being investigated – that results from single country studies, is seen as an essential part of the contribution that comparative education can make to our understanding of educational issues generally. Thus Noah argues that in comparative education 'a fundamental task [...] is to collect, classify and array data about the educational efforts of the nations of the world',[34] and Lauwerys saw the starting point as 'the collection and classification of information, both descriptive and quantitative, about schools and teaching'.[35] Such data collection and single country analysis has always been an important aspect of the work of comparativists, and it has been given added weight through the complex investigations and reporting now engaged in on a regular basis by such international bodies as UNESCO and the OECD.[36] The single country study, often undertaken by scholars with profound knowledge of the language, history and culture of the societies they are investigating, is indispensable in providing the essential data and interpretations on which secure comparisons can be based.

In citing the 'single country study', however, we should not create the impression that comparative inquiry involves only 'countries' in the sense of comparisons of individual nation-states. Intra-country comparative studies are a legitimate and fruitful area of inquiry; the nation-state provides the framework of common ground, while the sub-units of the state in question provide the basis for a study of similarities and contrasts. The UK would be a good example of a complex nation-state which lends itself to potentially informative comparisons between the various parts which together make up the nation. Within England, Scotland, Wales, and Northern Ireland further sub-regional units might be identified for comparison. In England, for example, we might compare the differing roles and challenges of local education authorities as between urban conglomerations and rural counties, or the education of members of ethnic minority groups in the industrial north and the rural south, or education and employment in the prosperous southern and the less wealthy northern regions.

As well as intra-country studies, comparativists are concerned with cross-regional investigation of educational issues. Processes of educational transition in the former eastern bloc might be compared with those in evidence in African states; language issues with cross-border implications can be investigated and compared in various parts of Europe and in all other continents; political and other kinds of grouping (as in the European Union) provide a rich source for inter-regional comparison.

In a widely quoted article in the *Harvard Educational Review*, Bray and Thomas proposed a 'framework for comparative education analyses' in the form of a cube which attempted to classify the various types of study undertaken by comparativists. Bray describes it as follows:

> Along one side were aspects of education and of society, and along another side were non-locational demographic groups. The front of the cube then presented seven geographical/locational levels. At the top were provinces, districts, schools, classrooms and individuals. We observed that comparisons could be made at each of these levels, and that the insights gained from such comparisons would differ at each level. We noted that in some respects patterns at each level were influenced by patterns at other levels. We made a

case for multilevel analysis of educational phenomena; and where resources did not permit such multilevel analysis, we suggested that researchers should at least be aware of the level at which they were operating and of the limitations imposed by focusing only on that level.[37]

The Bray and Thomas framework (Figure 2)[38] is useful in establishing clearly the multiple approaches possible in comparative studies which challenge tendencies to focus on the nation-state as the unit of analysis. An essential point in Bray and Thomas's article is that research often neglects the relationship between the 'lower' and 'higher' levels as depicted in the cube. Comparativists do indeed sometimes focus too much on the macro level of analysis and pay less attention to the micro level. While it is not always inappropriate to focus on the nation-state, other units of analysis are often more revealing and of greater value in our understanding of what is happening 'on the ground' in education.

But whatever the basis for comparison – between nations, within particular countries, across regions – there will be a number of questions that the comparativist will have to deal with at the outset of any inquiry. We shall consider problems of methods and methodology in detail in Chapter 6. Here we should note that in devising any scheme for the comparison of

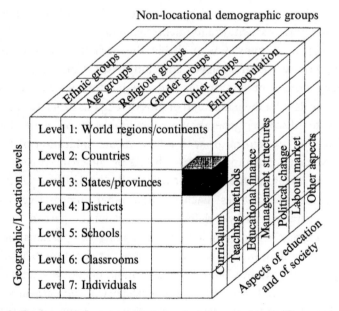

**Figure 2** Framework for comparative education analyses (Bray and Thomas)

educational phenomena attention should be paid to various equivalences on the basis of which comparisons can be sensibly undertaken. These equivalences typically relate to concepts, contexts, and functions. It is an important part of the comparativist's task to be certain that there is a proper basis for comparison, so that there is no 'so what?' factor in any response. The challenge here is to identify variables which will allow Noah's conditions for a comparative study:

> A comparative study is essentially an attempt as far as possible to replace the names of systems (countries) by the names of concepts (variables).[39]

Many of those working in comparative education will see themselves as belonging to various methodological traditions. Halls identifies several approaches: historico-philosophical; 'national character'; 'culturalist'; 'eclectic and pragmatic'; 'problem-solving'; quantitative; economic; and social science.[40] As we shall see, some of these determining methodological positions have been particularly associated with individuals whose work has made an impact on the way thinking has developed in the subject. There will be a wide variety of methods used, with their advocates and detractors. And this has led at times to a certain insecurity which is not so obvious in other comparative subject areas more closely associated with an established 'parent discipline'. There is a danger, indeed, that interdisciplinarity which is not controlled or determined by a parent discipline of some kind will languish in a sort of scientific and intellectual limbo.

Comparative anatomy was probably the earliest such subject area involving serious scientific analysis and comparison. Comparative religion has a long history of description and classification which has thrown considerable light on the nature and origins of religious belief. Comparative law aims 'to [discover] generalizations applicable to law generally, […] with a view to law reform, or with a view to the unification of law and the achievement of a universal law shared by all civilized humanity'.[41] Comparative literature attempts to identify similarities in literary endeavour across nations and cultures. Each of these other comparative fields of inquiry is characterized by a determined effort on the part of its practitioners to engage in the complex task of making comparisons, of using comparative methods in their research as opposed to limiting themselves to the single country study. Comparative education, of course – unlike some of these comparative fields – belongs to a category of comparison with the potential of identifying implications for policy in an important area of the social life of every nation.

Henk van Daele sees no agreement as to a definition of comparative education: '*Une définition précise, universellement acceptée, manque toujours*' ('A precise, universally accepted definition is still lacking').[42] But in the light of the analysis so far, we propose the following working definition of what we might understand by 'comparative education':

> The study of any aspects of educational phenomena in two or more different national or regional settings in which attempts are made to draw conclusions from a systematic comparison of the phenomena in question.

And we can conclude this introductory survey with Max Eckstein, who encapsulates in a couple of sentences the main purpose and justification of the study of comparative education:

> Varied and eclectic in subject matter, methods, concepts, and theories [comparative education] continues to perform two important functions. It is a source of both practical and theoretical knowledge for educational administrators, planners, and politicians, providing them with an array of case studies and alternatives, indications of possible outcomes (both intended and unintended) of specific programs or policies, and a context for understanding school practices and problems. At the same time, as a component in the education of teachers and others involved in professional education, comparative education serves to combat provincialism and ethnocentricity, to motivate study of the history and development of school systems, and to increase awareness of the interplay between schools and their social and cultural environments.[43]

In Chapter 2 we move to a consideration of the historical development of comparative education as a field of academic inquiry.

# Notes

1.   Debeauvais, 'Documentation in comparative education', p. 859.
2.   Hughes, *Schools at Home and Abroad*, p. 52.
3.   Epstein, 'Comparative and international education', p. 918.
4.   Ibid.
5.   Walker, 'Postscript', p. 275.
6.   Halls, *Comparative Education*, p. 23.
7.   Nóvoa, *Histoire et Comparaison*, p. 53. Present authors' translation from the French.
8.   Manzon, *Comparative Education: the Construction of a Field*, p. 2.

9.  Cowen & Kazamias (eds): *International Handbook of Comparative Education*.
10. Recorded interview in Steiner-Khamsi, *Comparatively Speaking*.
11. Broadfoot, 'The comparative contribution', p. 133.
12. Halls, 'Culture and education: The culturalist approach to comparative studies'.
13. Bereday, *Comparative Method in Education*.
14. See in this regard Schneider, *Triebkräfte der Pädagogik der Völker*, p. 9.
15. Magee, *Confessions of a Philosopher*, p. 168.
16. Durkheim, *The Rules of Sociological Method*, p. 147.
17. Ofsted: *Reading Recovery in New Zealand*.
18. Sadler, in Higginson, *Selections from Michael Sadler*, p. 50.
19. Lauwerys, in Blishen, *Blond's Encyclopaedia of Education*, p. 152.
20. Bereday, *Comparative Method*, p. 6.
21. Halls, *Comparative Education*, p. 23.
22. Jackson, 'Comparative education', p. 18.
23. Holmes, 'Comparative education', p. 357.
24. Farrell, *The Blackwell Handbook of Education*, p. 52.
25. Schneider, 'Vergleichende Erziehungswissenschaft', p. 771.
26. Collins et al., *Key Words in Education*, p. 44.
27. Halls, *Comparative Education*, p. 22.
28. Definition from *The Concise Oxford Dictionary*.
29. Phillips, 'Learning from elsewhere in education', p. 298.
30. Noah, *Use and Abuse*, p. 12.
31. Prais and Karin, 'Schooling standards in England and Germany', p. 68.
32. *TES*, 7 December 1990, p. 7.
33. Postlethwaite, 'Preface', p. xvii.
34. Noah, 'Comparative education: Methods', p. 869.
35. Lauwerys, 'Comparative education', p. 153.
36. Series like the OECD's *Education at a Glance*, for example, or UNESCO's *World Education Report*. The EURYDICE network also provides such data.
37. Bray, *Comparative Education: Traditions, applications, and the role of HKU*, p. 6.
38. Bray and Murray Thomas: 'Levels of comparison in educational studies'.
39. Noah, 'Defining comparative education: Conceptions', p. 114.
40. Halls, *Comparative Education*, pp. 31–2.
41. Walker, *Oxford Companion to Law*, p. 261.
42. Van Daele, *L'Éducation Comparée*, p. 15.
43. Eckstein, 'Concepts and theories', p. 9.

# 2

# How Comparative Education has Developed

Comparative education is as old as the custom of visiting countries other than one's own.

*Fraser and Brickman*[1]

## A brief history

'Comparative education' as a term has a long history, though the use of comparison in texts that make some reference to education (broadly understood) can be traced back many centuries before the term began to be employed. Some authors regard the *Histories* of Herodotus as the earliest text in which education is implicitly considered beyond the boundaries of the writer's own state (though Herodotus goes into very little detail: he records, briefly, that in Persia 'the period of a boy's education is between the ages of five and twenty, and they are taught three things only: to ride, to use the bow, and to speak the truth'[2]); others take Xenophon's *Cyropaedia*, with its comparisons of training for citizenship in Greece and Persia, as the earliest source in which education is specifically mentioned in a comparative context, though much of what is said about Persia has been seen as utopian fiction.[3]

We might argue that the dissemination – since the early modern period – of significant educational texts outside of the countries in which they were written contributed to the widespread comparison of educational ideas and therefore had an intrinsically comparative role. Rousseau's *Émile* (1762) would be a case in point, as might Locke's earlier work, *Some Thoughts Concerning Education* (1693). But it is in the early years of the nineteenth century that we can see the beginnings of a deliberate and systematic attempt to compare educational provision 'elsewhere' with that 'at home'. Increased travel opportunities and international communication – which had been interrupted in Europe by the Napoleonic wars – brought educational issues to the attention of commentators of all kinds who were interested in travelling to other countries and reporting in detail on what they observed.

Noah and Eckstein postulate five stages in the development of comparative education which, they argue, are not 'discrete in time':

1  travellers' tales
2  travellers with a specific educational focus; learning through example; improving circumstances at home
3  understanding of other nations; detailed accumulation of information; educational exchange
4  study of 'national character' and its deterministic role in shaping national systems of education
5  quantitative research; explanation of educational phenomena.[4]

Another way of looking at the phases of development in comparative inquiry in education, which complements Noah and Eckstein's approach, is to describe a sequential chain of emphases beginning at certain broadly defined historical points and continuing alongside the already existing emphases, while modifying them in various ways. This is attempted in Figure 3.

This chain of development begins with a limitation on the part of observers to description. It then moves to a period, from around the 1830s for the most part (though there are some earlier examples), when the investigation of foreign systems of education began to have an identifiable political purpose – to inform the national debate with both positive and negative examples of experience in other countries and to try to identify ideas and practices that might be imported or 'borrowed'. This general political purpose was strengthened when the collection of statistical information became more sophisticated: as the nineteenth century progressed, there was increasing effort to quantify and record, so that political arguments could be supported or attacked on the basis of 'hard' evidence. Much statistical information could in turn be used in analyses of socio-economic factors, and so our fourth phase introduces efforts to understand social phenomena and their relation to economic conditions. Much of the more significant early work of comparativists belongs to this tradition. More recently there has been a focus on international surveys of educational outcomes, most

description
- - - - - - - - ----------------------------------------------------------------------------->

        political analysis
        ------------------------------------------------------------------->

                use of statistical evidence, systematic data collection
                ------------------------------------------------->

                    socio-economic evidence/understanding
                    --------------------------------------------->

                        outcomes analysis
                        ------------------------------------->

                        globalized context
                        ------------------------------------->

                                postmodern approaches
                                ----------------------->

**Figure 3** Historical emphases in comparative analysis

notably manifest in large-scale comparisons of educational achievement. And at the same time there has been a tendency to look at education within an investigation of globalizing trends, where we find significant analyses of the tensions between global pressures for education to converge, and divergent local cultural and resource realities. Currently there are various theorists working in a generally postmodern context and developing new analytical approaches to the notion of comparison in education. We see each new phase as existing together with earlier traditions, so that the task of comparison becomes ever more sophisticated and diverse in approach. Each of our phases ('emphases') does not replace what has preceded it.

The first of Noah and Eckstein's five stages (recall that these stages are not 'discrete in time') – the 'description' phase in our Figure 3 – comprises the time when travellers brought back tales of what they had observed. These tales formed 'the most primitive [...] observations', originating in curiosity and emphasizing the exotic so as to produce stark contrast with the norm at home: 'Only the rare observer could extract systematic conclusions with explanatory value from a mass of indiscriminately reported impressions'.[5] The travellers who fall into Noah and Eckstein's first stage were visiting other countries out of cultural and general intellectual curiosity, and they constitute a very large group, writing with varying degrees of sophistication and providing sometimes rich descriptions of a wide range of aspects of education. They belong to a tradition which continues today, and it is a tradition which should not be glibly dismissed as having been superseded by later approaches.

One of the earliest of such travellers in the nineteenth century was John Quincy Adams (1767–1848), who wrote an account, published in 1804, devoted to his travels in Silesia in 1800–1. Adams was then the US Minister Plenipotentiary in Berlin. Himself the son of a president, he became the sixth US president in 1825. In a letter from Berlin of March 1801, Adams writes favourably of the educational policies of Frederick the Great; he argues that it was due to 'the zeal with which he pursued the purpose of spreading useful knowledge among all classes of his subjects' that, compared to the USA, 'probably, no country in Europe could so strongly contest our pre-eminence in [elementary education] as Germany'.[6] He highlights the training of teachers and covers various other details of educational provision in Silesia, and he initiates – with this attention to educational issues – a long process of serious examination of education in Prussia that was to exercise the minds of policy-makers in the USA, Great Britain, and France throughout the century.[7]

While Adams was representative of an intelligent and well-informed approach to educational questions, others who wrote travellers' tales reported on the more eye-catching aspects of what they had observed, or warned against any attempt to learn from foreign experience. Here is an arrogant warning from 1818, at the time the Continent was opening up to travellers again following the defeat of Napoleon:

> Let the traveller remember that *he is called not to import the principles or habits of foreign nations into his own, but to export to those less favoured countries the principles and practices he has learned at home.*[8]

The following is an example of a trivial observation expounded upon for effect; it is included in an account of travels in Westphalia in 1797:

> The Germans bring up their children with great tenderness, but in a manner to prevent the effects of effeminacy, or the ordinary ailments proceeding therefrom. I have seen the sons and daughters of gentlemen run through the dew of the morning without shoes, stockings, or any under garments, but shirts and shifts [...]. About noon, when there seems the less real necessity to wrap up, they begin to *put on*, just in the proportion as other children *throw off*; but they all look as healthy as if they were educated in the way of England.[9]

And we can see almost its mirror image in observations recorded earlier by Carl Philipp Moritz during his travels in England in 1782:

English boys remain true to nature until a certain age. What a contrast when I think of our six-year-old, pimpled, pampered Berlin boys, with great hair-nets and all the paraphernalia of an adult, even to being dressed in lace-trimmed coats, and compare these with the English boys in the flower of youth – lithe, red-cheeked, with open-breasted shirts, hair cut and curling naturally. Here in England it is unusual to meet a blotchy-faced boy or young man, or one with deformed features and disproportionate limbs. Were it so in Berlin a really handsome man would not be so conspicuous.[10]

These are typical early examples of travellers' tales which remain at the level of superficiality. They are subjective snapshots of observed phenomena, singled out for their bizarre or exotic character and with no serious implications for the transfer of notions and practices. Although they belong in Noah and Eckstein's first stage and our wholly descriptive first phase, we can still find examples today – particularly in the popular press – of sensational reporting of the perceived character of educational practice 'elsewhere'. Perhaps the most notorious example is the spurious story, reported *ad nauseam*, of the French minister of education looking at his watch and saying that at this exact time all French pupils are on page so-and-so of a particular textbook in whatever subject. The exaggeration here serves simply, of course, to illustrate the centralized nature of education in France. Here, for a change, is an example along the same lines from Hungary:

If one says 'So-and-so's son is in the fifth class of the Gymnasium', a Hungarian at once knows that the boy in question is about fourteen to fifteen years of age, […] and that at present he is encouraged to appreciate the beauties of Ovid and the lighter verse of Heine and Goethe.[11]

The early travellers who wrote so engagingly on their impressions of educational provision have left a rich source of description intended for the consumption of a wide popular readership. They were able at least to identify some of the themes – for example, the nature of the state's role in education and associated issues such as compulsory attendance and religious education – which would be the subject of more organized systematic inquiry by specialist observers as the century progressed.

Stage two of Noah and Eckstein's developmental division of comparative education – which overlaps with the first – introduces the notion of what can be learnt and assimilated from foreign systems, in effect what can be 'borrowed'. This is essentially a political objective, and so we see this stage as the beginning of a phase of political analysis (Figure 3) of the situation 'elsewhere', with the aim of informing policy 'at home'. Notions of policy borrowing remain a significant theme in the work of comparativists today.

We might cite here observations by Frances Trollope, a prolific and popular commentator on other countries (and mother of the novelist Anthony Trollope), who visited Germany in 1833 and reported enthusiastically on her perceptions of education in Prussia. She is remembered in particular for the indignant reaction her opinionated account of the United States, *Domestic Manners of the Americans* (1832), received. As far as her account of Germany is concerned, Trollope is representative of a bridging point between simple description and arguments in the direction of learning lessons from the foreign example.

> In this little village, as in every other part of the kingdom of Prussia, the education of the people is the business of the state. So deeply are the benevolent and philosophical lawgivers of this enlightened country impressed with the belief that the only sure method of rendering a people preeminently great and happy, is to spread the light of true knowledge among them, that the government leaves not the duty of providing instruction for the children of the land to the unthinking caprice of their ignorant parents; but provides for them teachers and books; selected with a degree of vigilant circumspection which would do honour to the affection and judgment of the tenderest father. Nor is this all:- not only are the means of instruction thus amply and admirably provided, but the children of the people are not permitted to absent themselves from school on any plea except that of sickness, which must be authenticated by the certificate of a physician.[12]

Trollope then contrasts this impression with educational provision in England:

> And how is this all-important business transacted with us? In some places, a teacher is appointed by the clergyman, who would regulate his parish school with the same anxious care which he exercises in the government of his own family. In others, some vain and canting Lady Bountiful has the power of nomination, – and selects a person who shall look sharply after the uniform, and take care that the children show themselves off well, upon all public occasions.
>
> In one village, a staunch constitutional Tory shall exert his utmost influence that the little people about him may be brought up to fear God and honour the king. He may watchfully see them led to the venerated church of their fathers, and teach them to look up, with equal love and respect, to the institutions of their country.
>
> In the very next, perhaps, a furious demagogue may insist that every

lesson shall inculcate the indefeasible right to rebel. And, if the poor rogues be taught any religion at all, it may be with the understanding that each and every of them, when they are big enough, will have as good a right to be paid for preaching as the parson of the parish.

What can that whole be, which is formed of such discordant elements? And would it not be better for our rulers even to enforce such a mode of instruction as might give a chance of something like a common national feeling among the people of England, instead of letting them be blown about with every wind of doctrine, as they are at present?[13]

Fanny Trollope was typical of a number of writers who commented on education alongside other aspects of the society of countries they visited as intelligent observers. Later in the century, for example, the French philosopher Hippolyte Taine recorded his impression of education in England, making contrasts with provision in France. He spent time at Eton and Harrow (from which generalizations should not have been possible) and at the University of Oxford. Here is his view of the character-forming aspects of the teaching he observed:

All the boys I saw in their class-rooms, in the fields and streets, have a 'healthy and active air'. Obviously, at least in my view, they are both more childish and more manly than our own boys: more childish in that they are fonder of games and less disposed to overstep the limits of their age, more manly in that they are more capable of decision and action and self-government. Whereas the French schoolboy, especially the boarders in our colleges, is bored, soured, fined-down, precocious, far too precocious. He is in a cage and his imagination ferments. In all these respects, and in what concerns the formation of character, English education is better; It is better preparation for the world and it turns out more wholesome spirits.[14]

At the same time as European and American comparativists were looking to other countries to understand their education systems, and to seek examples of education policy and practice to be 'borrowed', a related, but distinctly different, process was happening in parts of the world colonized by European powers. The perspectives of the time – which now appear distinctly ethnocentric and indeed racist – moved educationists to look for ways to provide what they deemed to be appropriate education for the 'natives' of these regions. Classic and illustrative examples of this process are found in the reports of the Phelps-Stokes Educational Commissions to West, South and Equatorial Africa and East Africa in the early 1920s. These commissions had the following descriptive and meliorist purposes:

1  To inquire as to the educational work being done at present in each of the areas to be studied.
2  To investigate the educational needs of the people in the light of the religious, social, hygienic and economic conditions.
3  To ascertain to what extent these needs are being met.
4  To assist in the formulation of plans designed to meet the educational needs of the Native races.
5  To make available the full results of this study.[15]

In the wake of the First World War, the commissions saw these aims as both altruistic and self-interested:

> … everything possible should be done to remove possible causes of serious friction or danger even in a continent so 'remote' from the great political capitals of the world as Africa. As long as any portion of it, or of any other continent, suffers because of disease or superstition or prejudice or ignorance, the elements are at hand out of which a conflagration, which might later gain world proportions, may be fanned into a flame.[16]

The areas deemed suitable for the educational development of the 'Negro masses' were character development, health and hygiene, agriculture and gardening, industrial skill, home economics, and 'healthful recreations', along with the 'three Rs' – reading, writing, and arithmetic. While there was a recognition that the type of education needed in Africa might be different from that needed in more 'civilized' nations, this verdict was guided not so much by an understanding of the context as by a low opinion of the capacities of Africans, a desire to bring what was perceived as the best of European and American culture to a selected elite, and the power of colonizers to impose policies on the colonies. Shaped by the attitudes of the time, the descriptions and recommendations of the Phelps-Stokes reports, while not commissioned or produced by colonizing nations, were influential in shaping colonial education policy.

But the notion of borrowing was gradually questioned as educational systems came to be regarded as interwoven in the fabric of their society. As we have seen, the person who did most to establish this principle in comparative education was Michael Sadler, who headed the Office of Special Inquiries and Reports in London from 1895 to 1903. Sadler oversaw an impressive effort at examining educational issues in other countries, with the intention of informing discussion in England. The poet and man of letters Matthew Arnold, an earlier official – he was an inspector of schools – who had played a significant role in bringing foreign practice in education to the attention of British policy-makers, had made it clear how he saw the notion of 'borrowing': 'I hope with time to convince people,' he wrote in 1868, 'that I do not care the least for importing this or that foreign machinery, whether it be French or German, but only for getting certain English deficiencies supplied.'[17] And the Oxford academic Mark Pattison, who served with Arnold as an assistant commissioner for the Newcastle Commission on the state of popular education in England (1858), recorded a similar view: 'Much rather is every one who has any information on foreign systems to give, called upon to come forward with it, not as precedent to be followed, but as material for deliberation.'[18]

Methods of data collection improved throughout the century, and informed observers had at their disposal a growing body of information which could be used to inform discussion based on comparison. And increasing numbers of influential people had spent time travelling or studying abroad.

Though he made little impact in his own day, an early investigator who has had lasting significance for comparativists is Marc-Antoine Jullien, whose *Esquisse d'un Ouvrage sur l'Éducation Comparée (Plan for a Work on Comparative Education)* appeared in 1816–17. Jullien is often regarded as the father of comparative education, principally because he used the term in his famous work and because he proposed a systematic empirical investigation, by means of a questionnaire, to facilitate comparison of educational provision between nations:

> Series of questions on each branch of education and instruction, drawn up in advance and classified under uniform headings, would be given to intellectual and active men of sound judgment, of known moral conduct, who would search for solutions in public and private educational institutions, which they would have the mission of visiting and observing on different points.[19]

Jullien's questionnaire is a remarkably thorough document, anticipating the kind of investigations which only became common much later. It was conceived as six series of questions, covering 'primary and common education', 'secondary and classical education', 'higher and scientific education', 'normal education', 'education of girls' and 'education as it is related to legislation and social institutions'. In the event, only the first two series appeared in Jullien's *Esquisse*. There is a note to the effect that the remaining four series 'will be published immediately', but they have not been discovered. Here is a sample of the questions included in the first series:

31. What is the number of students in the primary schools in the commune or in the district?
32. What is the proportion of the total number of these students to that of the population of the commune or of the district?
33. Approximately how many students are grouped under a single director or teacher?
34. At which age are children admitted to the primary schools?
35. Are children of both sexes admitted to the same school, and until what age?
36. Do children undergo, at the time of their entrance to primary school, and during the course of their studies, examinations adapted to produce an appreciation of their faculties and the progress of their instruction? How do these examinations take place?
37. Is care taken to separate the children of the same school into several classes or sections, and according to what basis is this division determined?
38. Are arrangements made among the [children] which allow them to mutually help and teach one another?
39. How much time is spent with an ordinary child to make him familiar with reading, writing, and mathematics?
40. At what age approximately do children leave primary school?[20]

Questions of such detail were to be asked later in the century in the course of various surveys undertaken in England in connection with the work of official committees charged with reporting on the state of educational provision in the country[21] and we shall return to them in Chapter 5. Jullien's questions remained theoretical, however, and so we have no systematically collected comparative data on the complex topics he wished to see addressed for the second decade of the nineteenth century.

Two significant early investigators of foreign systems of education, who lead us into Noah and Eckstein's third stage and our phase of systematic (including statistical) data collection, were the Frenchman Victor Cousin (1792–1867) and the American Horace Mann (1796–1859). They both produced influential texts based on thorough knowledge of what was happening in education in Germany and elsewhere.[22]

Cousin's book *Rapport sur l'état de l'Instruction Publique dans quelques pays de l'Allemagne (Report on the State of Public Education in Some Parts of Germany)* appeared in 1833 and was published in English translation in the following year.[23] It was to be frequently cited in contemporary and later writing in England and the USA, and it counts as one of the most influential texts in the context of the discussion of educational provision and the role of the state in the early nineteenth century. In his *Digest* of Cousin's Report, J. Orville Taylor, Professor of Popular Education at New York University, enthused over the 'lively interest' it had sparked in France and England, and argued that 'from the results of this great experiment in giving the *whole people* that *kind* and *degree* of instruction which they need, some of the most useful and practical lessons may be obtained'.[24]

Cousin's report focused on primary instruction, not unnaturally so at a time when the main topic of debate was how best to establish national systems of elementary education. The year 1833 saw the first financial support to educational provision on the part of the state in England, when Parliament voted £20,000 for the building of schools. This sum was reckoned to be about one-twentieth of the Prussian Government's annual expenditure on education, the equivalent to half the yearly cost of maintaining the King's stables …

And in America, Horace Mann's *Report on an Educational Tour in Germany, and Parts of Great Britain and Ireland*, originating in 1844, was also very influential:

> The heart of [Mann's] *Report* contained the message that the United States had fallen behind the Prussians in education, and in order to catch up and move ahead, it was now mandatory to create a truly professional corps of teachers, produce a systematic curriculum, and develop a more centralized and efficient supervision of the schools. The Prussians offered a model in practicality and efficiency which his own countrymen would be well advised to follow.[25]

The work of Cousin and Mann was built upon by those who produced some of the great official reports on education in Great Britain later in the century, in which the foreign example – and especially that of Prussia – figured prominently, and in which statistical evidence was systematically presented.

Noah and Eckstein's fourth stage – what we call 'socio-economic evidence/ understanding' – involves analysis of what has been termed 'national character'[26] and its influence on the shaping of institutions. Historical understanding was essential here to arrive at an appreciation of the 'factors' which had contributed to education systems being as they were and which helped with understanding of the socio-economic dimension of education. Prominent among those who represented this kind of approach were Isaac

Kandel, Vernon Mallinson, and Joseph Lauwerys, all of whom can still be read with profit today.[27]

With the fifth stage postulated by Noah and Eckstein, our stage of outcomes analysis and globalized context, we see the emphasis shift to detailed 'scientific' analysis of educational phenomena with the declared aim to provide explanation and therefore to point towards ways of improving performance. Developments in social science research generally helped to put comparative inquiry in education on a more secure basis, and in particular the work of the IEA (International Association for the Evaluation of Educational Achievement) and the OECD (Organisation for Economic Co-operation and Development) has led in recent years to the accumulation of huge amounts of data which enable us to describe educational provision internationally and to identify practice which might account for high levels of measured performance. There is currently much international interest in the education system of Finland, given that country's demonstrably high performance in the first two rounds of the OECD's PISA (Programme for International Student Assessment) survey.[28]

Not predicted by Noah and Eckstein's five stages is a contemporary movement which draws on postmodern perspectives in comparative education research. Postmodernism offers critiques of the 'grand narratives' that dominate what is accepted as knowledge, which consist mainly of white, male and western points of view, and therefore are seen to serve white, male and western interests. Instead, it favours a pluralistic view, which acknowledges and celebrates that individuals and groups of individuals have equally valid but different perspectives, and an equal right to constitute knowledge. Coulby and Jones[29] have noted three particular strands of postmodern critique: feminist, culturalist, and class.

It has been claimed that relative to other fields, comparative education 'has been late in addressing issues of postmodernity'.[30] Its increasing importance and redefining role is predicted by Gottlieb:

> The 'post-modern turn' in comparative education, if and when it takes place, will most likely result in a [different] construction of knowledge. The destabilisation of the dominant modernist genres of discourse and the opening up of space for the actors' voices and authority will introduce indigenous knowledge and new categories into the semantic universe of comparative education, through the typical interpretive underlying metaphors of culture as text, metaphor and game.[31]

Within international comparative studies in poorer parts of the world, post-colonial perspectives are sometimes associated with postmodernism because of their emphasis on a plurality of voices and a critical perspective on how the 'other' is construed in education and educational research. The dominant discourses of colonialism and neo-colonialism come under sharp critique and are offset by the diverse voices of those who have lived, and are living, under colonialism in all its forms.

One of the problems with many overarching theories, however, is that they tend on the one hand to be dogmatically embraced by their enthusiasts, and on the other to have only a limited life. There was a time, for example, when structuralism dominated and supposedly provided a key to understanding social phenomena that its proponents seemingly could not do without. Postmodernism – despite its semantic and conceptual problems as a term – has similarly dominated but slipped into decline as a guiding means of explaining and interpreting. The lesson here is that in a field of intellectual inquiry as diverse as comparative education there is no 'one size fits all' device with universal explanatory power. Instead the comparativist is better served by an appreciation of ways in which a variety of theoretical perspectives might be drawn upon to elucidate particular issues/problems/methodological approaches – essentially an eclectic approach not dissimilar from Edmund King's embracing of the concept of 'tools for the job'. Thus, if aspects of the work of Marx or Weber or Durkheim or Foucault (for instance) provide an illuminating perspective on a particular topic of inquiry, those theoretical features should of course be drawn upon with appropriate critical caution.

In observing the broad sweep of development in comparative education since its earliest origins, we can see that its progression has not been so much a series of discrete advances, each one replacing that which preceded it; instead there has been a slow accretion of layers of sophistication placed upon the early descriptive work so that we now have a multi-dimensional field of educational inquiry which, as we shall see in Chapter 5, draws on a wide range of expertise culled from other disciplines. We should make it clear that despite over-writing in terms of 'stages' or 'phases' or 'emphases' there is no implication that the later a stage, phase or emphasis begins, the more valuable it is regarded for the purposes of comparative inquiry. Long-established traditions have proved as rewarding as any of the latest nostrums.

# Organizations and publications

A number of societies in various countries and regions have made and still make a strong contribution to the development of comparative and international studies in education. These societies bring comparativists from around the world to regular conferences at which the full spectrum of topics in comparative and international education is discussed. They include the Comparative and International Education Society (CIES), the oldest and largest, founded in 1956; the Comparative Education Society in Europe (CESE), founded in 1961; the British Association for International and Comparative Education (BAICE) founded under another name in 1979 and before that the British Section of CESE, and many others. Comparative education societies are brought together in the World Council of Comparative Education Societies (WCCES, founded in 1970) which holds a regular World Congress, hosted in the country of one of the associated societies.

There are well-established journals in which a continuing debate about the nature of comparative education can be traced. These include: the *Comparative Education Review (CER)*, the journal of CIES; *Compare*, the BAICE journal, *Comparative Education*, an unaffiliated British publication; the *International Review of Education*, published by UNESCO; the *International Journal of Educational Development (IJED)*; the German journal *Tertium Comparationis*; *Current Issues in Comparative Education (CICE)*, an open-access online journal run from Teachers College, Columbia University; and a UK-based online journal, *Research in Comparative and International Education (RCIE)*. In addition there are various book series of long standing, including the *World Yearbook of Education*, which each year comprises a thematic volume, *Oxford Studies in Comparative Education*, published twice a year, and the Hong Kong Comparative Education Research Centre's *Studies in Comparative Education*.

Valuable sources of information include the *International Encyclopedia of Education*, edited by Torsten Husén and Neville Postlethwaite, and the various databases produced by UNESCO, the OECD, and EURYDICE, the EU information network.

The traditions of comparative studies in education are rich. Whatever discrete or overlapping stages we might identify in the development of the field, there is strength in the fact that each period of development has added incrementally to what had gone before, rather than wiping the slate clean following the latest new direction to be identified. There is a body of established literature produced by leading figures in comparative studies from the late nineteenth century onwards: some of the earlier texts (by Michael Sadler especially, but also by the scholars like Bereday, King and Holmes who did so much to set comparative education on a secure footing in the 1960s) deserve to be widely read today since they contain much wisdom about the nature of comparison and its methods. We shall return to methods in Chapters 6 and 7.

# Notes

1.  Fraser and Brickman, *History of International and Comparative Education*, p. 2.
2.  Herodotus, *Histories*, p. 70.
3.  Fraser and Brickman, op. cit., pp. 2–3. On Xenophon see Freeman, *Schools of Hellas*, pp. 259–72 and Castle, *Ancient Education and Today*, pp. 79–80.
4.  Noah and Eckstein, *Toward a Science of Comparative Education*, pp. 4–7.
5.  Ibid., pp. 4–5.
6.  Adams, *Letters on Silesia*, p. 362.
7.  See Phillips: *The German Example*, for a detailed study of the attraction to English policy-makers of educational provision in Germany since 1800.
8.  Cunningham, *Cautions to Continental Travellers*, p. 94. Emphasis in original text.
9.  Pratt, *Gleanings*, Vol. III, pp. 209–10.
10. Moritz, *Journeys of a German*, p. 68.
11. De Hegedüs, *Hungarian Background*, p. 95.
12. Trollope, *Belgium and Western Germany in 1833*, Vol. II, pp. 169–70. The village was St. Goar.
13. Ibid., pp. 172–3.
14. Taine, *Notes on England*, pp. 107–8.
15. Jones, *Education in East Africa*, p. xiii.
16. Ibid.
17. Murray, *Life of Matthew Arnold*, p. 240.
18. Pattison, 'Report', p. 168.
19. Fraser, *Jullien's Plan*, pp. 36–7.
20. Ibid., pp. 56–7.
21. For example, by the Royal Commission on the Elementary Education Acts (the Cross Commission) of 1888.
22. See, on Cousin: Brewer, *Victor Cousin as a Comparative Educator*; on Mann: Hinsdale, *Horace Mann*, and Messerli, *Horace Mann. A Biography*.

23. The translation was by Sarah Austin (1793–1867), who was herself a significant figure in the early history of comparative studies (see Goodman, 'A historiography of founding fathers?').

24. Taylor, *A Digest*, pp. iii–iv.

25. Messerli, *Horace Mann*, p. 407.

26. On national character see Barker, *National Character*; Vexliard, 'L'éducation comparée et la notion de caractère national'; Kay, 'National character – Concept, scope and uses'; Hans, *Comparative Education*; and Mallinson, *Introduction to the Study of Comparative Education*.

27. See Jones, *Comparative Education*, pp. 57–74, for summaries of the work of Kandel, Mallinson, and Lauwerys.

28. Among the factors that are said to account for the Finnish success in PISA are Finland's well-established nine-year comprehensive schools, the attention paid to pupils with special needs, degrees of local autonomy and – importantly – a committed, professional, and highly qualified teaching force, recruited from the successful ten per cent of applicants and educated to Master's level. (Sahlberg, *Finnish Lessons*.)

29. Coulby and Jones, 'Post-modernity and European Identities'.

30. Cowen, 'Last past the post: Comparative education, modernity and perhaps post-modernity', p. 151.

31. Gottlieb, 'Are we post-modern yet?', p. 171.

# 3
# Policy Transfer

As it moves, it morphs

*Cowen*[1]

In this chapter we shall be concerned with a fundamental aspect of the purpose of comparative inquiry in education, namely the question as to what might be learnt from an examination of educational provision 'elsewhere', and how this learning might be embedded in education systems. It is so central to the field that Cowen has argued '… it is the triad of transfer, and translation and transformation which stabilizes comparative education'.[2] There are perennial examples of nations whose educational success stories (however defined) have made them influential on the policies of other countries that seek to emulate them, and the intensification of globalization has introduced new patterns of policy movement to traditional notions of policy borrowing from one country to another. What implications does the example of the 'other' have for a particular nation or region? What ideas/policies might be successfully imported? What are the processes involved in such transfer? We begin with some historical examples which demonstrate the importance of education policy transfer as a theme over time.

## Meiji Japan and borrowing from the West

In the Edo-Tokyo Museum there is on display a board game dating from 1898 in which players – as school pupils – progress around the board from their first days at school, learning to read and write, through a variety of lessons and examinations and successes and failures which affect their relative positions on the board, to their eventual graduation. The aim is to reach the central rectangle, which shows a pupil (in Prussian-style uniform) bowing and stretching out both hands to receive a diploma handed to him by a school principal dressed in formal Western clothes, while admiring parents watch in the audience.[3] The image recalls the final moments of a notable BBC film on education in Japan, 'The Learning Machine', broadcast in 1990,[4] in which junior high school graduates are seen lining up with extraordinary military precision (and in uniforms still redolent of the nineteenth-century Prussian military academies) to be presented with their diplomas by a head teacher wearing a frock coat. Present-day traditions in education in Japan have a long history, much of their origin being evident in the reforming efforts in the early years of the Meiji Restoration.

The long Tokugawa Shogunate ended when power was transferred to the Emperor – the sixteen-year-old Mutsuhito – in 1868. Mutsuhito was given the posthumous name Meiji (Great Period) on his death in 1912. With the Meiji Restoration came a renewed effort at the opening-up of Japan. Some fifteen years earlier Commodore Perry had arrived off the coast of Japan with his 'black ships', demanding that the United States have access to Japanese ports and eventually succeeding in establishing diplomatic relations with a country that had been effectively closed to the West.[5] Soon after the Meiji Restoration the Japanese government engaged in a remarkable effort to investigate, and potentially learn from, the West.

Missions had been sent abroad in 1862 and in 1865–6 – and Japan had sought to benefit from Western learning in various ways over a long period[6] – but the 'embassy' that was convened in 1871 far surpassed the scope of those earlier efforts. Led by Iwakura Tomoni, the group that was to set sail for Europe and the United States and to spend a year and nine months away from Japan comprised half the government of the day. The delegation was huge (107 in all), and its objectives were wide-ranging: to present credentials to countries with which treaties had been concluded; to begin treaty revisions; and to observe and investigate advanced societies in order to determine what features of those societies might assist the moderni-zation of Japan. This latter objective became the principal aim of the mission. The Embassy visited the United States, Britain, France, Belgium, The Netherlands, Germany, Russia, Denmark, Sweden, Italy, Austria, and Switzerland. It included Tanaka Fujimaro and several inspectors from the Ministry of Education.[7]

A detailed report on the Embassy's travels and findings was put together by the Confucian scholar Kume Kunitake (1839–1931) and published in 1878 (*Tokumei zenken taishi Beiō kairan jikki*). We are fortunate to have a five-volume translation of Kume's text (*A True Account of the Ambassador*

*Extraordinary & Plenipotentiary's Journey of Observation Through the United States of America and Europe*[8]) which allows those not able to read Japanese to appreciate the extent of the Embassy's investigations. Let us focus, by way of example, on what Iwakura and his team did by way of exploring the nature of educational provision in the United States.

On 23 December 1871, the Embassy set sail from Yokohama en route for San Francisco, where they arrived on 15 January 1872. They were to visit Sacramento, travel through the Sierra Nevada mountains, detour for an unexpected stay in Salt Lake City, continue through Wyoming and Nebraska to Chicago, thence go on to Washington (where they met President Grant), tour New England, and spend time, among other places, in New York and Boston. They were able to visit many different types of school. They embarked from Boston on 6 August, having spent nearly seven months in the United States.

In Kume's general account of the United States there is mention of the effort put into elementary education, the over-riding principle of non-inter-ference on the part of the federal government, the habit of raising taxes at state level, and the importance of individual initiative. 'There are no laws forcing parents to send their children to school', he reported, but 'the reason parents do not neglect to send their children to school is that people feel ashamed if they are not educated'. Kume described the move from religious to secular control over educational provision and the reasons for it and concluded that state supervision had resulted in education in every state being 'more or less the same'. These features relate of course to issues which are familiar within the Japanese education system as it has evolved since the time of the Iwakura Embassy.

Here, as throughout his account of the Embassy, there is much factual and statistical information. As the translator puts it in an introductory essay:

> Although somewhat ad-hoc, it was still quite a systematic information-gathering effort – certainly not a junket. Kume declares in his Preface that they worked hard, and his narrative confirms it. Members of the Embassy, most of whom did not speak English well, came armed with books on the United States written in Chinese, or Japanese translations from Chinese and English; they also bought guide-books, maps, city directories and other sources of information as they travelled. They plied their guides and hosts with questions and asked for printed information, timetables and reports to study there and then, or to send back to Japan.[9]

The Embassy next sailed across the Atlantic to Britain to begin a tour of some seventeen weeks.

What is of especial interest in the Iwakura Embassy is its systematic attempt to gather data which would allow the group to learn from Western experience and so inform educational development in Japan. It serves as one of the clearest examples of a deliberate attempt at what has become known as 'policy borrowing'.

# 'The German example'

Japan serves as a pre-eminent example of a nation purposefully seeking to identify those features of education systems elsewhere that might be successfully imported into the home context: a 'borrower' country, in fact. An example of a 'lender' country, especially during the nineteenth century, would be that of Germany.

Germany had developed an embryonic system of compulsory state-supported schooling in the eighteenth century, far earlier than other developed nations. And it was not surprising that policy makers should look closely at what the Germans – specifically the Prussians – had been able to achieve. The German example therefore served to inform the educational policy debate, especially in England, France, and the United States, all of which countries commissioned lengthy reports on German provision in education.[10]

The principal interest was on the precise nature of the role of the state in legislating for school attendance (with fines for the parents of children who did not attend), in determining curricula, in dealing with the problem of religious education, and in educating teachers. As the century progressed, and as political relations changed, the German example could be seen as either positive or negative, as an ideal to be aimed at or a model to be avoided:

> There has been a consistent tendency over that long period to refer to the German example in education at one extreme to promote ideas for change and development ('do this and we shall be as good as the Prussians') and at the other extreme to warn against innovation and reform ('do that and you will end up as bad as the Prussians'), with various shades of attraction and repulsion in between.[11]

The German university, especially following the foundation of the University of Berlin in 1810, became a model for the development of research-based institutions in other countries. As Matthew Arnold, who had made several visits to Germany, famously put it: 'The French university has no liberty, and the English universities have no science; the German universities have both'.[12] German universities attracted large numbers of students from Britain and the United States, who wished to sit at the feet of professors who were pushing the scientific boundaries of their subjects, and especially in science and technology, where developments were supported by a remarkable German institution, the *technische Hochschule*. With the growth of Germany as an industrial nation, observers wished to profit from the evident quality of research and teaching in what were undoubtedly the leading higher education institutions of Europe. But alongside technological progress came increasing military power, and so warnings against emulating provision that might result in militarism were frequently heard, and during the two great conflicts of the twentieth century interest in education in Germany came to focus on how seriously wrong things could go.

The German economic miracle of the post-war period reignited interest in the potential benefits of sound educational provision for economic prosperity, and a particular focus was on the highly developed system of vocational training in place in Germany. This is still today an important area of interest for observers from other nations, while emulation of the German model in this particular area, dependent as it is on a remarkable compact between government and industry has proved mostly elusive.

# Analyzing policy borrowing

As we have intimated in Chapter 1, and as the work of the Iwakura Mission and the case of 'the German model' demonstrate, if we accept that one of the main purposes of comparative inquiry in education is to identify and learn from good practice elsewhere, such practice might then be adaptable for implementation 'at home'. The processes involved in policy transfer are very complex and have been a focus of attention for comparativists since the days of the 'father of comparative education, Marc-Antoine Jullien, to whose work we have referred in Chapter 2. The term 'policy *transfer*' is a broad descriptor of the phenomenon of which 'policy *borrowing*' is a part. The term 'policy borrowing' is now firmly established in the substantial literature on the subject.

Marc-Antoine Jullien had hoped that a 'special educational commission' might be established that would ask the detailed questions that his *Plan for Comparative Education* (*Esquisse d'un Ouvrage sur l'Education Comparée*) of

1816–1817 proposed. And he argued that the lessons to be learnt from other nations could be obviously beneficial: 'A wise and well-informed politician discovers in the development and prosperity of other nations a means of prosperity for his own country'.[13] The task, then as now, was to collect data and to identify aspects of good practice that might be transferable to another context.

We might see educational policy transfer as a spectrum involving various degrees of voluntary and involuntary cross-national influence, as depicted in Figure 4.

This spectrum sees educational transfer as a phenomenon ranging from extreme forms of imposition of ideas (as in an autocratic government demanding a new philosophy and new norms of provision), through policies required 'under constraint' (for example, in occupied countries, or in various post-crisis situations), policies 'negotiated under constraint' (as in conditions required by aid agencies or countries in receipt of their support), to aspects of educational transfer 'purposefully borrowed' (when policy makers deliberately seek to import ideas from elsewhere), and finally to the general influence which internationalization or globalization bring in terms of the spread of educational ideas and their associated methods.

The apparently simple three-stage process of: (i) identification of successful practice; (ii) introduction into the home context; and (iii) assimilation, is in fact extraordinarily complex and presents the comparativist with many problems. The *locus classicus* for a description of the basic dilemma is Sadler's much-quoted speech of 1900, 'How far can we learn anything of practical value from the study of foreign systems of education?' in which we find this passage, still worth repeating:

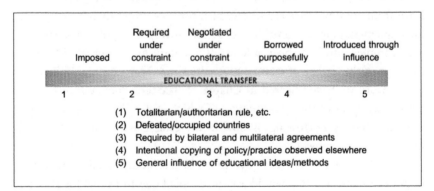

**Figure 4** Spectrum of educational transfer

In studying foreign systems of Education we should not forget that the things outside the schools matter even more than the things inside the schools, and govern and interpret the things inside. We cannot wander at pleasure among the educational systems of the world, like a child strolling through a garden, and pick off a flower from one bush and some leaves from another, and then expect that if we stick what we have gathered into the soil at home, we shall have a living plant. A national system of Education is a living thing, the outcome of forgotten struggles and difficulties, and 'of battles long ago'. It has in it some of the secret workings of national life.[14]

This famous injunction apparently undermines the very notion of the feasibility of policy borrowing. A similar position, with clear echoes of Sadler's text, was taken up by Isaac Kandel:

The comparative approach demands first an appreciation of the intangible, impalpable spiritual and cultural forces which underlie an educational system; the forces and factors outside the school matter even more than what goes on inside it. Hence the comparative study of education must be founded on an analysis of the social and political ideals which the school reflects, for the school epitomizes these for transmission and for progress. In order to understand, appreciate and evaluate the real meaning of the educational system of a nation, it is essential to know something of its history and traditions, of the forces and attitudes governing its social organization, of the political and economic conditions that determine its development.[15]

But it is precisely because of our awareness of the complexities of borrowing that it is a phenomenon which needs to be thoroughly analysed and understood. One of the tasks of comparativists is to unravel the processes which are involved in all aspects of educational transfer between nations, and to highlight the problems and warnings implicit in them. Paul Morris has described the starting point in graphic terms:

- Country A is an economic basket case (high levels of unemployment and low levels of economic growth) – this is portrayed as largely the result of the educational system which is not producing workers with appropriate skills.
- Country B is economically successful (low levels of unemployment and high levels of economic growth) – this is to a large degree the result of its possessing a well-educated workforce.
- Therefore, if country A adopts some of the features of the educational system of Country B it will improve the state of Country A's economy.[16]

The imperatives for policy transfer might of course develop from the very work of comparativists; more often they emerge from political decision-making of various kinds. They have been characterized as:

- serious scientific/academic investigation of the situation in a foreign environment
- popular conceptions of the superiority of other approaches to educational questions
- politically motivated endeavours to seek reform of provision by identifying clear contrasts with the situation elsewhere
- distortion (exaggeration), whether or not deliberate, of evidence from abroad to highlight perceived deficiencies at home.[17]

The task here is to produce checks and balances and to provide critical commentary – often commentary which warns against proposed courses of action based on models superficially observed elsewhere.

Policy borrowing within the spectrum of transfer described above involves complex processes of adoption and adaptation which can be analysed in stages. Phillips and Ochs[18] have proposed a circular model (Figure 5) which describes four stages in the borrowing process, from the events and conditions which spark off the initial 'cross-national attraction', through the decision-making procedures that led to the adoption of a particular policy and – in a third stage – its implementation, and then to the 'internalization' or 'indigenization' of the policy within the 'home' system.

The model in Figure 5 provides a framework for analysis of the phenomenon of policy borrowing. This is a promising and revealing research area which can throw light on topics ranging from the internationalization of certain types of knowledge to the development of common pedagogical techniques in, say, the teaching of mathematics. It facilitates understanding of 'the other' through close attention to the context in which policies and practices that attract attention exist, and it is concerned, too, with processes of educational change, an area of central importance in educational research. A model is not a method, and the full variety of investigative approaches would have to be used at every stage of analysis described. But this and similar frameworks for analysis assist the comparativist researcher in a number of ways. It seeks:

- to provide clear sequential stages for an analysis
- to underline the importance of context in comparative inquiry
- to suggest factors to be investigated within each stage

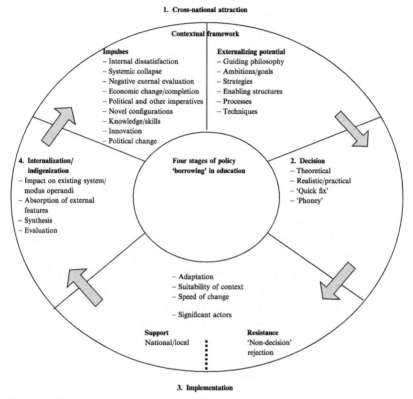

**1. Cross-national attraction**

**Contextual framework**

**Impulses**
– Internal dissatisfaction
– Systemic collapse
– Negative exernal evaluation
– Economic change/completion
– Political and other imperatives
– Novel configurations
– Knowledge/skills
– Innovation
– Political change

**Externalizing potential**
– Guiding philosophy
– Ambitions/goals
– Strategies
– Enabling structures
– Processes
– Techniques

**4. Internalization/
indigenization**
– Impact on existing system/
modus operandi
– Absorption of external
features
– Synthesis
– Evaluation

**Four stages of policy
'borrowing' in education**

**2. Decision**
– Theoretical
– Realistic/practical
– 'Quick fix'
– 'Phoney'

– Adaptation
– Suitability of context
– Speed of change

– Significant actors

**Support**
National/local

**Resistance**
'Non-decision'
rejection

**3. Implementation**

**Figure 5** Policy borrowing in education: Composite processes

- to establish the notion of a circularity of processes, in the Hegelian
  sense of thesis-antithesis-synthesis.

It aims, too, to remind us of the complexities involved in a phenomenon
which is often regarded simplistically by policy makers. Many are the politicians who pay a quick visit to another country and return with notions of
borrowing this or that policy perceived to be effective in quite a different
context. Often such notions are dropped with the passing of time after
they have been used for political effect at home. But where politicians and
administrators are persuasive enough to get a policy from elsewhere taken
on board 'at home', it is important for comparativists to use their expertise
in research to full effect to test the feasibility of the transfer of ideas in
question and then to analyse what happens as the stages of its adoption and
adaptation evolve.

It is in these and related areas that comparative research can be most
effective in terms of policy analysis, and it is here, too, that the full panoply

of methods can be brought together to produce findings that might warn of actual and potential problems. Research that results in warnings *against* certain courses of action can be as valuable as that which *encourages* change. This is not a new notion. Here is a rather flowery comment from Cloudesley Brereton, written before the First World War:

> We cannot go to school with any nation, or in other words we cannot blindly adopt the organization or methods of any of our neighbours, for each nation has evolved its own particular way of dealing with its educational flora, the result of long years of trial and experiment; but as ardent pueri-culturists, to use the French term, we can try to study and understand the methods and above all the loving care and insight that each nation lavishes on the coming generation. If we know our own country well, we can with a certain diffidence say what is practical in the way of imitation, whether it be adoption or adaptation; we can also see what it is advisable to safeguard against – for prevention is a large part of educational practice, and the teacher who says 'Don't' to himself saves himself from having to say many 'Don'ts' to the children; and, lastly, we may catch what is perhaps the most difficult, yet the most precious thing of all, a portion of that divine spirit or afflatus that pervades a great national system, and make it not merely our own, but communicate its inspiration to our fellow-countrymen, whether they be administrators, teachers, or parents.[19]

Finland has performed remarkably well in the OECD's PISA surveys of student performance. One of the results has been an influx of visitors (sometimes derogatively called 'PISA-tourists') anxious to learn the secrets of Finnish success and to identify what implications the Finnish educational recipe might have for other education systems. Pasi Sahlberg has suggested what might account for Finnish success in PISA: Finland's long experience with nine-year comprehensive schools, the focused attention to pupils with special needs, local autonomy in education, and a highly professional and well-qualified teaching force. In addition – and crucially – teaching in Finland is so attractive that only some ten per cent of applicants are accepted into teacher training, and the successful trainees are required to continue their professional education up to Master's level.[20] There is no magic formula that can be transferred to other contexts: in the case of Finland it is the special combination of the kind of factors Sahlberg identifies that creates the conditions that lead to educational success.

Analyses of policy transfer can also be seen within the context of 'World Systems Theory' and 'World Culture Theory', used in approaches to understanding globalizing trends in education that have engendered a huge but contested literature, produced by faithful adherents[21] on the one hand and sceptical critics on the other.[22] Adherents report a number of drivers for what they conclude to be increasing global policy convergence. These include human rights agreements, and global competition in terms of educational performance and its understood relationship to the development of human capital. Policy movement under these conditions is not so much a matter of national governments taking ideas from other national governments as it is everyone working towards a shared global script. However, even under these conditions there are perceived leaders and perceived followers, and local interpretations of global norms. A useful summary of the issues is provided by Arnove, who sees benefit for comparative education in the confluence of these 'systematically evolving intellectual currents': 'It has stimulated further inquiry to refine and elaborate the theories and methodologies that will enable scholars, policy makers, and practitioners to better understand the multidimensional, transnational trends shaping the workings and outcomes of education systems everywhere'.[23]

Important work on policy borrowing can be found in edited volumes by Steiner Khamsi[24] and by Steiner-Khamsi and Waldow.[25]

# Notes

1.  Cowen, 'The transfer, translation and transformation of educational processes', p. 315.
2.  Cowen, 'The national, the international, and the global', p. 339.
3.  *Esugorokuten* ('Exhibition of Board Games'), Edo Tokyo Hakubutsukan, Tokyo, 1998, p. 77.
4.  BBC2, first broadcast 11 November 1990.
5.  See Wiley, *Yankees in the Land of the Gods*; Barr: *The Coming of the Barbarians*.
6.  Keene, *The Japanese Discovery of Europe, 1720–1830*.
7.  Nish (ed.), *The Iwakura Mission in America and Europe*, pp. 1–2.
8.  Kunitake, *The Iwakura Embassy, 1871–73*.
9.  Ibid, Vol. 1, p. xxxv.
10. See, for example: Cousin, *Report on the State of Public Instruction in Prussia*; Mann, *Report of an Educational Tour*; Arnold, *Schools and Universities on the Continent*; and for an overview of the attraction to Germany on the part of English policy makers, Phillips, *The German Example*.
11. Phillips, *The German Example*, p. 1.

12. Arnold, *Schools and Universities on the Continent*, p. 232.
13. Fraser, *Jullien's Plan*, p. 37. The original has 'Une politique judicieuse ...': so, 'a wise and well-informed *policy*', rather than *politician*.
14. Sadler, in Higginson, *Selections from Michael Sadler*, p. 49.
15. Kandel, *Studies in Comparative Education*, p. xix.
16. Morris, 'Comparative Education and Educational Reform: Beware of Prophets Returning from the Far East', p. 4.
17. Phillips, 'Learning from elsewhere', p. 299.
18. Phillips and Ochs, 'Researching Policy Borrowing', p. 779.
19. Brereton, *Studies in Foreign Education*, p. ix.
20. Sahlberg, *Finnish Lessons*.
21. Schriewer (ed.), *Re-Conceptualising the Global/Local Nexus*.
22. Carney, Rappleye and Silova: 'Between Faith and Science'.
23. Arnove, 'World-Systems Analysis and Comparative Education in the Age of Globalization', p. 114.
24. Steiner-Khamsi, *The Global Politics of Educational Borrowing and Lending*.
25. Steiner-Khamsi and Waldow, *Policy Borrowing and Lending in Education*.

# 4

# International Education: Meanings, Practice, and Research

International: Existing, constituted or carried on between different nations; pertaining to the relations between nations.

*Oxford English Dictionary*

Comparative education and international education have been called 'twin fields',[1] and the two fields are indeed closely related. It is not always possible to tell where one ends and the other begins, and they are highly complementary. However, in this chapter we shall attempt to tease apart further the two components of that rather awkward label 'Comparative and International Education', and to explore the range of educational practices and research associated with international education.

The term 'international' in relation to education has a veritable plethora of meanings. As we see in the definition above, 'international' means, literally, 'between nations', implying a potentially comparative relationship from the outset. As an essential starting point, while comparative education traditionally involves the direct comparison of two or more systems of education, or units within systems, most uses of the term 'international education' suggest a more implicitly comparative and often applied approach. Intentional or not, arguably, education is inherently international in the contemporary era. Many educational institutions adopt an explicitly international perspective in their approach, with a view to offering qualifications with international currency, or creating 'global citizens' among learners. Forces of globalization have acted inexorably on education, creating greater standardization or what World Culture theorists have termed 'convergence' (although, importantly, equal and opposite effects are also in evidence).[2]

There has always been considerable similarity between schools across contexts: the curriculum, for example, has been shown to be divided between language, mathematics, science and the arts in a comparable way in schools around the world, but empirical studies point to increasing convergence.[3] Likewise, school buildings in terms of their architecture share remarkable similarities internationally, as a result of shared patterns of teaching and learning (although facilities and resources differ significantly). Some of this transfer of ideas and norms has been purposeful and cross-national as we have seen in the previous chapter; some of it has been shaped by international agencies including UNESCO and International NGOs (non-governmental organisations); some of it results from competitive global league tables on everything from national enrolment ratios to university standings which use common indicators and therefore create common pressures; and some of it is a result of technologies which bring distant practices closer, more accessible, and more 'normal' through the compression of space and time. Historically, colonialism and other influences spread western models of schooling to much of the developing world, and these models have persisted into the present with little obvious change.

In this chapter, we shall explore the international in terms of educational practice, and also consider what we mean by the international in educational research, considering the relationship between international education researchers and their subjects, along with some of the characteristics that people bring to the endeavour.

# Internationalization

Nowhere has the internationalization of education been more apparent than in the higher education sector, and internationalization is one of the most significant movements in higher education globally. The practice was initially driven by increased student mobility, and the desire of universities to attract students from overseas. This is still a significant driver and the impressive numbers of students who travel to study at universities outside their own countries has increased by over 50% in the past decade to about 3.7 million in 2009.[4] So, each year a student population the size of a medium-sized state is on the move, and the trend shows no sign of slowing down, although patterns change over who goes where. While the internationalization movement started from this platform, in OECD countries, by the mid-1990s:

... a need was recognized to extend the analysis of internationalization from simply the physical mobility of students to the more complex issues of internationalization for all faculty and students through curricular, co-curricular, and other institutional adaptations.[5]

International curricula are defined as: 'curricula with an international orientation in content, aimed at preparing students for performing (professionally/socially) in an international and multi-cultural context, and designed for domestic students and/or foreign students'.[6]

Internationalization extends also to research activities, with a growing emphasis on international collaborations (facilitating, of course, comparative work). A range of contemporary imperatives creates the environment for internationalization in higher education globally, including social/cultural, political, academic, and economic factors. International league tables of universities help to sustain the momentum by including indicators which reflect an international environment, and by facilitating comparisons which inform student mobility and academic partnerships.

Europe provides examples of this homogenizing trend in higher education, not only in terms of curricula, but also in terms of creating comparability across qualifications, with a strong emphasis on mobility of learners. Attempts to create greater conformity in higher education in Europe are evident in the so-called 'Bologna Process' of 1999, the aim of which is to encourage EU member states and other countries to move towards a common framework of qualifications based on the three cycles of bachelor, master and doctorate degrees. The European Ministers of Education who signed the Bologna Declaration agreed on various objectives in terms of the coordination of policy:

- the adoption of a system of easily readable and comparable degrees (to promote employability and international competitiveness)
- the adoption of a system essentially based on two main cycles, undergraduate and graduate
- the establishment of a system of credits, such as in the European Credit Transfer System (ECTS) (as a means of promoting student mobility)
- the promotion of mobility by overcoming obstacles to the effective exercise of free movement (for students: access to study and training opportunities; for academics and administrators: recognition and valorization of periods spent in another European context)

- the promotion of European cooperation in quality assurance (comparable criteria and methodologies)
- the promotion of the necessary European dimensions in higher education (curricular development, inter-institutional cooperation, mobility schemes and integrated programmes of study, training and research).[7]

Exchanges play another role in creating the international scholar. The EU's European Region Action Scheme for the Mobility of University Students (ERASMUS) 'seeks to enhance the quality and reinforce the European dimension of higher education by encouraging transnational cooperation between universities, boosting European mobility and improving the transparency and full academic recognition of studies and qualifications throughout the Union'.[8] It does so through student and teacher exchanges, through the joint development of study programmes, through international intensive programmes and thematic networks in higher education, through language courses, and through the ECTS. It includes students and staff in the 25 member states of the EU, together with Iceland, Liechtenstein and Norway and the three (2006) candidate countries, Bulgaria, Romania and Turkey. Some 1.2 million students have participated in the various activities subsumed by ERASMUS.

Forms of 'borderless education' are another force of internationalization. Satellite campuses of existing universities – such as the University of Nottingham's Chinese campus – and overseas-accredited institutions – such as the British University in Dubai – are becoming more prevalent. There is a very wide range of provision of this type, from so-called 'accreditation mills' with very low standards, to more rigorously monitored institutions accountable to both their home universities and their hosts. Another form of increasingly borderless education is that offered through distance learning. The use of new technologies, such as Internet-learning packages, video-conferencing and on-line discussion fora, where students from many different contexts share ideas and experiences, has allowed learners to have diverse pedagogical experiences while registered for degrees at universities in other countries which they never physically visit.

Both advantages and disadvantages are perceived in the context of this increased internationalization. Among the advantages are the development of internationally oriented and interculturally competent individuals and civil society; improved quality of higher education through innovations; and increased opportunities for graduates for networking and working abroad.

On the downside, there is a risk of brain drain from poorer countries when talented nationals are readily trained abroad: increased resource requirements; curtailing of the development of local higher education; a loss of national control over quality, curriculum and standards; and a potential loss of cultural identity.[9] The result of this process of internationalization is that 'the scholar is becoming less and less a citizen of one nation alone and more a citizen of the academic world'.[10]

# International schools

International schools have existed since Victorian times[11] but a clear definition of them remains elusive.[12] They share some pedagogical, ideological and practical purposes and concerns. Ideologically, they seek to promote international understanding through the development of requisite skills, knowledge and attitudes[13] – similar to global citizenship education as described below, and with similar pedagogical practices. Skelton describes the 'international' aspect of these schools' curricula as follows:

> ... it is an approach that sets out to develop understandings of our similarities, in addition to an acceptance of our differences [...] [and] accepts the need to define the knowledge, skills and understanding that lead to an international mindset as rigorously as it accepts the need to define the learning outcomes for individual curriculum subjects [...].[14]

From a practical perspective, international schools offer school-leaving qualifications recognized all over the world for university entrance. This is a practical necessity for international school students, many of whom are transient expatriates whose best chance of a coherent education and a school-leaving diploma of international currency is through these schools and the International Baccalaureate (IB) Diploma Programme. The IB is an internationally recognized qualification offered by more than 3,500 schools – although not exclusively by international schools – in over 140 countries,[15] and its credentials remain essentially unchallenged.[16] Despite many international schools across the world sharing aspects of ethos and a qualifications structure, they are very different from each other, and are affected by their host countries and communities as well as their own individual histories and staff and student populations.[17] By their natures they tend to have a diverse student body and staff members from different countries, enhancing their international character, wherever they may be located.

On a regional level, there are also 'European Schools' (and the associated 'European Baccalaureate'), catering for pupils in EU member states. These schools have multilingual curricula and accept children from the international community. The UK European School in Culham, Oxfordshire, for example, founded in 1975 to provide education for the families of people involved with the Joint European Torus (JET) project, has five language sections which offer tuition in the various mother tongues of its pupils: Dutch, English, French, German and Italian.

# Global Citizenship Education

Global Citizenship Education (GCE) explicitly seeks to inculcate in learners an international outlook and a sense of belonging to, and responsibility towards, the global community. In this it shares some of the purposes of the IB, and of the general internationalization of curricula, as outlined above. GCE is sometimes known as global education[18] or, confusingly, international education.[19] It acknowledges the increasingly interconnected nature of nations, and so in that sense is international (i.e. between nations), and also recognizes the importance of a level of responsibility and of governance above and beyond individual countries, at the global level. It can incorporate development education, which focuses on less developed parts of the world. While being integrated into citizenship or civics education in the curricula of many countries, it is also a potential antidote to the nationalistic aims which may underpin these subject areas. In addition to being part of some formal curricula, either as a subject or as a cross-curricular theme, it is further promoted through a number of non-governmental organizations (e.g. Oxfam), adult and community education programmes (e.g. the Development Education Association's 'Global Learning in Action') and formalized networks (e.g. UNESCO's Associated Schools Project Network). GCE can be considered in terms of the knowledge, skills, attitudes, and behaviours it seeks to develop in learners.

On one level, the requisite knowledge for global citizenship includes facts about the world, and a wide understanding of physical and social geography. In England, it also includes a 'core of learning' around the key concepts of citizenship, sustainable development, social justice, values and perceptions, diversity, interdependence, conflict resolution, and human rights.[20] For example, a student should be aware of the contents and implications of the Universal Declaration of Human Rights, should be able to describe the ways in which acting on the environment in one part of the world affects others, and should know how colonial practices of the past have impacted on development in richer and poorer areas of the globe.

In terms of skills, global citizenship learners should, for example, possess the ability to communicate interculturally in an effective manner. Other examples of key skills include the ability to analyse critically, and potentially to challenge their own role and the role of their countries in the international arena, and the ability to explore the nature of conflicts (at all levels) and to provide solutions for their resolution.

It is possible to conceive of a global citizenship education which encourages blind patriotism and xenophobic attitudes, and no doubt there are accidental examples of this. However, GCE is intended to encourage a questioning of such parochial attitudes. Among the attitudes most commonly held to underpin GCE are: empathy for people of other cultures; a sense of social justice; and what Pike and Selby[21] call 'world-mindedness'. Behaviours which enact these values, use these skills, and are informed by this knowledge are also objectives of GCE; examples include shopping as a responsible consumer (including buying Fairtrade products), recycling waste, and lobbying on global justice issues.

GCE implies a core set of values which transcend national boundaries. Interestingly, studies have shown that how GCE is conceptualized and delivered is country-specific.[22] Even in this ostensibly global domain, comparative research illustrates how national and school cultures can mediate in the teaching and learning process. Studies in England and Canada, for example, show how issues such as the prescriptiveness of the curriculum, the attitudes of teachers, and the status of the subject in relation to others in the curriculum all impact on what takes place in GCE classrooms, and on how conservative or radical that version of GCE can be.[23]

# When is educational research international?

Which of the following research scenarios – none of which is explicitly comparative – might we consider to constitute international educational research?

1  A researcher conducting research on educational policy-making outside of his or her own country of residence.

2  A researcher from country A, registered for doctoral studies in country B, conducting fieldwork on adult literacy in country A.

3  A group of Masters students from different national contexts, studying together in country C, collaborating on a project on assessment practices in Country C schools.

4  A researcher from country A, writing about pedagogical practices in country A, publishing in an international journal of pedagogy.

5  A researcher using conceptual or theoretical frameworks, generated from data analysis conducted elsewhere, to analyse educational change in his or her own country. An example would be the application of Bîrzea's[24] model of educational change, arising from analysis of transitions in Eastern Europe, to changes in another country.[25]

6  A group of researchers monitoring global efforts towards the achievement of Education for All around the world.[26]

7  An explication of the impact of globalization on language policy in country D.

8  A study of the cultural aspects of girls' schooling in a developing country.[27]

9  A consultant from a richer country advising a ministry of education in a poorer country on policies for increasing access to schooling.

An inclusive definition of international educational research would incorporate all of the above. In each, a particular educational phenomenon is being examined through a lens which brings an international perspective to the study. We shall discuss the nature of each of these lenses below, and link them to the wider field of international education.

## Insider and outsider research

In the first three cases, the lenses focused on the educational phenomena arise from the researchers' own perspectives. As we have seen in Chapter 1, regardless of whether the aim of the research is comparative, the study of education from an outsider's perspective will inevitably involve implicit comparisons as the researcher's frame of reference is his or her own cultural and educational experience. The outcome may look like broadly descriptive accounts of education policy or practice in a country or region, as in area studies. However, there are methodological issues which need attention in order to control for rigour and quality in the enterprise, no matter how broad a church we might consider international educational research to be. One important methodological consideration is the foregrounding and bracketing of the researcher's assumptions through a process of reflection and comparison. This entails the researcher coming to understand his or her own perspective to the point where its influence on the research process can be controlled, if never eliminated. The processes and outcomes of international research can be enriched by the perspectives of cultural outsiders; equally, they can bring ethnocentric notions about educational norms that can lead to rather biased interpretations. There has been strong advocacy of the combination of insider and outsider perspectives, in order to address this methodological concern and enhance learning on the parts of all researchers involved.[28] Increasingly, individuals also have transnational identities which mean they may be both an insider and an outsider or occupy a space between, owing to their own personal history of migration or international travel and research.

In the second example above, the researcher is examining his or her own national context, but while studying elsewhere. This process is inevitably different from researching one's own education system from a purely insider perspective: the lens has been adjusted through the process of studying in another country. As part of the process of studying abroad – and we would hope this would be part of a student's motivation in doing so – there is exposure to different ways of working in education, as well as opportunities to read works by authors from different national contexts and to compare perspectives with students from other countries. Such experiences 'make the familiar strange'. They have a considerable impact on the fieldwork process, and later work attitudes, as researchers return to their home context. International students would have to resist the comparative impulse, or learn within programmes that isolate individuals and do not invite comparisons, if they manage to maintain their original perspectives on educational issues without beginning to question what they originally perceived as 'normal'.

Similarly, in the third example, even if the research question is not posed in an explicitly comparative manner, the lenses brought to bear upon the question of assessment practices by the students from different countries will result in an international piece of research. By virtue of their educational experiences, they will notice different things, emphasize divergent aspects, find some practices more or less surprising, and possibly approve or disapprove of some characteristics of the system being examined. For example, a student from mainland China might find the emphasis on continuous assessment in the German *Abitur* unusual, while a student from

Canada might be surprised at the importance placed on common examinations and the 'league tabling' of examination results in England. The
process of collaborating on this project is almost certain to generate a more
international piece of work than a similar study by students from within the
country being studied.

In the fourth example, dissemination to an international target audience,
for example through publishing in international journals or giving papers
at international conferences, invites a cumulation of related area studies
and ultimately comparison. The lens of the individual researcher may not
be international, but an international lens will be brought to bear upon it
as referees and other researchers examine and critique the research, and
place it within the comparative context of related cases. Many international
journals would expect some reference to wider international literature, or
the use of international frameworks, to enhance this potential.

# Research employing international frameworks

The next two examples in the list are international in that they employ international frameworks for the research. The first is theoretical or conceptual
in nature, based on models derived from empirical data generated in a
particular context, and the second is based on international goals that have
been multilaterally agreed by a large majority of the world's nations. The
second is also international in that the data used are international.

Some models used in educational research internationally have been
derived from a comparative research process. They have therefore become
the sorts of abstractions referred to in Chapter 1, and have been tested
against a range of contextual realities. Examples of these include models
of transition in education in countries moving from authoritarian systems
to democratic government; in addition to that of Bîrzea, others include
models created by Fullan, and McLeish and others, further elaborated
in Chapter 8.[29] Other examples include Human Capital Theory,[30] which
theorizes the relationship between education and economic development,
and the 'Diploma Disease',[31] which describes and explains the devaluing
of qualifications in a context of increasing uptake of education (these and
other theories will be discussed in Chapter 5 in relation to education in
developing countries). Research which uses these frameworks to study one
or more countries might be considered to be international, especially if the

international nature of the framework is acknowledged and its global applicability explicitly tested as part of the process.

A second kind of international framework for educational research arises from international agreements, such as the commitment to Education for All, the Millennium Development Goals, or the Declaration of the Rights of the Child (see Chapter 5). As with theoretical frameworks, when these form the basis for research they can serve to internationalize even single-country studies.

## Globalization studies

The seventh example above uses globalization as a framework for research into language policy. Globalization has been defined as:

> The growing interdependence and interconnectedness of the modern world through increased flows of goods, services, capital, people and information.[32]

Globalization might be considered just another concept to be used in educational studies, but its current importance justifies its inclusion as a branch of the field of international education research. The phenomenon of globalization has had enormous implications for the fields of comparative education and international education:

> Intensified globalisation, and its implications for the social sciences in general, has recently helped to stimulate both a revitalisation of the field [of comparative and international education] and a widening of interest in international enquiry from the mainstream of educational and broader social science research communities.[33]

Additionally, the phenomenon of globalization and its implications for education internationally has become a subject of research and much discussion in itself. The establishment of a successful journal in this area – *Globalisation, Societies and Education* – and the rapid growth of special interest groups on this theme such as that found in the Comparative and International Education Society of North America illustrate how central this theme has become to international education research.

As the relationship between education and globalization becomes a more prominent dimension of international educational inquiry, understandings of different forms of globalization inform the debates. Economic globalization involves integration of all nations into global economic networks, including poorer countries, although the division of labour and profit tends to favour richer countries inequitably. Political globalization reflects the changing role of the nation-state, with global and local forces pulling in opposing directions. So, on the one hand, countries are joining larger units, such as the EU and the Organisation for Eastern and Southern African Economic Co-operation, but at the same time, smaller units of countries are breaking away from nation-states, as evidenced in the break-up of the former Yugoslavia. Cultural globalization is manifested in changing cultural identities, through, for example: migration and the formation of diaspora, such as the large educated African population living in developed countries; other forms of transnationalism, including migrant students with diverse networks of contacts and diverse cultural interests; post-colonial legacies, such as the prevalence of English as an international language; and hybridization of formerly distinct categories, for example through intermarrying. All of these carry national education policy implications for issues such as language and the rights of indigenous people. They also invite the development of new units of analysis in comparative studies and there has been considerable and important recent work on these themes.[34]

# Education and development studies

The eighth example is situated in the education and development branch of international education. Traditionally, particularly in the UK, the term international education has been strongly associated with the study of education in developing countries, to the point where for some, international education and the study of education in developing countries are synonymous. Several important international frameworks have been generated and employed in this part of the field. A number of universities (e.g. the Institute of Education, University of London, and Harvard University) offer international education Masters degree courses which focus on aspects of education and developing countries, and journals exist which specialize in this area (e.g. the *International Journal of Educational Development*). As in the final example above, international education research in this branch often has a strong applied dimension, through consultancy and other forms of cross-fertilization of ideas. International frameworks are brought to bear on international and local questions of policy and practice.

Key issues, theories, terms, and research in this area will be explored further in the chapter on education and national development (Chapter 5). However, before proceeding to this discussion, it will be useful here to problematize the concept of a developing country – and therefore to problematize this area, or at least this label, as part of the field of international education.

The terms 'developing' country and 'developed' country imply that countries may be classified into one of these two categories.[35] This is a false dichotomy for a number of reasons. A large proportion of the world's nations falls into the category of 'middle-income' countries and do not fit either label. In most countries, there are also relatively developed areas, and other areas which are less developed – and so regions of the same country may fall into different categories. Similarly, there may be vast differences between different ethnic groups, or between men and women. Much also depends on how we define 'development' – some populations which are economically poor may have good systems of health and education (such as Cuba); some or all of the population in other, richer countries may suffer from violence and oppression (such as the Palestinian population living in disputed Israeli territories, or the Roma of Europe), and some relatively wealthy countries may not have a democratic political system (such as Brunei). The UN compiles an annual Human Development Index to combine a number of indicators of development to enable more meaningful comparisons – the result is a continuum of countries from the 2013 number one (Norway) to number 186 (Niger).[36, 37] Such tables allow comparison between countries along with monitoring of progress of individual countries. However, to draw a line somewhere on this continuum and declare those above it to be developed and those below to be developing would be nonsense.

The terms 'developing' and 'developed' themselves suggest that some countries have achieved development while others are still in the process. Any country that would like to improve any aspect of its national wellbeing needs to be considered still 'developing' – that is, all of them. Some writers get around these labels by talking about *development*, or the *developing world*[38] without implicating the nation-state as the primary unit of analysis.

Substitutions for these terms fare little better. Those based on geography, such as south/north or east/west,[39] are simply inaccurate. Australia would then be in the same category as Sierra Leone. Industrialized/non-industrialized or rich/poor suffer from the same problems of dichotomization. The category 'post-colonial' is made problematic by the rare examples of poorer countries never officially colonized (e.g. Thailand), by examples of richer countries that were (e.g. Canada), and by the handful of still-colonized nations (e.g. the Turks and Caicos Islands, a British 'protectorate'). The term 'third world', is also in fairly common usage, but suffers from the same problems of labelling, and creates a questionable hierarchy among countries based on perceived stages of development.[40]

Given that there are educational issues shared by the countries and regions traditionally categorized as 'developing', and that it is such an important part of the field of international education, with some reluctance we will use this term in this book, and focus on these issues in Chapters 4 and 6 – while keeping in mind its weaknesses as a category, term and concept.

# The crux of comparative and international education inquiry: The relationship between the researcher and the researched

We have suggested above that international education research is implicitly comparative. It is so by virtue of the position of the researcher or practitioner in relation to the context being examined. How familiar are they with it? How similar or different from their 'home' context is it? How well equipped are they to learn from similarities and differences?

If we think of the range of possible answers to these questions as continua, the possible dimensions look like this:

Familiar context —————————————————▶ Unfamiliar context

'Context' here can refer to the national context, but regional, local, and institutional contexts may be equally important, as these may vary considerably within countries. Familiarity may come from time spent living and/or working in a given situation. The length of time spent is significant, but other factors may intervene, such as a reflexive approach to experience, or whether language difference is an issue. Additionally, there is much that researchers can do in terms of familiarizing themselves with an environment in advance of fieldwork, by reading primary and secondary sources and/or discussing the context with key informants, in order to enhance their depth of understanding.

Another significant factor in the researcher's perspective is the extent to which the context under study is similar to the researcher's own.

Similar to home culture ───────────► Different from home culture

The degree of similarity or difference may be related to cultural patterns, including language, traditions, and gender relationships. Differences in any major indicators of development between the home and study context are also likely to be significant. Someone from an industrialized country will find a poor, agrarian context very different; a researcher used to an authoritarian government will require adjustment to a liberal democracy.

If we combine these continua into a matrix, a typology is created of four different research circumstances in the four quadrants.

In the first quadrant, where the research context is both familiar and similar to the researcher's home context, the research process is likely to be relatively straightforward. The extreme case is 'international' research conducted by researchers in their own contexts, informed by international frameworks or a comparative perspective.

In the second quadrant, the context being studied is similar to what the researcher is most accustomed to, but is new to the researcher. This situation has the advantage that the similarities may facilitate interpretation of the new data: linguistic and cultural similarities, for example, may serve to highlight small but significant differences, and may make the researcher more at ease and able to understand what is going on. The dangers are twofold: firstly, small differences can be highlighted insofar as the extent of similarity will be neglected. For example, in classroom observation, what inevitably stands out to observers is what is perceived as unusual;

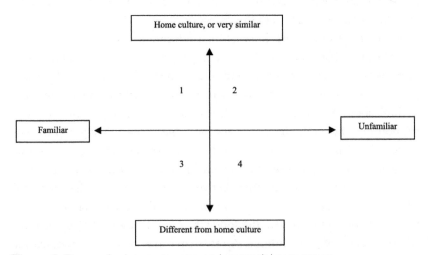

**Figure 6** Research circumstances and potential responses

much of what is happening may be overlooked because of the attraction of minor differences. The second danger is that the researcher might project familiar explanations on to the new context. The researcher can be lulled into thinking that situations that appear similar superficially are the same. An example might be the existence of subject areas with the same names, but which in reality have different emphases and purposes. 'Citizenship education', for example, in one context may be content-driven, with an emphasis on learning by rote the national structures of governance and law; a subject with the same name within another national curriculum may emphasize a more active and radical citizenship, where critical analysis and intercultural communication are developed as skills, and questioning attitudes to government policies are inculcated.

In the third quadrant, the researcher has a depth of understanding of a context which is very different from his or her own. The classic example is of the academic who becomes an expert on education in one specific country or a region. Such a researcher gains depth of expertise, an obvious advantage; for better or worse, the context can become almost as familiar as the home situation. The challenge for this researcher may be to produce reports which sufficiently contextualize the research findings for the less initiated: the strange may become too familiar. The final category, where the researcher is working in an educational context both unfamiliar and very different from the home culture, invites culture shock. The value of this situation is this very novelty, which can potentially heighten sensitivity. However, data can be difficult to interpret and the exoticism of the context may be unduly emphasized in the outcomes of the research. Historically, 'travellers' tales' would fit into this category.

All four quadrants are international education research milieux and describe international researchers, yet they represent very different relationships between the researcher and the context, and lead to divergent processes and likely outcomes. Researchers could use this matrix reflexively to think about themselves, or in evaluating studies by mapping out different relationships between the researcher and the context being researched: more or less familiar, more or less similar to the researchers' 'home' context. These may have implications for the reliability and validity of any research.

In considering the relationship between comparative and international education, and the nature of the comparative and international researcher, we might add to this matrix the following considerations, based again on an intersection of two continua. A researcher may accrue the material for a comparative perspective through experiencing a number of different contexts. We might thus classify researchers as being more or less well informed in terms of their range of experiences. The more contexts researchers have experienced and investigated, the wider their comparative perspectives may be, as they can draw on a wider repertoire of observations, phenomena and explanations. At one extreme, a researcher could have experienced only one education context in his or her own birthplace. At the other extreme, we find experienced educationists who have learned, taught or researched in a divergent range of contexts, potentially resulting in a comparative perspective. The two extremes generate the continuum below, and all international researchers would fit somewhere along the line.

Monocultural perspective ⎯⎯⎯⎯⎯⎯⎯▶ Comparative perspective

As desirable as a comparative perspective may be, it is a necessary but not sufficient precondition for successful international research. Just as there are teachers with 20 years of experience who, in reality, have one year of experience repeated 20 times, there are unfortunate examples of experienced international education researchers or consultants, who, despite possessing the raw ingredients of a comparative perspective, have managed to preserve an ethnocentric or single-solution outlook. Apart from research skills, a major factor in this is the intercultural competence of the researcher. This, too, is a question of degree, ranging from the unskilled to the highly skilled.

Interculturally unskilled ⎯⎯⎯⎯⎯⎯⎯▶ Interculturally highly skilled

Drawing on the work of Alred[41] and Byram,[42] we might argue that skills contributing to intercultural competence include the following: critical reflection on one's own culture; curiosity about other cultures; empathy for people from other cultures; linguistic skills; and analytical awareness that allows understanding beyond superficial representations. These may develop through experience of other cultures – but not necessarily.

If we combine these two continua, we can create the matrix in Figure 7 (see page 70).

The resulting categories range from the ideal international researcher who is interculturally competent and possesses enough experience to have a sound comparative perspective (2), to the monocultural researcher possessing no intercultural skills (extreme of 3). Category 1 researchers have more potential than experience, and may be able to extract meaning effectively from subjects very different from themselves, and write empathetically

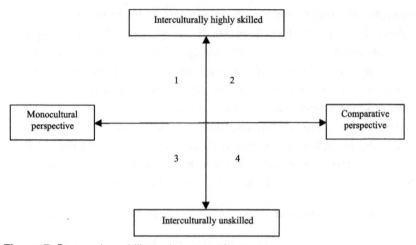

**Figure 7** Researcher skills and perspectives

about them. In contrast, category 4 researchers may not be able to gather data that reflect the insider reality of other cultures, and are likely to be ethnocentric in their analysis, no matter how much experience they have had.

There are, of course, other factors which affect the research process when conducted internationally, such as the rigour of the research and the nature of the informants in the process. However, these two matrices introduce some important dimensions of the relationship between the researcher and the researched in such studies, and may also reinforce the importance of the relationship between comparison and internationalism. They also suggest a relationship between international domains of practice in education and international research, as the sorts of intercultural and self-questioning skills demanded of the international researcher can be developed through 'international pedagogy'. The Indian poet Rabindranath Tagore made intriguing reference to the power that comes from learning to be international in outlook: 'This Giant-Killer, the international mind – though small in size – is real'.[43]

# International education – weakness in ambiguity, or strength in diversity?

We have here been very inclusive in how international education is interpreted, in both its research and applied dimensions. We see no reason not to be; no writer has a monopoly on how the phrase may be used. Within comparative and international education as a field, there have been long debates about its nature and status, and efforts to pin down clear parameters of where it begins and ends. It might be argued that these vague boundaries are a weakness, and have encouraged something of an identity crisis within the field. From a quite different perspective, in interview, the late Edmund King compared the field to other, more established disciplines:

> Suppose you take another field, say animal biology. Some people will classify all the animals into various types, invertebrates and so on. I have no problem with people specialising in, say, worms. But other biologists will be ecologists, and others will be concerned with the physiology of the animals. All that's necessary to say is that my investigation is partial, and leave the rest.[44]

In the same interview, he noted the importance of the field's ability to respond to changes in the wider environment, to be what he called 'ecological'.

The frontiers delineated here are wide and permeable, and unapologetically so. However, unthinking use of any terms should be avoided. When working within these domains, reflection is to be encouraged on which particular meaning of international education is being evoked. The categories delineated in this chapter may be helpful for that purpose.

# Notes

1. Crossley and Watson, *Comparative and International Research in Education.*
2. Schriewer, *Reconceptualising the Local/Global Nexus.*
3. Baker and LeTendre, *National Differences, Global Similarities.*
4. OECD, *How many students study abroad?*
5. Windham, 'Overview and Main Conclusions', p. 8.
6. Ibid., p. 13.

7. 'Joint Declaration of the European Ministers of Education convened in Bologna on the 19th of June 1999'.
8. 'Socrates-ERASMUS: The European Community Programme in Higher Education'.
9. Van der Wende, 'Internationalising the curriculum'.
10. Kerr, 'The internationalisation of learning', p. 18.
11. Sylvester, 'The first international school'.
12. Hayden and Thompson, 'International schools and international education'.
13. Hill, 'The history of international education', and Skelton, 'Deining "international" in an international curriculum'.
14. Skelton, 'Defining "international" in an international curriculum', p. 53.
15. http://www.ibo.org/school/
16. Garton, 'International schools and their wider community'.
17. Ibid.
18. Examples are Pike and Selby, *Global Teacher, Global Learner*, and Tye, *Global Education*.
19. For example, Scottish Executive, *Think Global, Act Local*.
20. DfEE, *Developing a Global Dimension*.
21. Pike and Selby, *Global Teacher, Global Learner*.
22. Pike, 'Re-evaluating global education'.
23. Schweisfurth, 'Education for Global Citizenship: Teacher agency and curricular structure', and Yamashita, 'Global citizenship education and war'.
24. Bîrzea, *Educational Politics of Countries in Transition*.
25. Polyzoi and Cerna, 'Educational change in the Czech Republic'.
26. See UNESCO 2002 and 2004, *EFA Global Monitoring Report*.
27. For example, Stephens, *Girls and Basic Education*.
28. For example, Choksi and Dyer, 'North-South collaboration'.
29. Fullan, 'The emergence of a conceptual framework', and McLeish and Phillips, *Processes of Transition in Education Systems*.
30. Schultz, 'Investment in Human Capital'.
31. Dore, *Diploma Disease*.
32. Tikly et al., 'Globalisation and Skills'.
33. Crossley, 'Bridging cultures and traditions in comparative and international education'.
34. For a succinct review and list of references in relation to globalisation, see Tikly et al., *Globalisation and Skills for Development*. Recent work on units of analysis includes for example Robertson, Bonal and Dale, GATS and the education service industry, and Ozga and Lingard, Globalisation, Education Policy and Politics.
35. See, for example, Harber and Davies, *School Management and*

*Effectiveness in Developing Countries* and Crossley and Vulliamy, *Qualitative Research in Developing Countries*.

36. UNDP, *Human Development Report 2013*. The report divides nations into four categories of human development: very high, high, medium, and low, and also adjusts the HDI for equality.

37. These examples were contemporary at the time of writing but we acknowledge that their status as useful illustrations may change.

38. For example, Hallak, *Investing in the Future: Setting educational priorities in the Developing World*, and Graham-Brown, *Education in the Developing World*, and the UKFIET (United Kingdom Forum for International Education and Training) Oxford Conference on Education and Development (www.cfbt.com/oxford conference).

39. For example, Buchert, *Education Reform in the South*, and Epskamp, *Education in the South*.

40. For example, the following quotations: '... During the 1980s in much of the Third World agricultural production stagnated or even declined' (Samoff, *Coping with Crisis*, p. 5); '... It is the purpose of the *International Journal of Educational Development* to bring these developments to the attention of professionals in the field of education, with particular focus upon issues and problems of concern to those in the Third World' (*International Journal of Educational Development*, Aims and Scope).

41. Alred, 'Becoming a better stranger'.

42. Byram, 'On being bicultural and intercultural'.

43. Tagore in Murray and Tagore, 'East–West understanding'.

44. Interview with Edmund King by Michele Schweisfurth, 1996.

# 5

# Education and National Development: An Introduction to Key Ideas and Questions

So development is for Man, by Man, and of Man. The same is true of education. Its purpose is the liberation of Man from the restraints and limitations of ignorance and dependency. Education has to increase men's physical and mental freedom to increase their control over themselves, their own lives, the environment in which they live.

*Julius Nyerere*[1]

Education is a weapon, whose effects depend on who holds it in his hand and at whom it is aimed.

*Joseph Stalin*[2]

The study of the relationship between education and development has long been an important dimension of comparative and international education. In fact, as we have seen, the term 'international education' has at times been used to delineate that part of the field devoted to education in the developing world. Within this area of inquiry, a number of important theories linked to the broader field of development studies have been developed.

Underpinning the existence of this sub-field is the assumption that there is a positive relationship between an educated population and national development in all its forms, and that education can be used as a 'weapon' against poverty and other forms of underdevelopment. Education is seen as contributing to the public good, and therefore as deserving of the allocation of public investment, and in need of public control. This ideological stance needs to be unpacked. What do we mean by development? Who should define what we mean by progress, and what power issues are at stake? In what ways can education contribute to the development process? What kind of education is likely to do this? What theories help to explain these intersections of education, development, and power? The quotations above suggest two very different purposes for education. Note also the gendered language of both of the famous men cited, as a reminder of the changing discourses and hegemonies around these questions over time.

These questions are of academic interest, but in application their resolution has literally life or death implications for people in poorer parts of the world. Research findings and theories generated within different branches of the education and development sub-field feed into the policy process at many levels. Perhaps the most significant of these is the international 'business' of aid to education, which is both a consumer and a producer of educational research linked to development and developing countries.

This chapter serves as a general introduction to key theories and debates concerning the nature of the link between education and national development. It is necessarily brief, but it seeks to ask questions as well as to map some of the major landmarks of the field. A few of these questions will be explored further in Chapter 7, which examines research perspectives on education in developing countries, as well as some of the practical issues of this kind of research. As we stated in the Introduction, we will concentrate primarily (but not exclusively) on issues related to formal schooling rather than the diverse world of out-of-school and adult education. This is by no means to suggest these latter areas are less significant.

The dichotomization of developing versus developed countries has already been problematized in Chapter 4. Throughout this chapter, the reader should keep this dilemma in mind: it is extremely difficult to discuss this topic without falling into the trap of dividing the world into two along these highly questionable lines, but this sub-field is sufficiently significant that the special issues of education in developing countries and regions need to be explored. It is important to note that the observations and theories pertaining to development discussed here are of significance to all nations, less or more developed, although the nature of that significance may vary. How investment in education may lead to national economic growth, for example, is a process that all governments would dearly love to control. However, for a more developed country at one end of the spectrum, the United States or United Kingdom for example, the main concern may be a matter of its own national policy on access to higher education, with a view to fuelling growth in highly skilled employment in post-industrial sectors. In contrast, for a less developed country, towards the other end of the spectrum, including most states in Sub-Saharan Africa for example, the focus may be on negotiations with aid donor agencies on how to increase access to primary school, in line with global pressures regarding Education for All, in order to raise basic standards of literacy in the majority of the population, with the reduction of poverty as a primary goal. Increasingly, as primary enrolments increase, the next stages of education, particularly lower secondary schooling, come into focus of attention.

While individuals feel the impact of development, it is generally analysed as a phenomenon for the common national good and as a goal for governments to pursue through their own policies (sometimes in partnership with international donors). This discussion therefore uses the nation-state as the main unit of development. This, of course, is also problematic. As we have noted before, there are pockets of relative wealth and privilege in under-developed countries, and pockets of poverty and social deprivation in the wealthiest states. Using the examples cited above: in the UK and US, parts of the population are known to be functionally illiterate and living in poverty, and the likelihood is that children from this group, while not denied access to schooling in basic terms, are underachieving or unable to engage with school.[3] The preoccupation with widening access to higher education is of marginal significance to these members of society. Meanwhile, in Sub-Saharan Africa, where access to basic education has improved for the majority, for the poorest it remains elusive,[4] but a small elite can afford to send their children to study in the private schools and universities of the UK and US.

A further weakness of using the nation-state as the unit of analysis is evident in the phenomenon of globalization. As the world figuratively becomes smaller, the policies and development successes and failures of each nation depend more and more on those of other states. The impact of changes on national or aid policy on individual countries becomes more and more dependent on global connections and flows of trade and aid: 87 per cent of developing countries are categorized as 'globally integrated'.[5] Despite these caveats, both development and education still largely matter for the state, and so it is national development which we will address in the main.

We begin by interrogating the nature of development, setting out its economic and social dimensions as a framework, and looking at various indicators of development and their implications for education. We then introduce a number of key theories and concepts that are used within the sub-field of education and development, along with their main critiques. The next section briefly examines issues in aid to education, and how the theories and assumptions discussed help to drive policy. Finally, basic education – currently a major international driver and indicator of development of all kinds, and an important part of national and aid policies – is examined as a case study which brings together many of these definitions, theories and goals.

# What is development?

How we define development has significant implications for how we conceptualize the role of education within it, and how policy might be shaped in order to achieve development goals. How developed or under-developed a country is judged to be depends on the indicators used to measure this; therefore the selection of indicators is a key aspect of the study of development, and a value-laden one. If we decide that development is about increased wealth and growth generated within the economy, we will set indicators to measure this, such as those used to calculate gross national product, and monitor changes accordingly. On the other hand, if we think development is about people feeling that they can trust their neighbours, our indicators will reflect this, and data on feelings of trust will be gathered, analysed, and compared in order to inform policy. Both of these are examples of factors that most people would consider important for the public good, but, as indicators, one is in common usage, one is very rare. Development, like poverty, is experienced subjectively and so means different things to different people,[6] but the drive at national and international levels to control, manage and cultivate it belie this. Indicators which are most measurable and which are used by powerful players such as the World Bank are likely to be taken seriously, which helps to explain why economic goals for development have been dominant.

In order to understand development, it may be helpful to consider what we mean by underdevelopment, and its implications for education. Harber and Davies[7] distinguish between six different dimensions of the education context in developing countries:

- The demographic context. Demographic trends such as high birth rates, high teenage pregnancy rates, and rural–urban migration contribute to problems in the provision of schooling, and enrolment and retention rates.

- The economic context. A range of economic stringencies affect developing nations' capacities to offer sufficient education of high quality. These include low income, structural adjustment (see below), and vulnerability to changes in international markets.
- The resource context. Low levels of expenditure resulting from economic difficulties affect human and material resources in schools. A shortage of funds to pay teachers, for example, impacts on pupil: teacher ratios (PTR), levels of qualification, teacher shortages, and teachers taking second or third jobs. It is not uncommon in classrooms in poor communities to find whole classes sharing one or two textbooks.
- The context of violence. Developing countries are more likely to be affected by war and violent unrest. This has devastating effects on the continuity of schooling, on the physical and psychological well-being of teachers and learners, and on the culture of teaching and learning in schools.
- The health context. Poverty makes citizens much more vulnerable to illnesses, including water-borne and other infectious diseases, and malnutrition. Even mild hunger or a poorly-balanced diet can affect children's capacity to learn. Of particular concern at this time is the prevalence of HIV/AIDS, the consequences of which have been horrendous in the most affected countries, where more than a quarter of adults are infected.[8] The presence of AIDS orphans and infected children, and the loss of a large part of the teaching population, are among the issues affecting schools.
- The cultural context. The developing world represents a massive diversity of countries, and these clearly do not share cultural beliefs, but they do tend to hold a mixture of traditional (mainly indigenous) and modern (mainly imported) values. The co-existence of these factors may affect schools in a range of ways, including attitudes to the education of girls, and the interruption of schooling for initiation rites.

Goals for development will here be clustered into two very broad categories: economic and social. Clearly there is considerable overlap between these categories, and causal relationships may exist: greater economic development may facilitate the achievement of social goals, such as improved health, for example. In turn, a healthier population can fuel economic growth. Additionally, how these forms of development are manifested is partly determined by the political development underpinning them in a given country. Economic development takes on very different forms in capitalist societies as compared to those with socialist policies; social development is unlikely to be prioritized in the same way under authoritarian regimes as it is in a democracy.[9]

# Economic development

'Both theoretically and empirically the notion of economic growth has been at the heart of development thinking and has dominated policy and research at national and international levels'.[10] Thirty years have passed since this was written; since then the emphasis on different aspects of development has become more balanced, but the hegemony of economic discourses within development studies and its educational branches largely prevails. Indicators used in assessing the economic development of a country include per capita gross national product, percentage of people existing below the poverty line, and unemployment statistics.

While economic development is not a linear phenomenon, until recent years most industrialized countries have enjoyed sustained periods of economic growth, as evidenced by increases in per capita income. They are also marked by a growth in non-farming sectors of the economy, including industry and, increasingly post-industrial, 'knowledge economy' sectors, an exponential growth in the use of transport and communications technology, and an attendant increase in energy consumption. There are more telephones, televisions, and computers in use; more newspapers read; and more cars on a better developed road infrastructure. Countries at the poorer end of the economic development spectrum tend to be agrarian in nature (i.e. having farming as the base of the economy). Since the end of the colonial period, such countries have in the main experienced very inconsistent periods of growth and recession, compounded by their dependence on fickle and self-interested western markets for their goods, and by the economic policies of international bodies such as the World Bank and the International Monetary Fund (IMF).

One policy which has had enormous impact on the economies of developing countries, and on their educational provision, is structural adjustment. Structural adjustment is an extensive economic reorganization, whose aim is to:

> ... overcome economic crisis and imbalance caused by internal or external shocks and past mismanagement of the economy [...] The *immediate objective* of structural adjustment policies is to restore balance in the country's income and expenditure (fiscal) account and in the trade account. The *longer term objectives* are to improve resource allocation, economic incentives (i.e. prices, wages and salaries) and to increase competition in the market by reducing or eliminating protectionism and factors that tend towards market distortions.[11]

Such policies were often prescribed by the World Bank or IMF as a condition for provision of assistance, and are a shock treatment whose value has been questioned. Part of the agenda often includes reduced public expenditure, reduced subsidies, user charges for public services, and privatization: all of which have enormous implications for the provision of education.[12]

There is a strong correlation between education and economic development. The more economically developed a nation is, generally speaking, the more educationally developed it will be, with increased levels of literacy and a higher average level of qualifications. The question is: which comes first? Human capital theory (see below) posits that investment in education creates a workforce able to drive economic growth. On the other hand, it is clear that a country able to afford high-quality mass education is also able to sustain the economic growth which facilitated educational expansion in the first place. In contrast, poor countries which face economic and resource stringencies have schools such as these described from the Zambian context.

> Classrooms are overcrowded; teachers are overworked and underpaid, sometimes not paid at all for months on end; the books used in classrooms are often long out of date, and not enough to go around [...] and the school equipment and buildings are in such a state of neglect, due to lack of funds for maintenance and repair, that even the most basic functions, such as keeping out inclement weather, have been severely compromised. For long periods of time, students and teachers have to go without the most rudimentary of classroom learning tools such as paper, pencils and chalk [...] That any kind of learning takes place in such circumstances is a miracle in itself.[13]

The average PTR internationally in 2011 ranged from six (San Marino) to 81 (Central African Republic),[14] with strong correlations between poverty and a high PTR. Bear in mind that these averages can mask extremes – such as up to 200 in Sub-Saharan African contexts of poverty and rapid enrolment growth.[15] Additionally, teachers' salaries in developing countries have declined in real terms – a situation which affects morale and forces many teachers to take second jobs. Under these conditions, whatever efforts individuals may make to use human and material resources to facilitate learning, education is in a poor position to develop the skills and attitudes in the population that can lead to successful participation in an increasingly sophisticated labour market. In many such countries, in order to meet increasing demand for schooling while controlling public spending, government policy has demanded community input into the funding of local schools – although communities can ill afford to contribute. In some contexts, such as India, there has been an attendant growth in private education, with some providers offering a low-fee, reasonable quality alternative to state-funded schools. The savings to government, mixed outcomes, and mixed models regarding private schooling make it an increasingly intriguing policy option with old public vs private polarized understandings breaking down.[16]

Critics of the 'development as economic growth' school of thought include those concerned with the sustainability of infinite economic growth and its effects on the environment. Tellingly, among the indices of economic development of a country are those measuring use of communications and transportation technology, industrialization and urbanization. The implication of some of this is that the more economically developed a nation is, the more likely its population is to do harm to the environment. With energy consumption as an indicator of economic development, in a world of dwindling energy resources, dangerous levels of pollution and global warming, ever-increasing development of this kind could have disastrous repercussions. A second major critique notes that the benefits of economic growth are rarely felt evenly throughout a country. To varying degrees, in every country there are geographic, ethnic, religious, and gender divides which demarcate the 'haves' from the 'have-nots'. A fiscal policy concerned with economic growth and its attendant capitalist underpinnings sits uncomfortably with the sorts of redistribution or equity-enhancing policies necessary for the benefits of economic development to be experienced justly by all citizens. Despite their prominence in the discourse of development, it is widely acknowledged that to limit analyses of development strictly to questions of economic growth and productivity is a reductionist approach which belies the importance of social and political parameters.

# Social development

Beyond purely economic analyses of development are a cluster of goals which could broadly be categorized as social development. Social development as a goal emphasizes the improvement of quality of life through focusing on improvements to social factors of well-being such as health, law and order, stability and security, and social cohesion. Furthermore, it can incorporate broader issues of equality and social justice as goals and indicators of development. Equality is about the distribution of goods and opportunities among individuals. Ideally, each individual would have equal access to resources, but the compromise position is to emphasize that the variation between social strata should be reduced.[17] Concern for equality and social development generally can be seen as independent of concern for economic development, but they are in many ways complementary.

Indicators that fall within this category might include some of the following: rates of crime; numbers of refugees and armaments; doctors per capita; female participation in the public sphere, including schooling; and the Gini coefficient,[18] which measures the gap between rich and poor in a country.

Education is seen as a vehicle to promote social development. It has the potential to do this through direct instruction, for example through science lessons on HIV/AIDS. Where due attention is paid to equity in access to schooling, it has the potential to even out disparities and promote equality. It can also shape attitudes through the modelling of desired outcomes. For example, where greater female participation is desired among the population in general, schools can model this through the equitable treatment of women and girls. This could be in terms of promotion possibilities for female teachers, creating role models, and through opportunities for girls to participate successfully in learning activities. Of course, as theories discussed below suggest, schooling can also do the opposite: reinforcing the status quo, or even encouraging the sorts of attitudes and behaviours that are antithetical to social development.

As an example of the contribution of education to social goals of development, there is considerable evidence that an educated population, particularly an educated female population, is a healthier one. Consider the following claims:[19]

- Educated mothers have smaller families, using contraception to space pregnancies. This reduces maternal and infant mortality, and increases investment in the health of the smaller number of individual children.

It also reduces overall population growth rates, facilitating economic development.

- The greatest number of deaths among children is caused by preventable diseases, and ignorance of prevention and simple methods of treatment (such as oral rehydration therapy) is a major contributing factor.
- UNICEF studies have shown that education about basic health information could halve the rate of childhood malnutrition.

Female education is of course not just about educating mothers, but also about human rights and empowerment, as writers such as Stromquist, Kelly, Unterhalter, Leach and others have argued. Education as a right in itself (see Chapter 7) dictates attention to the equal participation of girls and where access for them is most restricted this reflects and exacerbates their lack of agency and social position – and vice versa. Beyond access, the empowerment agenda demands equal opportunities to achieve, gender analysis of curriculum and pedagogical processes, and a supportive environment safe from exploitation and the threat of violence.

# Holistic approaches

The human development paradigm embraces elements of all of the above perspectives, while putting people at the centre of its concerns.

According to one view, development is a process of economic growth, a rapid and sustained expansion of production, productivity and income per head (sometimes qualified by insistence on a wide spread of the benefits of this growth). According to the other, espoused by UNDP [United Nations Development Programme]'s annual *Human Development Report* and by many distinguished economists, development is seen as a process that enhances the effective freedom of the people involved to pursue whatever they have reason to value. This view of human development (in contrast to narrowly economic development) is a culturally conditioned view of economic and human progress. Poverty, in this view, implies not only lack of essential goods and services, but also lack of opportunities to choose a fuller, more satisfying, more valuable and valued existence. The choice can also be for a different style of development, a different path, based on different values from those of the highest income countries.[20]

The four pillars of human development are equity, sustainability, productivity and empowerment.[21] The Human Development Index (HDI) employed by the UNDP uses a wide range of indicators, both economic and social, to compare and rank the level of human development within countries. The main indicators since 2010 include life expectancy; combined primary, years and expected years of schooling; and gross national income adjusted for purchasing power. Note the prevalence of indicators related to education. The UNDP also monitors a diverse range of aspects of human development, including access to clean water; percentage of population living on low incomes; fertility rates; public health expenditure; people living with HIV/ AIDS; scientists and engineers in research and development; inequality measures between rich and poor in the country; unemployment; flows of aid; women's political participation; military spending; voter turnout; and the status of human rights conventions, among many others. The good news is that 40 developing countries have recently experienced unpredictably high HDI gains, along a range of indicators including reduced inequalities. A formula for how this was achieved, however, remains elusive, although increased public spending is one element.[22]

Within this human development paradigm, two particular approaches emerge: development as human rights, and development as freedom. The Declaration of Human Rights, adopted by the UN General Assembly in 1948, sets out a list of fundamental entitlements common to people in all contexts. These include, for example, for everyone, without discrimination: freedom from torture and slavery; freedom of movement; access to public services; right to work and to equal pay for that work; and the right to a free basic education.

> Human rights and human development are both about securing basic freedoms. Human rights express the bold idea that all people have claims to social arrangements that protect them from the worst abuses and deprivations – and that secure freedom for a life of dignity [...] When human development and human rights advance together, they reinforce one another – expanding people's capabilities and protecting their rights and fundamental freedoms [...] In short, human development is essential for realizing rights, and human rights are essential for full human development.[23]

In *Development as Freedom*,[24] Amartya Sen sets out powerful arguments showing how economic development is only truly possible in a context of human freedom from oppression, while also arguing that a nation can only be judged to be developed if citizens are able to exercise freedom. Thus, freedom is both the means and the end to development. He points out, for example, that there has never been a famine in a democratic country, showing that where governments are accountable to citizens they have the will and capacity to intervene in ways that prevent the worst kinds of poverty. Increasingly, research evidence and rights based arguments align in emphasizing the importance of voice and agency among the poor in facilitating development of all kinds.[25]

# Theoretical links between education and development

Education is perceived as a key social institution that can affect the values and behaviours of individuals, shaping the citizens and workforce of the future, and therefore impacting on national development. This process has been theorized in different ways in the post-Second World War era. Some of the dominant theories are briefly discussed here.

## Human capital theory

Human capital theory has its origins in the work of Adam Smith in the eighteenth century,[26] but more recently it has come into prominence starting with Theodore Schultz's analysis of the effects of education on development in the 1960s.[27] The basic premise of the theory is that investing in human beings is a way of increasing the overall economic productivity of a nation. Education is assumed to be a good means of doing this, instilling skills, knowledge, and motivations for economic productivity. This contributes to the wealth of individuals, leading to higher wages and salaries, for example, and, in agrarian societies, more efficient farming techniques. The whole nation's economic development is then seen to be dependent upon these skills, knowledge, and motivations for productive behaviours in the whole population. People with higher personal wealth also spend more – contributing further to overall economic growth.

Education is believed to be a sound investment both for the individual and the nation. Traditional rates of return analysis differentiates between these two beneficiaries, specifying individual and social rates of return for investment in education. While individuals benefit from education at all levels, overall, the higher the level of education, the greater the proportionate benefit to the individual, while at the lower end, the social returns are at their highest. Thus, public investment in primary education through taxation benefits everyone by increasing literacy and thereby improving socially beneficial factors such as health and basic productivity. On the other hand, tertiary education, which brings high returns to the individual, through the potential for securing high-paying employment, tends to be perceived as a sector less deserving of high levels of public expenditure, with greater cost-sharing by the ultimate beneficiary, the individual.[28] Critics of human capital theory[29] focus on the one hand on the problems of establishing cause and effect. If someone earns a higher salary, the theory is that this is in direct correlation to their productivity and their education: a perfect fit between education and the labour market. However, there are other reasons why they may be so blessed: their own family and personal connections, for example; or a tendency in society to discriminate in this person's favour, perhaps because of their race or gender. Likewise, at the level of the state, the direction of causality is methodologically difficult to establish. While there is a clear correlation between an educated population and economic development, it could equally be that economic development facilitates public and private investment in education, rather than the other way around. Many poorer countries, South Africa being a good example, actually spend a higher proportion of their government budget on education than many developed countries, but many of these same countries are marked by chronic unemployment and low – or even negative – rates of growth. These problems may not be of their own making – international markets, for example, may be to blame – and purposeful investment may not be able to control them.

'Screening theory' introduces another cause and effect conundrum into the human capital critique. It suggests that the main purpose of schools is not to instil the requisite skills for productivity. Rather, they measure – often through examinations between phases of the system – what is already present in an individual and bar from the next phase those people who are not deemed right for the highest qualifications and the best jobs. Hurdles at the end or beginning of each new phase of schooling serve to identify the winners and take the weaker candidates out of the race.

Another key critique of human capital theory comes in the form of what Ronald Dore[30] called 'the diploma disease'. When the value of education is perceived as high by a given population, people strive to attain the top qualifications they can. Of course, once most of a country's population has a particular qualification, that qualification loses much of its cachet, and no longer guarantees a good job. In a country where few people have a secondary school diploma, one might expect to get a management job in a bank by completing secondary school. In a country where almost everyone has one, employers might demand such qualifications before considering people as bus drivers. Dore uses the example of India, where mass education was introduced and taken up at great pace, to illustrate these issues. Qualification escalation becomes certificate devaluation – again confounding the link between education and wealth.

# Modernization theory

Modernization theory, which was a particularly popular perspective in the 1970s, is based on the premise that development is conditional upon members of a society holding 'modern' values. The prevalence of these values facilitates working behaviours and personal priorities that allow industrialization and economic growth to take place. 'Modern' values are seen to be substantively different from 'traditional' values. Examples of these, based on ideas developed and studied comparatively by McLelland[31] and Inkeles and Smith,[32] include the following:

**Figure 8** Traditional versus modern values

| Traditional values | Modern values |
| --- | --- |
| Fatalism | Sense of control over one's destiny<br>Motivation to work for success |
| Deep respect for traditional authority | Respect for evidence |
| Flexible approach to time | Punctuality |
| Conservatism – desire for a homogeneous society and little desire for change | Acceptance of diversity and change |
| Particularism – belief that one should treat people in one's inner circle differently from other people | Universalism – belief that everyone should be treated according to a set of principles |

Schooling is seen to inculcate modern values in learners by virtue of the 'hidden curriculum' that is an integral part of the bureaucratic nature of school routines:

> School stops and starts at fixed times each day. Within the school day there is generally a regular sequence for ordering activities: singing, reading, writing, drawing, all have their scheduled and usually invariant times. Teachers

generally work according to this plan, a pattern they are rather rigorously taught at normal school. The pupils may have no direct knowledge of the plan, but its influence palpably pervades the course of their work through school day and school year. Thus, principles directly embedded in the daily routine of the school teach the value of planning ahead and the importance of maintaining a regular schedule.[33]

Critiques of modernization theory include the obvious fact that it uses values currently dominant in western industrial societies as a model for traditional societies to follow, leading to charges of ethnocentrism. The correlation between modern values and economic development is extended to causation: such societies are seen to be developed – and therefore to be imitated – because of their modernity. But which comes first – modern values or industrialization? Is this the only route to economic development, or can respect for existing cultural values be upheld in a development process qualitatively different from that which has taken place in industrialized nations?

The traditional/modern dichotomy also belies the contemporary reality of less developed countries. Institutions based on modern values – such as schools – exist throughout the developing world, but the values embedded in them do not simply replace long-standing traditional ones. Rather, the two co-exist, not always harmoniously. Riggs[34] refers to such societies as 'prismatic', where post-colonial and indigenous values exist side-by-side in the same culture and in organizations. Harber and Davies[35] cite a number of examples from schools, such as teachers who are obligated by family and community ties to favour certain students, or headteachers required to leave their duties constantly to attend all weddings and funerals that take place in the community.

Dependency theory offers a further critique of the human capital and modernization perspectives by locating the reasons for underdevelopment in the exploitation of poorer nations by the rich. Richer northern countries control world markets and the means of production and use these to benefit their own economies at the expense of the south, for example, by buying raw materials at very low prices for conversion to expensive goods by northern-based multinational corporations. Modernization or human capital investment would not be able to have an impact on development, because this would alter the balance of power, and this is not in the interests of the rich.

# Liberation theory, conscientization, and the capability approach

Liberation theory prioritizes the moral obligation to side with the oppressed of the world, and to seek development through freedom from this domination. Education can play a role in oppression, by dulling minds and reinforcing the status quo. Freire[36] labelled this approach the 'banking' concept of education:

> The teacher talks about reality as if it were motionless, static, compartmentalized and predictable. Or else he expounds on a topic completely alien to the existential experience of the students. His task is to 'fill' the students with the contents of his narration – contents which are detached from reality, disconnected from the totality that engendered them and could give them significance. Words are emptied of their concreteness and become a hollow, alienated and alienating verbosity [...] Narration (with the teacher as narrator) leads the students to memorize mechanically the narrated content. Worse still, it turns them into 'containers', into receptacles to be filled by the teacher [...] The capacity of banking education to minimize or annul the students' creative power and to stimulate their credulity serves the interests of the oppressors, who care neither to have the world revealed, nor to see it transformed.[37]

Equally, the right kind of education can serve to 'conscientize' the oppressed, giving them the opportunity and skills of analysis, through dialogic approaches to learning, to awaken critical consciousness and ultimately to reconstruct society. Freire focused on adult education, and indeed his approaches have been very influential in shaping approaches to adult learning in developing countries, including the 'REFLECT' literacy programme practised by the NGO ActionAid in communities in developing countries. This programme is based on core elements which include democratic space, grounding in existing knowledge, power awareness, and the use of participatory tools. It stresses communication rather than literacy in the narrow sense. It is described as:

> ... an approach to learning and social change [...] REFLECT aims to improve the meaningful participation of people in decisions that affect their lives, through strengthening their ability to communicate.[38]

A less politicized approach, but with an emphasis on individual emancipation, the capability approach as a framework for understanding development has become increasingly widely-employed in recent years.[39] It helps to explain the link between education's role in nurturing freedom for individuals, and democracy for a country/society. The concept of capability within this theory is not the narrow understandings associated with skills such as literacy or numeracy (as useful as these might be). Capabilities are defined as the functions, opportunities and freedoms people possess that enable them to pursue goals they value and to bring about changes that are meaningful to them. It is therefore, like liberation theory concerned with the development of personal agency, as a key to the improvement of quality of life. The capabilities approach

> ...has implications for the way that education is understood and evaluated because a key role for good quality education becomes one of supporting the development of autonomy and the ability to make choices in later life rather than simply providing individuals with the necessary resources to learn.[40]

# Correspondence theory, reproduction theory and perpetration theory

Human capital theory, modernization theory and liberation theory all construe at least partially positive links between education and development: crudely put, more education leads to greater development, economic or otherwise. However, there are theories which question schooling as a medium of positive change.

Correspondence and reproduction theories illustrate the ways in which opportunities in schooling mirror those in life. Working-class or poor children often receive a different education from those of middle- and upper-class homes, as a result of settlement patterns, selective entry, private education opportunities, or streaming within schools. The different forms of education prepare them for their role in life – in correspondence with their backgrounds. Children from poorer homes learn pre-vocational and vocational skills, while children of the elite learn confidence and independence of thought, preparing them to take charge. Thus, the class system is reproduced. Likewise, unequal gender roles are reproduced through differing access to education and experiences within it. Rather than the system gearing towards national development for everyone, it is seen to perpetuate the status quo and ensure the dominance of those already living at the high end of the development spectrum.

In developing countries, forms of schooling which were imposed during colonial times persist to the present day. In former British colonies, a small number of elite (often boarding) schools have replicated the structures, curricula and values of traditional 'public' schools in the UK, such as Kamuzu Academy in Malawi, the 'Eton of Africa'. Meanwhile, mass schooling creates a compliant workforce that has learned to sit still and behave. Equally, the poorest find it most difficult to access and stay in education[41] and are least likely to have highly skilled, qualified teachers, who often prefer to work in cosmopolitan centres because of the amenities on offer.[42] This affects their future employment potential, so perpetuating the intergenerational cycle of poverty.

Harber[43] has gone further than accusations of reproduction in examining the role of schooling in the socialization process, and ultimately in contributing to human development. 'Perpetration theory' posits a more sinister relationship, with schools taking an active role in teaching children hatred, intolerance, and violence:

> By doing nothing or ignoring a negative or dangerous aspect of the surrounding society – bullying, infection of HIV/AIDS, racism, gendered sexual violence and violence itself – the role of schools can be said to be reproductive. However, all too often, given that schooling is supposed to be an enlightened and beneficial institution, schooling isn't only reproductive. In terms of schooling as a violent institution we need to go beyond schooling as reproduction to look at schooling as *perpetration*. This is because schooling not only reproduces some significant forms of violence that exist in the wider society, it actively perpetrates them thereby adding to the problem, making it worse and multiplying it. Indeed, in relation to schooling it is possible to borrow from economics and talk of a 'multiplier effect' in relation to violence.[44]

Harber uses examples of incidents and common practice from all over the world, including many from developing countries, to argue the case that schooling is anti-developmental. Among the issues raised are corporal punishment, racism, gender violence, stress, and anxiety generated by testing, and militarization.

# Development assistance to education

Aid or official development assistance to education involves financial or technical support for education from richer donors to poorer recipients. Where aid flow is from one national government to another, it is known as bilateral; where there are multiple sources of funding coordinated by an international agency (such as UNESCO or the World Bank), this is known as multilateral aid. Non-governmental Organizations (NGOs) have also played a very significant role in aid to education, from large international NGOs such as Oxfam, to much smaller organizations.

In taking an overview of historical trends and priorities in the post-colonial era in bilateral and multilateral aid to education, patterns emerge which broadly parallel evolution in the conceptualization of development, and the relationship between more and less developed parts of the world. While early forms of aid were open to accusations of neo-colonialism,

> Current trends in international development co-operation suggest that there should be a rethinking of relationships between the north and the south [...] Many international agencies, including UNESCO, have emphasized the primary responsibility of southern countries for their own development, while both the north and the south recognize the need for a genuine partnership in tackling issues of poverty alleviation, sustainable development and debt relief. Equity and especially gender equity are now a priority [...] [along with] emphasis upon the protection of the environment, human rights and multi-party politics [...] [Agencies] have also been stressing the need for a new code of conduct for international agencies in their development co-operation with governments to the south – to be expressed in clear contractual standards and principles of ethics among equal partners.[45]

King characterizes the main changes to international development cooperation as the following: decline in the proportion of official development assistance, with many countries reducing their aid budgets in real terms; the emergence of the partnership discourse, as suggested above; coherence and consistency in partnership, with governments giving bilateral aid that is consistent with their own policies across ministries; global sustainability and development targets for both north and south, with a growing awareness of global responsibilities of all nations; and, in terms of modalities of delivery, a movement from donor projects to sector development and sector-wide approaches to aid (SWAPs).[46]

The prevalence of SWAPs as the preferred modality of aid reflects the imperative for donors in the development cooperation to allow recipients to own the development process. Aid to education was once characterized by projects designed, staffed and resourced by the north – for example, the placement of an expatriate northern 'expert' in a region of a developing country, to introduce a new textbook and to provide in-service teacher education to facilitate its use. It is now more likely to involve transfers of funds directly to government departments, with the southern partner driving the process and making key spending decisions, in consultation with donors.[47]

A further trend in development assistance has been a unified front among different countries to work towards shared development goals, such as the Millennium Development Goals (MDGs), with foundations in the large data sets that are increasingly available. This globalization has facilitated concerted efforts in chosen areas, but is not without its critics, some of whom argue that the power balance still resides in the north and with powerful multilateral agencies such as the World Bank and IMF,[48] and that innovation is stifled within a paradigm based on current information, understandings and hegemonies. Education for All is one of these shared goals, and for many donors the attendant focus on access and quality in basic education has dominated their priorities, for example through sector-wide assistance to primary education in recipient countries.

# Education for All: A case study

The global movement toward Education for All (EFA) makes a good case study to illuminate the concepts and theories in this chapter, as so many of them are relevant to its origins and current status.

Education for All is normally defined as six years of basic education. For most people, this means completion of the primary phase of schooling. As a global movement, it has its origins in the 1990 World Conference on EFA in Jomtien, Thailand, where consensus was achieved on its definitions, and on national and donor commitment to it as a goal. Since then, this commitment has been extended through two major agreements: the Dakar Framework for Action, and the UN's Millennium Development Goals. The World Education Forum meeting in Dakar, Senegal, in April 2000, attended by representatives from governments of most of the world's countries and by multilateral and bilateral donor agencies and NGOs, agreed to the following six goals:

> We hereby collectively commit ourselves to the attainment of the following goals:
> - Expanding and improving comprehensive early childhood care and education, especially for the most vulnerable and disadvantaged children.
> - Ensuring that by 2015 all children, particularly girls, children in difficult circumstances, and those belonging to ethnic minorities, have access to and complete free and compulsory primary education of good quality.
> - Ensuring that the learning needs of all young people and adults are met through equitable access to appropriate learning and life skills programmes.
> - Achieving a 50% improvement in levels of adult literacy by 2015, especially for women, and equitable access to basic and continuing education for all adults.
> - Eliminating gender disparities in primary and secondary education by 2005, and achieving gender equality in education by 2015, with a focus on ensuring girls' full and equal access to and achievement in basic education of good quality.
> - Improving all aspects of the quality of education and ensuring excellence of all so that recognised and measurable learning outcomes are achieved by all, especially in literacy, numeracy and essential life skills.[49]

These aims were further taken up through the MDGs, passed as a resolution at the UN General Assembly in 2001, two of which directly relate to EFA:

> Goal 2: Achieve universal primary education
> [...] Ensure that, by 2015, children everywhere, boys and girls alike, will be able to complete a full course of primary schooling.
> Goal 3: Promote gender equality and empower women
> [...] Eliminate gender disparity in primary and secondary education, preferably by 2005, and to all levels of education no later than 2015.[50]

Why such a powerful and unified focus on EFA as a goal? The unified stand is in itself evidence of a globalizing of education goals in a more interconnected world. As for the reasons behind the movement, as Lewin and Akyeampong put it: 'Access to education lies at the heart of development [...] Determined efforts to improve health, nutrition, agriculture, industry, commerce and environmental conditions [... ] have to start from a position where access to both basic and secondary education is equitable and what is provided is of appropriate quality.'[51] Human capital theory's connection between investment in education, especially primary education, and national economic growth has played a very important role in earning the consensus. Additionally, arguments about the social benefits of education, especially those related to health, were instrumental in securing the Jomtien agreement.[52] It is also underpinned by another, earlier international agreement, the 1948 UN Convention on Human Rights, which posits free and compulsory elementary education as a right. Within the rights framework it is also characterized as an enabling right: one that makes other rights possible. As the UNESCO EFA Monitoring Team put it: 'The right to education straddles the division between civil and political rights on the one hand, and economic, social and cultural rights on the other'. [53] The language of the Dakar Framework and the MDGs draws attention to the focus on issues of equity, and gender equity in particular, reflecting the growing importance of social and human development models.

The annual UNESCO Global Monitoring Report collates current statistics of progress towards the EFA MDGs. The themes of these reports reflect the topics of concern with regard to progress as well as the processes and outcomes of education. They have become increasingly specific and focused since the initial broad analysis and baseline of 2002:

> 2002: Education for All: is the world on track?
> 2003/4: Gender and Education for All: the leap to equality
> 2005: Education for All: the quality imperative
> 2006: Literacy for Life
> 2007: Strong Foundations: early childhood care and education
> 2008: Education for All by 2015: will we make it?
> 2009: Overcoming Inequality: why governance matters
> 2010: Reaching the Marginalised
> 2011: The Hidden Crisis: armed conflict and education
> 2012: Youth and Skills: putting education to work
> 2013: Learning and teaching for development.

As the deadline for achievement of the MDGs draws nearer, it is evident that while significant progress has been made in terms of overall enrolment and female participation, the goals will not be attained, as the most recent report attests:

> Unfortunately, this year's *EFA Global Monitoring Report* shows that progress towards many of the goals is slowing down, and that most EFA goals are unlikely to be met. Despite the gloomy outlook overall, progress in some of the world's poorest countries shows what can be achieved with the commitment of national governments and aid donors, including greater

numbers of children attending pre-school, completing primary school and making the transition to secondary education.[54]

Reaching the most marginalized has been the main barrier, and where access is improved, problems with retention and quality persist. The seeds have also been sown for aspirations for education beyond the primary phase for those who have successfully achieved it, and for jobs that reflect these aspirations – these will create new funding and development challenges.

Of course, one could use correspondence, dependency and reproduction theories to argue that the real and more sinister goals of education are obscured by such discourse, and that the drive to EFA is in the interests of the powerful. The role of primary schooling in reproducing social inequalities within societies, and in creating a compliant workforce in the less developed world to be exploited by wealthier nations, is an alternative perspective on the issue. Household wealth continues to be the most powerful predictor of participation in schooling, perpetuating cycles of poverty.[55] Proponents of the development of higher phases of education, secondary and tertiary, have argued that these have suffered as a result of the focus on EFA, to the detriment of local control of development in poorer nations. Additionally, the practicalities of actually achieving the targets[56] have been widely debated, and the evidence is mounting that either the targets are unrealistic, there is not sufficient political will to achieve them, or that the diversity of challenges in developing countries is too great to make them possible. One significant barrier is the costs to parents of sending children to school – even school which is 'free' – as there are hidden costs (such as books and uniforms) and indirect costs (such as the loss of household labour).[57] There are ongoing debates on what should constitute 'basic education', and hints at a pendulum swing through a re-emerging interest in secondary education in agencies such as the World Bank.

Whatever the critiques and challenges, the drive for EFA, at the time of writing, continues to be the main force in donor commitment and strategies in aid to education. As well as bilateral and multilateral forms of aid, international NGOs such as Oxfam have taken up the call for EFA, reflecting further the extent of the globalization of support for shared goals.[58]

# Conclusion

In conclusion, let us return briefly to the questions posed in the introduction. In terms of what we mean by development, the plethora of models and indicators of development suggests that this is shifting territory. While definitions of development based on economic indicators remain in the ascendant, there is increasing attention to issues of social and human development, with gender equity priorities and human rights perspectives on education reflecting a shift away from strict economic models. International movements and new modes of development cooperation also emphasize these goals, and also suggest new perspectives on the question: who should define what we mean by progress, and what power issues are at stake? The answer is that, more and more, there is recognition of the importance of stakeholders in the developing world defining and controlling development. There is far to go on this front, though, and critical theories and perspectives point to a continuing power struggle.

In relation to education's contribution to the development process: we have seen that, theoretically at least, education has the potential to contribute to economic growth and social and human well-being, and is itself a human right. What kind of education is likely to do this? This is a complex question which we have barely started to answer. A starting point is the question of basic quality – meaningful learning is likely to be compromised in contexts of stringency, in poorly equipped classrooms of a hundred pupils, staffed by underpaid and unqualified teachers. But it is important, particularly in goals of social and human development, to look beyond these basic indicators to questions of curriculum and human relationships in schools. Schools, it must be remembered, can do harm as well as good in the development of people and societies.

We have explored a number of theories which help to explain these intersections of education, development, and power, including human capital theory, modernization theory, liberation theory, and reproduction and perpetration theories. We shall be returning to some of these questions and these theories in Chapter 7, when we examine a range of perspectives used in educational research in and on developing countries.

# Notes

1.  Nyerere in 'Development is for man, by man and of man', p. 28.
2.  Stalin, in Meighan, *The Freethinkers' Guide to the Educational Universe*, p. 4.
3.  Pye, 'Poor children, poor results'.
4.  Dyer, Educating the poorest.
5.  UNDP, Human Development Index 2013.
6.  Dyer, 'Educating the poorest'; Robinson-Pant, *Why Eat Green Cucumbers?*
7.  Harber and Davies, *School Management and Effectiveness in Developing Countries*.
8.  www.avert.org/aafrica.htm
9.  Other writers, for example, Fägerlind and Saha in *Education and National Development*, and Harber in *Education and Theories of Development*, have included political development as a category of analysis in addition to economic and social development. It is here treated as underpinning the others, but is understood to be a significant dimension on its own as well.
10. Fägerlind and Saha, *Education and National Development*, p. 63.
11. Woodhall, *Education and Training*.
12. Samoff, *Coping with Crisis*.
13. Lulat, 'Education and national development', p. 318.
14. World Bank, *Pupil Teacher Ratios*.
15. Harber and Davies, *School Management and Effectiveness in Developing Countries*.
16. Bangay and Latham, Are we asking the right questions?
17. Fägerlind and Saha, *Education and National Development*.
18. For a more detailed discussion of the Gini coefficient and company rankings, see http://hdr.undp.org/statistics/data/indicators
19. Lewin, *Education and Development*.
20. Haq, *Reflections on Human Development*, p. 22.
21. Ibid.
22. UNDP, *Human Development Report 2012*.
23. UNDP, *Human Development Report 2000*.
24. Sen, *Development as Freedom*.
25. Chronic Poverty Research Centre 2008, *The Chronic Poverty Report 2008–2009*; UNDP, *Human Development Index 2012*.
26. Smith, *The Wealth of Nations*.
27. Schultz, 'Investment in human capital'.
28. Psacharopoulos and Patrinos, Returns to investment in education.
29. This discussion of critiques draws on Little, 'Motivating learning and the development of capital'.

30. Dore, *The Diploma Disease*.
31. McLelland, *The Achieving Society*.
32. Inkeles and Smith, *Becoming Modern*.
33. Ibid., p. 141.
34. Riggs, *Administration in Developing Countries*.
35. Harber and Davies, *School Management and School Effectiveness*.
36. Freire, *Pedagogy of the Oppressed*.
37. Ibid., pp. 45–7.
38. www.actionaid.org.uk
39. Sen, *Development as Freedom*; Nussbaum, *Women and Human Development*.
40. Tikly and Barrett, Social justice, capabilities and the quality of education, p. 7.
41. Dyer, Educating the poorest.
42. Schweisfurth, *Learner-centred education in international perspective*.
43. Harber, *Schooling as Violence*.
44. Ibid.
45. Colin Power, in Preface to King and Buchert, *Changing International Aid to Education*. For a critique of the effects of aid on education in Africa, see Samoff .
46. King, 'New challenges to international development co-operation'.
47. See, for example, Epskamp, *Education in the South*.
48. See, for example, Stiglitz, *Globalization and its Discontents,* and Klees et al, *The World Bank and Education*.
49. UNESCO, *Dakar Framework for Action*, paragraph 7.
50. UN Resolution A/56/326, in UNESCO *EFA Global Monitoring Report*.
51. Lewin and Akyeampong, Education in sub-Saharan Africa, p. 143.
52. Little et al., *Beyond Jomtien*.
53. UNESCO, *EFA Global Monitoring Report*.
54. UNESCO, *EFA Global Monitoring Report* 2012.
55. Lewin and Akeampong, Education in sub-Saharan Africa.
56. See, for example, Goldstein, 'Education for All'.
57. See, for example, Boyle et al., *Reaching the Poor*.
58. Watkins, *Education Now*.

# 6

# Comparative Education: Method

The comparison of the educational systems of several countries lends itself to a variety of methods of treatment, depending somewhat on its purpose.

*Kandel*[1]

We turn now to a consideration of method. Much effort has been expended on discussion of appropriate methods in comparative education, and there has been considerable dispute among those taking differing positions on the subject. As we were discussing this chapter a prominent British comparativist asked us 'Is there a method?'

What distinguishes the work of comparativists from that of other educationists – and what therefore distinguishes the approaches they use to research – is the obvious fact that for the most part they are concerned essentially with other cultures/countries. Aside from this concern with education 'elsewhere' and the question as to how comparisons might realistically be made, comparativists use all the research methods that other investigators of aspects of education employ in their research. They can therefore call upon a huge body of established approaches to investigation in education and must then add to that body approaches specific to the particular task of comparison. The essential questions are: What methods and conditions are appropriate to ensure adequate understanding of other cultures from a vantage point outside of those cultures? What does the act of comparison consist in and how might it best be undertaken? These questions in turn revolve around the issues of purpose we have discussed in Chapter 1.

In considering the methods of comparative education we might cite two leading British comparativists, Edmund King (1914–2002) and Brian Holmes (1920–93), as representative of polarized approaches to the possibilities. King was a classicist by origin, trained in the humanities and demonstrably a proficient linguist. Holmes was a physicist, used to the rigours of scientific method and with an uncompromising insistence on structured analysis. Their different backgrounds led them to adopt more or less incompatible stances on how to undertake comparative inquiry. 'Holmes wanted to define a research framework which should always be adhered to [...], while King took a pragmatic approach characteristic of much research in the arts'.[2] Holmes was prescriptive; King argued that comparative researchers should use what he would call 'tools for the job' – that is to say, whatever approaches were deemed most appropriate to any particular investigation.

The fundamental issue that lay behind the different positions of King and Holmes is one with which all social scientists grapple: it has to do with the possibility, viability, and desirability of seeking to establish laws which will enable us to make predictions. Some (like Holmes) see this as indeed possible, viable and desirable; others (like King) argue that the social sciences are concerned with matters that are dependent on human behaviour – which they assert is intrinsically unpredictable. Turner develops the Holmes position like this:

> Holmes argued that studies of educational systems should be based on sociological laws in the form, 'If we do this, then that will follow.' Of course [...] I do not intend the term 'sociological law' to be imbued with that kind of certainty which once might have been attached to the laws of physics. 'Sociological law' is no more than a hypothesis which enables a study to be conducted.
>
> However, sociological laws are important because they provide the social policy maker with a framework for linking means with ends. They provide a hypothesis that the mechanisms of educational institutions function in particular ways. They specify the kinds of actions which will produce the results which the policy makers desire.[3]

King, too, insisted that 'a "sociological law" – if it exists – is a description and not a prescription. It is a hypothesis on present evidence, and no more'.[4] And he criticized Holmes for his belief in the certainties of sociological laws:

> [Holmes's] writing shows a marked tendency to talk of so-called sociological laws not only as if they were physical laws, but also as though they carried the compulsive powers of positive law produced by legislation.[5]

Holmes responded with a dismissive reference to King's 'rather eclectic methodology'.[6] Disputes of this kind are rarely ever resolved. The stances of both men are reflected in the approaches of others to comparative inquiry in education. In connection with the Holmes position, we might record a point made by Christopher Winch: '[T]he fascination science has for us makes it easy for us to adopt its scientific form as a paradigm against which to measure other modes of discourse'.[7] The danger lies in imposing on such a multidimensional and essentially interdisciplinary area of inquiry as comparative education methods of the kind which have proved useful and appropriate for more well-defined disciplines, whether in the physical, natural or social sciences.

As far as a more scientific approach is concerned, the titles of two important publications by Harold Noah and Max Eckstein, their co-authored book *Toward a Science of Comparative Education* and an edited collection of papers ('illustrating the strategy and tactics of comparative education'), *Scientific Investigations in Comparative Education*, both published in 1969, reflect attempts in the late 1960s to put the house of comparative education in order through the establishment and use of quasi-scientific methods. Their aim was to move away from the historical–philosophical tradition and to draw on approaches common in the social sciences. As the preface to *Scientific Investigations in Comparative Education* puts it,

> The new approach demands the application of complex techniques of investigation and is predicated on a number of crucial assertions: a priori assumptions about the nature of man and his institutions are to be avoided; facts in and of themselves are meaningless, for only in the context of explanation can facts take on significance; research should be concerned with systematic attempts to test hypotheses within a more general framework of theory; and theory bereft of the possibility of empirical testing is little more than metaphysics.[8]

Before we consider what such a new approach implied, we must review various types of research that have characterized comparative studies in education.

Watson usefully talks of descriptive, analytical, evaluative, exploratory, and predictive research types.[9] And Theisen and Adams[10] propose a classification of comparative education research, shown in Figure 9, which includes analysis, description, evaluation, and exploration as research types. We shall synthesize these types into description and analysis, and explanation and prediction, and then discuss some research problems peculiar to the business of comparison. We shall return to evaluation in Chapter 7, since both in industrialized societies and in developing countries considerable progress has been made in evaluation in recent decades and its importance merits separate consideration.

**Figure 9** Theisen and Adams: Classification of comparative research

| | | |
|---|---|---|
| Analytical | What are the explanations for relationships between components? | Description of roles. |
| | Why do actors or systems behave in the way they do? | Specification of cause-and-effect relations or explanation of relations and consequences. |
| Descriptive | What is the current status of the phenomena? | Description of phenomena or conditions. |
| | What are the relationships between variables? | Description of relations between variables. |
| Evaluative | Is programme A better or more cost effective than programme B? | Judgement of the merit, value or worth of any given programme or technique. |
| | Is the programme or policy appropriate for a particular context? | Interpretations useful for decision-making. |
| Exploratory | What issues pertaining to roles, relationships and processes exist which are worthy of examination by other modes of research? | Generating new hypotheses or questions. |
| | What models, paradigms or methods might be useful in designing future research? | Exploration of relationships and functions with potential for in-depth research. |

# Description and analysis

The main criticism of earlier approaches was that though they excelled in description and attempts at explanation they failed to predict outcomes and hence to be of practical use in policy-making. We can pass over the early examples of 'travellers' tales'; interesting though a lot of them were, many were the result of superficial observation, with only the odd *aperçu* of value, and almost none was the result of detailed and systematic inquiry. Their principal worth lies in their creating awareness in their readership of different approaches to educational provision. It is with the work of the French philosopher Victor Cousin and the American administrator Horace Mann, and later that of Matthew Arnold in England, that we begin to see more thorough analysis, some of it using statistical evidence (as we have noted, huge progress was made in collecting statistics as the nineteenth century progressed), though it is very much within the historical–philosophical tradition.

This tradition was added to in the work of Michael Sadler, starting towards the end of the nineteenth century. His writings were both thorough and scholarly. They built on the nineteenth-century predilection for the assembling of masses of carefully recorded data, as in the papers which emerged from the Office of Special Inquiries and Reports (which Sadler directed) or in William Torrey Harris's huge 'International Education Series' in the USA. The meticulous attention to detail which was Sadler's forte is evident, for example, in an impressive handwritten document he produced for internal use in the Education Department in London and which survives in the National Archives. This 'Memorandum on the Constitution & Financial Powers of Local Educational Authorities in Various Countries'[11] consists of 78 folio sheets ruled into two columns, and covers France, Belgium, Prussia, Bavaria, Saxony, Baden, Switzerland, The Netherlands, Norway, the Dominion of Canada (with separate entries for various provinces), the Commonwealth of Australia (various states), New Zealand, and the USA (various states and cities). The first column in each case deals with the constitution of the local authority and the second with its financial powers. Here is a wealth of detail about the precise constitutional and financial positions of local authorities in a remarkable range of other societies.

Sadler spent eight years as Director of the Office of Special Inquiries and Reports and oversaw the production of 11 volumes of 'Special Reports on Educational Subjects' which 'made available for English readers a large amount of useful information otherwise difficult to get at, but served an even more valuable purpose in the way of suggestion and inspiration'.[12] The first volume (1896–7) contained a comprehensive array of papers, many of them written by Sadler as sole or co-author. Here is the full list of contents:

1  Public Elementary Education in England and Wales, 1870–1895
2  English Students in Foreign Training Colleges
3  Brush Work in an Elementary School (with illustrations)
4  The ABC of Drawing: an inquiry into the principles underlying elementary instruction in Drawing (with illustrations)
5  Domestic Economy Teaching in England
6  Technical Education for Girls

7 The Secondary Day School attached to the Battersea Polytechnic, London – an experiment in the co-education of boys and girls

8 The History of the Irish System of Elementary Education

9 The National System of Education in Ireland

10 Recent Legislation in Elementary Education in Belgium

11 The Housewifery Schools and Classes of Belgium

12 The French System of Higher Primary Schools

13 The Realschulen in Berlin and their bearing on modern Secondary and Commercial Education

14 The Ober-Realschulen of Prussia with special reference to the Ober-Realschule at Charlottenburg

15 The Prussian Elementary School Code

16 The Continuation Schools in Saxony

17 The School Journey in Germany

18 The Teaching of the Mother Tongue in Germany

19 Holiday Courses in France and Germany for Instruction in Modern Languages

20 Recent Educational Progress in Denmark (with maps)

21 Education in Egypt

22 The Education of Girls and Women in Spain

23 The National Bureau of Education of the United States

24 The History of the Manitoba School System and the Issues of the Recent Controversy

25 Arrangements for the admission of Women to the chief Universities in the British Empire and in Foreign Countries

26 Appendix giving a list of the chief official papers bearing on Education in Great Britain and Ireland

As with the work of the great commissions on education earlier in the nineteenth century, the foreign example was being systematically investigated and reported on. The phenomena observed were analysed in terms of how they had emerged historically and philosophically. How they might be used in any practical sense in policy-making is less clear, but the documentation provided policy makers with a valuable source through which they could be fully informed about practice elsewhere.

The same question about possible usefulness might be asked of some of the data collected by commissioners appointed to report on education earlier in the nineteenth century. Here, for example, are the first ten questions in a schedule produced in 1887 in connection with the inquiries undertaken by the Royal Commission on the Elementary Education Acts (the Cross Commission) which reported in 1888.[13] The concern in this part of the schedule has largely to do with compulsory school attendance:

Inquiries

1. What is the date of the School Law now in force?
2. What is the Estimated Population of the Country?
3. Give the number of Children –
   a. Of School Age – i.e., from – to – years of age.
   b. On the School Rolls of
      Public schools – i.e. under Public Management
      Non-public schools – i.e. under Private or Voluntary Management
   c. In Regular Attendance
4. Is Elementary Education Compulsory?
5. If so,
   a. Between what ages?
   b. What minimum of Attendances satisfies the law?
   c. What penalties are imposed for Non-Attendance?
   d. What Exemptions are allowed?
   e. How and by whom is Compulsion enforced?
6. Are there any Rewards on the part of State or the Locality for Good Attendance?
7. Is there any class of Vagrant or Destitute children where the ordinary school system fails to reach? If so, how is that class dealt with?
8. What are the prescribed Hours per day and per week of School Attendance? Do they vary with the age of the scholar or with the season of the year?
9. For how many Days during the year must the School be Open? Is this minimum usually exceeded, and by how much?
10. Is there any system of Half-Time or Partial Exemption from attendance of scholars for the purpose of enabling them to go to work?
    a. If so, what is the system?
    b. What is the Law as to Juvenile Labour?

The detail evident here provided the basis for description and the analysis which could emerge from it, and the questionnaire is reminiscent in general style of Jullien's proposed questions in his much earlier *Plan for Comparative Education* of 1816–17.[14]

The collection of descriptive data remains, of course, an important function within comparative education. Now, through more sophisticated electronic and other data collection methods, we have at our disposal huge banks of information on education systems around the world. Apart from the data made available by individual governments, organizations such as UNESCO, the OECD and the EU (through EURYDICE) provide detailed descriptive information in a form which facilitates comparison.

The EURYDICE network, initiated in 1980 as part of the Community's action programme Socrates, describes itself as 'working on behalf of policy makers and the world of education', publishing:

- regularly updated descriptive analyses of the organization of education systems
- comparative studies on specific topics of European interest
- indicators on the various levels of education from pre-primary to tertiary education.[15]

Its database (EURYBASE) provides further information. EURYDICE is the major source for current reliable data on education in Europe.

The OECD's regularly published compendium *Education at a Glance* has become a valuable and widely discussed source of comparative data on the performance of education systems. This document typically covers 'the output of educational institutions and the impact of learning'; 'financial and human resources invested in education'; 'access to education, participation and progression'; and 'the learning environment and organisation of schools', each of which broad areas contains a number of 'indicators'. The latter area, for example, subsumes six such indicators: total intended instruction time for students in primary and secondary education; class size and ratio of students to teaching staff; teachers' salaries; teaching time and teachers' working time; student admission, placement and grouping policies in upper secondary schools; and decision-making in education systems.[16]

But it is one thing to collect data, quite another to begin the process of comparison and analysis, to explain similarities and differences, and to attempt predictions: Taine's maxim 'Après la collection des faits, la recherche des causes' ('After the collection of facts, research into causes')[17] takes us to the next step.

# Explanation and prediction

Explanation involves the complex issue – of central concern to philosophy (and especially to the philosophy of science) – of causality. Causality involves what are called *universal statements* in the form of hypotheses, and *singular statements* which relate to the specific conditions of phenomena.[18] In a field like education, both types of statement are particularly problematic since proofs are difficult to determine. If, in a given set of circumstances ($x$), there are a clear set of results ($y$), it is not logically the case that $y$ is explained by x. The results ($y$) might be chance results, or they might be explained by factors that have nothing to do with $x$. Observations and experiments which purport to demonstrate that certain conditions produce certain results and that the results are therefore explained by the conditions are in danger of falling prey to the *post hoc ergo propter hoc* fallacy or are susceptible to the so-called 'Hawthorne effect' (which says, in effect, that experiments succeed by virtue of their being experiments).

Comparative studies that present series of disconnected data easily fall into the trap of implying that certain observable features of educational provision are in some way the result of certain other observable features. Typical here is the association of economic performance with aspects of education systems. If a country is performing well economically (something that can be demonstrated by means of hard data), investigators might try to identify aspects of educational provision in that country which appear interestingly different from what can be observed in other, less economically successful countries. Such an aspect might be a developed system of vocational education and training. It is then an easy step to argue that economic success (the output) is the consequence of vocational education and training (the input), especially if, over time, there is no other obvious explanation for the successful economy. The high scores of pupils in some countries in the OECD's PISA surveys naturally provoke attempts at explanation in terms, for example, of the structures of secondary education (a common system? diversified provision?), but we should be very wary of explanations that depend on the association of such variables with outcomes. It might well be the case, for example, that Germany's relatively poor performance in PISA is a consequence of that federal country's hierarchical – for the most part tripartite – secondary school systems, but this has to remain at the level of speculation rather than proof. We should also be wary of the judgement of researchers who do not have intimate knowledge or experience of the processes of education: there is indeed a worrying tendency following publication of large-scale studies of pupil attainment to focus on the outcomes and to attempt to explain them in simplistic terms, rather than through detailed attention to the processes of teaching and learning that have preceded the tests (and which the tests might not in fact be measuring in all cases).

Prediction, which relies on powers of explanation, has occupied the minds of philosophers since the beginnings of science. But the bottom line of discussion within the philosophy of science remains the position that there can be no absolute predictability of observed phenomena. No matter how many times the behaviour of a phenomenon is observed within a particular set of circumstances, there can be no guarantee that the phenomenon in question will behave similarly when those circumstances are replicated. That said, however, it is also clear that there can be some fairly reliable 'laws' on which scientific theory depends and which are generally accepted; there are even such relative certainties in the social sciences, especially (for example) in economics or behavioural psychology. We seem happy to accommodate the fact that the 'certainties' involved here are not absolute but constitute reasonable hypotheses.

It seems therefore acceptable to assume that certain types of outcome will in most cases be observed if certain types of condition are in place. If this were not the case, much work at a practical level in education would be haphazard; in fact, present and future practice is informed by past practice deemed to have been successful. But, as Popper has observed, prediction is problematic insofar as it can both cause and prevent future events:

> A prediction is a social happening which may interact with other social happenings, and among them with the one which it predicts. It may […] help to precipitate this event […]. It may, in an extreme case, even *cause* the happening it predicts: the happening might not have occurred at all if it had not been predicted. At the other extreme the prediction of an impending event may lead to its *prevention*. […] The action of predicting something, and that of abstaining from prediction, might both have all sorts of consequences.[19]

The warning here is that a too narrow focus on a 'scientific' approach to comparative inquiry might attach too much importance to notions of explanation and prediction, and that while it is natural to seek to explain, and to predict on the basis of explanation, any conclusions must be treated with considerable caution.

# 'Scientific' and other approaches

Given these problems with analysis, explanation and prediction, is it feasible to speak of a 'scientific' approach to comparative education such as that conceived by Noah and Eckstein? In some respects the answer is an obvious 'Yes'. Developments in data gathering and analysis have become more and more 'scientific' in nature. In comparative studies of aspects of education, techniques can be used that are not dissimilar from those used by investigators in more conventionally 'scientific' areas – psychology and medicine, for example – as well as in other social sciences. Comparativists have at their disposal all the sophisticated techniques of investigation and analysis employed by researchers in a wide range of cognate areas.

At the same time, however, they still bring to comparative inquiry the advantages (and some of the disadvantages) of their 'original' disciplines. Thus the physicist will tend towards the rigorous testing of hypotheses and the replication of results typical of scientific research; the economist is likely to look for complex inter-relationships between educational input and economic output and will focus on statistical information; the historian – or the linguist as cultural analyst – might rather use a more speculative philosophical approach, drawing on a range of essentially non-quantifiable evidence.

There is still a strong case to be made for a historical dimension to comparative studies. With a focus on approaches within the scientific tradition, the potential of *understanding* the present through the past has tended to be relatively neglected. This is the result, too, of scepticism as to the predictive power of past experience, or of what might be learnt from 'the lessons of history'. Hegel made a powerful case against attempting to learn anything from history:

> Rulers, Statesmen, Nations, are wont to be emphatically commended to the teaching which experience offers in history. But what experience and history teach is this – that peoples and governments never have learned anything from history, or acted on principles deduced from it. Each period is involved in such peculiar circumstances, exhibits a condition of things so strictly idiosyncratic, that its conduct must be regulated by considerations connected with itself, and itself alone. Amid the pressure of great events, a general principle gives no help. It is useless to revert to similar circumstances in the Past. The pallid shades of memory struggle in vain with the life and freedom of the Present.[20]

This is an unpromising judgement. Whether history provides us with usable lessons is a much debated question, and there are those who would take an opposing view to Hegel's. What is important, however, is to understand how things in education have come to be as they are, i.e. to go deeper than an analysis of purely present-day phenomena. The historicist argument is that all cultures are shaped by events of the past and that 'nothing can be understood in isolation from its past'.[21] A comparative study which neglects an analysis of the historical antecedents to any present-day phenomena in education is not covering the whole story and will lack an important dimension to any explanatory power it might otherwise have. This is not to argue against research which provides us with up-to-the-minute data on such matters as pupil attainment or access to higher education, or special needs provision. But in our view, in any attempt to explain such data the historical background should be an essential part of the analysis, and to dismiss the Sadlerian notion, exemplified in the work of Hans and Kandel, that 'the national system of education embodied the historical roots and philosophical wisdom of their own society' as 'simplistic, subjective, and totalistic'[22] is as blinkered as a blanket dismissal of 'scientific' approaches to comparative education would be.

# Other problems

## Ethnocentricity

A problem faced by comparativists at every stage of an investigation is that of ethnocentricity. It is important to recognize that we come with many preconceptions based on long personal experience of a particular way of looking at things in education, and thus to try to create a kind of neutrality in attempting to understand other systems of education and the issues that are of interest or concern in them. Seeing things through an ethnocentric filter can have distorting effects as far as our understanding of educational phenomena in other countries is concerned.

It is only by a process of determined objectivity that the scope for analysis of concepts such as, for example, 'professionalism' or 'autonomy', can be properly exploited in more than one national (or sometimes sub- or intra-national) context. When we talk of school reports, examinations or homework, or even headteachers, ministries or schools, we cannot easily ignore the mental image, the notions, which they stimulate. A school in France is a very different 'idea' from the notion of a school in Britain, and schools in Germany or India or the Sudan will be different again by varying degrees. The important issue here is not to impose alien constructs on foreign systems, in whatever context.

Yoneyama has addressed this question and proposed a matrix to describe the factors which researchers bring to any analysis of aspects of educational reform.[23] The schema is constructed in Figure 10, based on her description.

This kind of analysis is particularly useful inasmuch as it draws attention to the multiple possibilities for distortion which can result from a researcher's conditioned perspectives. The 'factors the researcher brings to the analysis' (on the vertical axis) dissect with the 'stages of a specific aspect of reform' (on the horizontal axis) and help both to explain the reform and to condition it. So that, if, for example, the disciplinary background of the researcher is in psychology, it might be expected that proposed 'methods of implementation' might have rather more to do with teaching and learning than with administration or finance. Yoneyama has a nice image, in the context of her article reviewing a book on educational reform in Japan: 'The discourse on education reform in Japan may perhaps be likened to the colour of a cuttlefish which changes depending on the touch of the analysts'. One of Edmund King's favourite images was of a 'subject' perceiving an 'object' in different ways:

> [T]he subject who sees an object is directly or unconsciously aware of himself looking at it. That is to say, a man seeing a fish in a pond looks at it as an angler, as a zoologist, as an aquarist, as an aesthete, or as someone

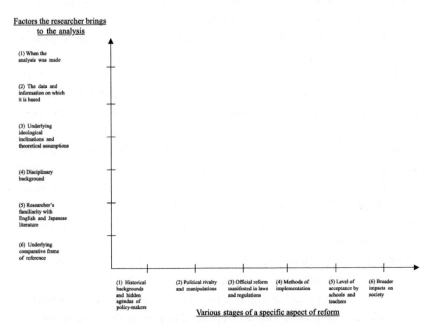

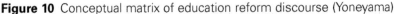

**Figure 10** Conceptual matrix of education reform discourse (Yoneyama)

thinking of his supper. In other words, he is conscious of what Whitehead calls 'the occasion' of which he himself is a part. That is to say, a great deal more than the transmission of light from the object to the retina goes into anyone's perception of an object.[24]

Objectivity, of course, is a quality required of any researcher, but it is particularly necessary in comparative studies to 'be aware of ourselves looking at' an educational phenomenon in another country and to neutralize as far as possible the preconceptions our individual backgrounds have formed in us.

# Language

The problems with language are not unconnected to matters of ethnocentricity, since language 'fixes' concepts. Let us take some examples from German. There are two principal words for 'education' in German: *Erziehung* and *Bildung*. Often the two are linked together as *Bildung und Erziehung*. This creates problems for translators, and there are no easy solutions that can successfully isolate the precise nuance evident in the deliberate use of one of these terms rather than the other in any particular context. Another example would be the nomenclature used for various types of school. The academic type of secondary school in Germany, the *Gymnasium*, is often translated as 'grammar school', but that links the German concept of an academic secondary school to a particular English version of such a school, and – to complicate matters – in American usage a 'grammar school' is an institution at the primary level. The main problem here is that a wrong translation will lock the English reader into a conceptual framework from which it is difficult to escape. The most straightforward solution is to define and use the foreign terms without translation, as we do with the word *Kindergarten* in English.

There is potential for considerable confusion. The word 'state', for example, has a different immediate interpretation (invokes a different kind of concept) in the USA from its interpretation in the UK. 'Higher education' will include different categories of institution, depending on national context. The term 'professor' will imply different kinds of status in the USA, the UK, and Germany.

Differences in language use are associated with differences in conceptual approach to the kinds of issues with which comparativists deal. 'Teacher professionalism', for example, is a term that would have to be subjected to considerable linguistic and conceptual analysis in the context of any comparative study involving, say, France and England.[25]

Language is also a problem in the context of empirical investigations involving interviews or questionnaires.[26] Bereday argued that comparativists must be competent in the languages of the countries they investigate,[27] but this remains unrealistic for many researchers. If there is reliance on translation and interpretation, safeguards must be in place to ensure accuracy and reliability. 'Back translation' is a technique used in the construction of interview schedules and questionnaires: the original language is first translated, then retranslated into the original language. If differences emerge, they can point to problems with the interpretation of concepts germane to the particular research project.

## Units of analysis

There is a tendency, as we have seen in Chapter 1, to regard the nation-state as the basic unit of analysis and comparison. And so comparativists have compared, for example, Britain and France, or Germany and America. There are considerable problems here. Firstly, the nation-state is not necessarily a coherent entity in educational terms. 'Britain' is 'Great Britain' and consists of England, Wales and Scotland (but not Northern Ireland). England and Scotland have quite separate education systems. 'Germany' is the Federal Republic of Germany, which comprises 16 individual 'states' (*Länder*), each with its own education system; 'America' is the United States of America, a federal system with a variety of governing structures from state to state. Secondly, and following on from these problems, *intra-national* investigation has been relatively neglected, despite its potential to result in our learning about best or better practice from analogous situations (from state to state in the USA, for example, or from *Land* to *Land* in Germany). Thirdly, there are problems, too, with regional groupings such as 'Latin America', or 'Eastern Europe', or 'The Caribbean', or the 'Central Asian Republics': to lump nations with rich individual cultures and traditions together on the basis of geographical proximity, or one-time political allegiance, or former colonial administration, is to deny that individuality and to create an often spurious comparability. Rather, as we have seen from the work of Bray and Thomas described in Chapter 1, comparativists should seek out units of analysis that are intrinsically appropriate to the task in hand. An investigation of modes of school-based assessment, for example, might well be based on a local education authority in one county of England and an initiative in one board of education in Canada; a study of bullying might look at policies in individual schools in a number of local or national or regional settings; an inquiry into the teaching of reading might look at what individual teachers do, rather than what curricular regulations at higher levels prescribe.

# Gathering comparative data

The full range of empirical methods that are available to the social science researcher can be used in comparative studies, but the nature of comparative inquiry creates particular issues for each. We consider here a few illustrative examples.

*Interviewing* is perhaps one of the most commonly-used methods for gathering information and understanding the perspectives of individuals or groups. In its less structured forms, the interview is a purposeful conversation with the flexibility to allow probing of key points as they arise. In comparative research, a number of issues arise. Firstly, the interview process may be understood differently in different cultural and political contexts. For example, where government oppression is an historical or contemporary concern, the interview situation can be perceived as threatening and data gathered may lack validity if the subject is reluctant to be truthful. Equally, in hierarchical or high power-distance societies, the desire to please an interviewer perceived as an authority may result in less than truthful responses, or in the case where the interviewee is a powerful person, the interview may not be taken seriously or prioritized, and the interviewer considered a 'time-waster'.[28] Obviously language as discussed above can be an issue, particularly for outsider researchers, but this extends also to body language and other non-verbal forms of communication. The intercultural skills referred to in Chapter 4 are crucial, whether it is a question of a language, of appropriate dress, or intensity of eye contact. All of these affect the comparability of data across contexts as well as their validity internal to one setting.

*Questionnaires* used to gather quantitative or qualitative data for comparative analysis are also in common usage, and a number of the same cautions are in order as for interviews. Data on controversial issues can be particularly sensitive if they are in writing. Language issues can be compounded with problems of illiteracy in some contexts. In our experience of working with students researching in a range of settings, response rates to written or on-line questionnaires have varied widely, and it is evident that some national or cultural groups are simply more likely to respond. This might be because survey fatigue is more common in some parts of the world than others, or perhaps because of differing levels of trust and respect for academic research, or because of a lesser or greater willingness to help strangers, acquaintances, authorities, students, or friends. This can create differences in samples which raise issues for comparison.

*Document analysis* can be a fruitful method for comparative analysis, not least for practical reasons: it becomes possible to research from a distance if policy documents, or textbooks, or school prospectuses for example, are the primary objects of study, and the question of cross-cultural human inter-action does not have the same immediacy. However, behind the document lies a human writer or writers, with particular instructions or pressures, and the real and symbolic purposes of such documents can vary greatly – the researcher needs to be alert to questions of equivalence (see below).

Increasing access through internet sites to international data sets on every-thing from expenditure to enrolments facilitates secondary data analysis, another comparative-research-at-a-distance possibility. In such cases, comparative statistical analysis of existing data replaces the fieldwork process (although the data will still need to be contextualized, as per the framework below). One of the most commonly-used of these tools in the comparative toolkit is the data from cross-national tests of achievement such as PISA, which will be explored in greater depth in Chapter 8.

Some of the ethical implications of using various methods in interna-tional research (particularly in developing countries) will be discussed in Chapter 7.

# Research design and analysis

We have mentioned in Chapter 1 that comparisons are typically made on the basis of various equivalences. Nowak refers to types of 'relationally equivalent phenomena' in terms – among others – of:

- cultural equivalence
- contextual equivalence
- structural equivalence
- functional equivalence.[29]

Once researchers establish such equivalences (constants) between societies they can then begin to identify differences (variables). This might be the neatest way to conduct comparative studies, but it is not the commonest. Indeed, it is often the cultural, contextual, structural and functional aspects of education systems (or parts of them) that are so fundamentally different as to provide the initial impetus for comparison, and it is the immediate contrasts evident in the lack of 'equivalence' that cause the researcher to seek explanations for them in terms of differences in 'culture' and 'context'. For example, in comparing a particular aspect of education in California and Massachusetts, we would identify all sort of equivalences, and any differences would be explainable through phenomena outside of those equivalences: the constants would throw light on the variables. If, on the other hand, we were comparing education in, say, Albania and Switzerland, the equivalences would be for the most part minimal, and so the variables would cause us to question the viability of any imagined constants on the educational phenomena in question.

Once criteria have been established for the task of comparison, and data have been 'juxtaposed' (to use Bereday's term), attempts to postulate explanations for differences or similarities can begin.

The following structure for comparative inquiry (Figure 11)[30] develops a model proposed by Bereday insofar as it includes a 'juxtaposition'[31] stage and recognizes the centrality of context. The first stage is termed 'conceptualization' and represents the essential initial attempts in any investigation to identify the research questions and to 'neutralize' them from any particular context. Questions of the kind 'What is the nature of?' are the most useful at this stage.

The second stage (at which point Bereday's model is very informative) comprises detailed description of educational phenomena in the countries to be investigated with full attention paid to the local context in terms of its historical, geographical, cultural, political, religious, linguistic (etc.) features. The principal question here is 'What is the situation of $x$ in the context of $y$?'

The third stage involves an attempt to isolate differences through direct comparison of the phenomena observed or the data collected. 'How different/similar – in terms of $x$, is $a$ from $b$ in the context of $y$?'

The fourth stage comprises explanation through the development of hypotheses: 'Given that we can observe differences in terms of $x$, between $a$ and $b$ in the context of $y$, what might explain those differences/similarities?'

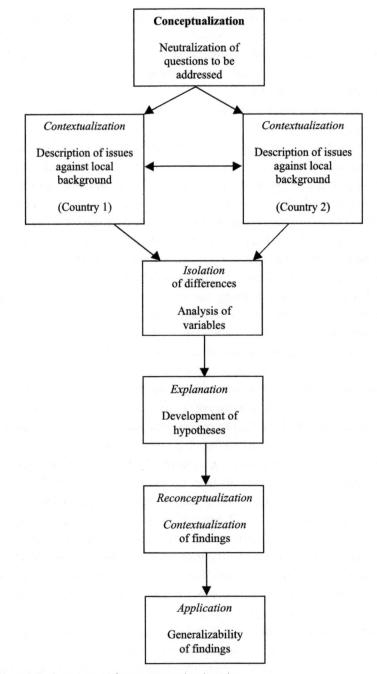

**Figure 11** A structure for comparative inquiry

The fifth and final stage then considers the applicability of the findings to other situations, i.e. the extent to which they might be generalizable: 'Given that there are such similarities/differences (in terms of $x$, between $a$ and $b$ in the context of $y$) what are the implications of such similarities/differences for the separate context of $z$?'

This approach is offered as a possible structure for comparative inquiry where the researcher seeks to put a particular problem into comparative perspective across more than one context. It suggests a systematic procedure for comparison which takes into account the essential requirements of proper conceptual analysis of a problem, the isolation of variables to be investigated after a thorough study of context, the development of hypotheses based on attempts at explanation, a revisiting of the conceptual analysis based on the findings, and a consideration of any applicability of the findings. It assumes that a proper comparative study will first and foremost address a clearly defined issue in education which is to be analysed, and then, having established a strong theoretical basis for such analysis, will proceed to examine the issue in question in two or more contexts.

As we have tried to show, comparative education is a very broad area within the huge range of topics and research approaches subsumed under 'educational studies'. There can be no single approach to comparison that will be agreed upon or that will be appropriate even to the majority of circumstances: as Rust et al. have put it, 'no single research methodology has ever characterized the field of comparative education'.[32] Some contemporary research in comparative education takes a broader, 'bird's-eye' view by focusing on the global context; examples include important work on world culture and world systems (see, for example, recent texts by Baker and LeTendre and Schriewer[33]). Findings from this approach suggest that beyond national and local contextualized differences lie convergent universal patterns. This poses its own methodological challenges and brings large data sets as well as specific theories to bear on questions of education from an international perspective. But at the cross-national level, at the very least there should be attempts to produce a systematic framework for analysis which uses techniques of what Bereday called 'juxtaposition' of data for comparison and which includes a full consideration of context in any attempts to reach conclusions or to generalize from the findings.

We turn now to aspects of research in comparative education in the specific context of developing countries.

# Notes

1.  Kandel, *Studies in Comparative Education*, p. xi.
2.  Obituary of Edmund King, *The Times*, 26 March 2002. Holmes 'had no ear for languages, an uneasy sense of sociology, and some indifference to history' (Robert Cowen, obituary of Brian Holmes, *The Independent*, 30 August 1993).
3.  Turner, *Theory of Education*, p. 101. The reference to Holmes is to his 1981 study, *Comparative Education: Some Considerations of Method*.
4.  King, *Comparative Studies and Educational Decision*, p. 52.
5.  Ibid., p. 53.
6.  Holmes, *Comparative Education*, p. 57.
7.  Winch, 'Understanding a Primitive Society', p. 308.
8.  Eckstein and Noah, *Scientific Investigations*, p. vii.
9.  Watson, 'Comparative Education', pp. 382–3.
10. Theisen and Adams, 'Comparative education research', p. 281.
11. National Archives: Ed 24/1880.
12. Selby-Bigge, *The Board of Education*, p. 214.
13. National Archives: FO 83/978. Initial capitalization of individual words as in original. The full text is reproduced in Phillips, *Reflections on British Interest in Education in Germany*, pp. 39–42.
14. Jullien asks (in connection with school attendance): What are the conditions of admission for children to primary schools? Do all parents send their children and are they invited or obligated by legislative arrangements or local administration, to send them? Jullien, *Plan for Comparative Education*, p. 54.
15. European Commission, 'EURYDICE, the Information Network on Education in Europe', p. 1.
16. Taken from *Education at a Glance, OECD Indicators 2004*.
17. 'After the collection of facts, research on causes', quoted in Gardiner, *The Nature of Historical Explanation*, p. 70.
18. Popper, *Logic of Scientific Discovery*, p. 60.
19. Popper, *Poverty of Historicism*, p. 15.
20. Hegel, *The Philosophy of History*, p. 6.
21. Bebbington, *Patterns in History*, p. 92. Popper's use of the term 'historicism' is idiosyncratic: he used it to refer to what he argued was the mistaken belief that the past allows the prediction of future events.
22. Gottlieb, 'Are we post-modern yet?', pp. 154–5.
23. Yoneyama, review of *Can the Japanese Change Their Education System?*, in *Japanese Studies*, Vol. 24, No. 1, May 2004, pp. 139–42.
24. King, *Comparative Studies and Educational Decision*, pp. 29–30.

25. See Broadfoot and Osborn, *Perceptions of Teaching*, pp. 77–87.
26. See Laczik, unpublished D.Phil. thesis, Oxford, 2005.
27. Bereday, *Comparative Method in Education*, p. 10.
28. Razak in Robinson-Pant, *Cross-Cultural Perspectives on Educational Research*, p. 85.
29. Nowak, 'The strategy of cross-national survey research', pp. 42–3.
30. Taken from Phillips, 'Comparative education: An approach to educational inquiry'.
31. Bereday develops his concept of 'juxtaposition' in 'Reflections on comparative methodology in education', pp. 5–9.
32. Rust et al., 'Research strategies in comparative education', p. 89.
33. Baker and LeTendre, *National Differences, Global Similarities*; Schriewer, *Re-conceptualising the Global/Local Nexus*.

# 7

# Researching Education and Development: Perspectives, Practicalities, and Ethics

I've looked at clouds from both sides now

*Joni Mitchell, Both Sides Now*[1]

Researchers studying education in poorer parts of the world approach their questions from very different starting points, depending on from which 'side' they look at education and development. The focus in this chapter is on research issues in relation to education and national development. We begin by considering some of the social science perspectives within which researchers in this field situate themselves and their studies. Any of the perspectives used in social science may be used to study education and development; however, we will focus here on a selection of perspectives which have particular salience for research on education in less developed parts of the world. Brief outlines of some of the main characteristics of these perspectives are provided, related to theories of education and development.

All of the perspectives outlined here remain in use at the time of writing, but in parallel with changing ways of looking at development, and an evolving relationship between the north and the south, there are discernible shifts in the prevalence of certain perspectives in comparative and international research. The world of international research on education and development has become more pluralistic. This also parallels shifts in the social sciences generally, from an unquestioning faith in the power of rationality and the quest for a single truth, to the inclusion of more nuanced and subject-sensitive perspectives that acknowledge the complexity of societies and the diversity of worldviews. Many of these perspectives are based on the premise that development, developing countries, and many people affected by development processes have been marginalized by the dominant discourses around development.[2] Put another way, the manner in which development has been conceptualized and discussed has actually contributed to maintaining the status quo, and silencing the voices of the less powerful. Current thinking promotes greater sensitivity to these voices, and, as is also true for development assistance, a different relationship with the research subjects:

> As the field of comparative and international education has become increasingly sensitive to the need to take context into account in exploring the lessons to be learned from the experience of other countries, so those involved in research in developing countries have recognized the particular importance of partnership in the research endeavour; of not imposing values and goals generated elsewhere on their colleagues working in very different circumstances.[3]

Other emergent perspectives challenge linear models of development and its relationship to other processes, such as education. In viewing the development process through these lenses, researchers critically question views of development which posit these relationships as straightforward and controllable.

There is a fine line between theories and perspectives, and specific theories are associated with certain perspectives. As a way of differentiating between them, while the theories outlined in Chapter 5 may help to explain relationships between education and development, each of the perspectives sketched in this chapter might be viewed as a distinctive 'lens' through which researchers examine these relationships. Here, examples of influential studies serve to illustrate these perspectives in use, and the section on perspectives closes by comparing the sorts of research questions that might be generated within each of them.

This chapter finishes by highlighting some of the practical and ethical aspects of conducting research in less developed parts of the world. Studies of this kind face the same constraints and can be subject to the same 'abuses' as all comparative studies. However, for 'outsiders', the process of planning and conducting research in developing country contexts demands sensitivity to a cluster of factors related to such issues as power, culture, capacity, and resources and infrastructure.

# Perspectives

## Economic

As we have already noted, economics has dominated understandings of development for some time; Stirrat, for example, refers to 'the hegemony of economics as a discipline' and points to economists' roles as 'legitimators of policies'.[4] In researching education from this perspective, the lens is focused on '... the implications of resource allocation and distribution for relations between educational variables and between these and the external environment'.[5] Examples include the contribution of education to economic growth, or how to provide public education that is cost-effective and efficient. The emphasis is on quantitative data and macro-level studies, within a broadly (and usually) positivist view of the power of numbers to measure and ultimately to promote development. Neo-liberal economics, associated with policies such as structural adjustment and reduced public expenditure, is a particular angle to this perspective, emphasizing free markets and competition as key to increased growth and therefore development. Human capital theory also fits within this perspective, in relation to education's potential to offer both personal and social wealth returns. The assumption is that the relationship between education and development is a largely linear and controllable one, and that economic resources and outcomes are the keys.

An example of an influential study rooted in this perspective is Psacharapoulos and Woodhall's 1985 and Psacharapoulos's 1993 study of the rates of return of different phases of education in terms of their contribution to an individual's private benefit and wider social benefits. Their general conclusion was that in developing countries the benefits of education to

**Figure 12** Average social and private rates of return to education in the developing world[6]

| Region | Social | | | Private | | |
|--------|---------|-----------|--------|---------|-----------|--------|
| | Primary | Secondary | Higher | Primary | Secondary | Higher |
| Africa | 27 | 19 | 14 | 45 | 28 | 33 |
| Asia | 18 | 14 | 12 | 34 | 15 | 18 |
| Latin America | 35 | 19 | 16 | 61 | 28 | 26 |

the individual and his or her family more than compensate for any costs incurred, real or hidden, and that the same holds true for a society: the social benefit of educating the population is enjoyed by everyone. They also determined that primary education offers the best social rate of return, as illustrated by the summary table (Figure 12).

More recent evidence shows changes to these returns, with secondary and higher education now increasingly important both to individuals and society.[7] While there have been many critiques of the analysis,[8] the implications of the basic findings have influenced national policies and donor tendencies. The three main implications are:

> First, the evidence that education is socially and privately profitable suggests that the costs of education need to be shared by society and individuals (government and households). Second, the high social rates of return to primary education indicate that top priority for public financing should be given to the primary level. Third, the difference between high private rates of return and low social rates of return for higher education suggests that a greater part of the cost burden for the tertiary level should be borne by individuals.[9]

These implications have been drivers of the international movement for Education for All. The use of human capital theory has not only been influential in analysing relationships in the developing world. Another more recent study taking a long-term comparative view of economic development in France and Germany has concluded that the conundrum of cause and effect persists:

> The role played by education in economic growth is not as clear as it would seem. The question whether the key to this is the level of education or, on the other hand, the result of economic development, is far from having been settled by the specialists, and the two hypotheses are still opposed.[10]

## Marxist and neo-Marxist perspectives

In contrast to the economic perspective, which is based on optimism that economic growth will deliver development, Marxist and neo-Marxist perspectives emphasize the uneven nature of this growth and how it polarizes society into groups based on their socio-economic status. As in Karl Marx's original theory of class conflict,[11] studies situated within these perspectives emphasize the exploitative relationship between the advantaged rich and the disadvantaged poor, either within a given national context or between developed and developing countries. Using a Marxist or neo-Marxist lens to examine relationships between education and development tends to focus the researcher on economic inequalities and their roots, and reveals the social justice problems attendant in capitalist faith in free markets.

From the international perspective, dependency theory is rooted in the Marxist view of the world. Harber describes the dependency relationship between richer and poorer countries:

> ... dependency theory does not see all poorer countries as 'developing' towards some future developed goal. It argues that they are underdeveloped because other, industrial countries are developed. It posits that the relationship between the 'metropole' or rich and powerful northern countries and the 'periphery' of poorer, southern countries is based on exploitation and domination. Rather than poor countries being poor because they are not 'modern', they remain poor because the more powerful capitalist countries of the metropole (Western Europe and North America) can use their financial, organisational and technological supremacy to control the terms of trade. This means that they can buy primary goods (agricultural and mining products) at low prices and sell manufactured goods at prices favourable to themselves.[12]

Studies using these perspectives highlight how this dependency keeps economically poorer countries poor, and some studies – such as Carnoy's study of education as cultural imperialism[13] – have extended the analysis beyond economic dependency to cultural dependency. The policy implications of this perspective are for intervention in free markets to ensure equitable distribution, and for aid agendas to be examined through this lens in order to ensure that they do not reproduce or exacerbate exploitative and dependency-creating tendencies. A neo-Marxist perspective is also complemented in single-country or comparative studies by the use of reproduction or correspondence theories to explain how schools reproduce social inequalities in a given society. Bowles and Gintis's[14] influential study of how American students are taught their appropriate function as compliant workers through the overt and the hidden curricula in schools is an example of the use of this theory within this perspective.

## Anthropological perspectives

Studies employing an anthropological perspective focus on deep understanding of the cultural context, and how it shapes the meanings that people give to phenomena such as schooling or being an educated person. The emphasis is on qualitative, and in particular, ethnographic research approaches, with a focus on understanding how the people being studied see and experience the world from their points of view: 'the goal is to formulate a *pattern* of analysis that makes reasonable sense of human actions within the *context* of a given place and time'.[15]

Examples of the use of anthropological perspectives and the methodology appropriate to them can be found in literature on adult literacy, which has drawn heavily on ethnography in order to understand in nuanced ways what literacy means to people and how they experience it, the lack of it, or the acquisition of it in their lived worlds. Robinson-Pant's work on Nepal, for example, demonstrates how community attitudes to aging shape older women's participation and valuing of learning.[16] Maddox, in another example, uses ethnographic approaches to understand one woman's perspectives on literacy, contextualized within her family and community relationships, and the vulnerable livelihoods of her and her family.[17] In both cases, extended periods of fieldwork enabled the researchers to make sense of individuals' views of what literacy means to them. These understandings facilitated questioning of the theoretical divide between two camps in the field of adult literacy, by illustrating that the cognitive, functional, and 'situated' aspects of literacy were all significant in their lives and worldviews, and these and similar studies draw on the work of Brian Street on these themes.[18]

## Post-colonialism

According to Crossley and Tikly, post-colonial perspectives '... place centre stage the continuing implications of Europe's expansion into Africa, Asia, Australasia and the Americas from the fifteenth century onwards'.[19] The history of the colonial encounter, and its ongoing manifestations, is told ('renarrativized') from the perspective of those formerly colonized by European powers. The post-colonial lens tends to focus on the legacy of colonial inequalities, and their philosophical, political, economic, social and cultural consequences.[20] In its interest in discourse, pluralism, voice, and the construction of the 'other', post-colonialism is sometimes linked to postmodernism. Given the desire to understand the colonial and post-colonial experience from this perspective, topics typically approached include:

> ... slavery, migration and diaspora formation; the effects of race, culture, class

and gender in post-colonial settings; histories of resistance against colonial and neo-colonial domination; the complexities of identity formation and hybridity; language and language rights; the ongoing struggles of indigenous peoples for recognition of their rights.[21]

The implications of this perspective and these topics for education are vast.[22] Two recent edited collections on post-colonialism and education include studies of the following:

- the discourses of ethnicity in the schooling of American and Australian indigenous children[23]
- the use of multicultural literature in education as a preferred alternative to the 'classics'[24]
- pedagogy and identity in 'offshore' higher education[25]
- advocacy for acknowledging all kinds of hybrids in the curriculum, including a combination of post-colonial and the non-heterosexual ('queer') identities[26]
- language attitudes and choices in second generation immigrant children in the UK, and the tension between 'world languages' such as English and linguistic diversity.[27]

# Gender

Gender has been at the forefront of development studies for decades, and the Millennium Development Goals highlighted its prominence: of the eight goals three have an explicit gender-related component. Goal 2, to achieve universal primary education, singles out the need to address the imbalance between boys and girls in terms of school access and enrolment. Goal 3 is to promote gender equality and empower women, and the target is to 'eliminate gender disparity in primary and secondary education, preferably by 2005, and at all levels by 2015'. Goal 5 is to improve maternal health. As one UNESCO publication puts it:

> The removal of gender gaps should have first priority in all programmes of school expansion and quality improvements. The state [...] must create an enabling environment for promoting gender equality, invest in redistribution strategies and mitigate the burden of conflict, economic crisis and HIV/AIDS. The international community must boldly accompany this process, using a gender lens as a focus for all aid to education programmes.[28]

Gender is one of many dimensions of equality, which development programmes within this paradigm seek to address, but it has been central to education and development agendas in recent years – note, for example, that half of the papers in a recent special issue on Education Outcomes and Poverty[29] are on gender themes. As might be expected, within the context of education and development, gender frameworks include feminism, focusing on the emancipation of females, and the danger and potential of education in this area. From this perspective, studies related to education and development constitute a vast and rapidly growing field of literature. A selective list of research areas from an annotated bibliography on the field[30] includes the following topics: gender bias in policy-making; the social gains from the impact of schooling on girls; comparisons of educational attainment of boys and girls; women in education management; barriers to access to schooling; and the interaction of gender, culture, and learning. This resource focuses on girls; however, gender studies are increasingly concerned with masculinities as an essential part of the equation, and the attendant issues of gendered violence in schools (such as a study of the extent and nature of the abuse of schoolgirls in several African countries[31]) and the problem of some groups of boys' disengagement from schooling.

# Human rights

A human rights perspective in education is framed by international agreements about the rights and freedoms that all humans share. Education is thus conceptualized not as a means for people to contribute to the development of their society but as a fundamental entitlement. To contradict John F. Kennedy, ask not what citizens can do for their country; ask what their country must do for them.

This perspective in education has been categorized into three main approaches: rights *in* education; rights *to* education; and rights *through* education. Rights in education refer to the ways in which education is provided in such a way that respects the learners' rights as guaranteed in the UN Universal Declaration of Human Rights (UNDHR) or the UN Convention on the Rights of the Child (UNCRC), to which almost all countries are signatories. For example, the right not to be discriminated against on the basis of race, language or religion (Article 2, UNDHR and UNCRC); the right to express opinions freely (Article 19, UNDHR and Article 12, UNCRC); and the right to be protected from violence and abuse, which is usually interpreted to include corporal punishment (Article

19, UNCRC). In terms of rights to education, these are enshrined in the UNDHR, Article 26:

1. Everyone has the right to education. Education shall be free, at least in the elementary and fundamental stages. Elementary education shall be compulsory. Technical and professional education shall be made generally available and higher education shall be equally accessible to all on the basis of merit.

Rights through education refers to the rights that are more accessible to people who are educated, including such rights as the right to equal pay for equal work (UNDHR Article 23); and the right to participate in the cultural life of the community, and enjoy the benefits of the arts and scientific advancement (UNDHR Article 27).

To this we would add learning *about* rights in education. One important role that education can play is in teaching about and promoting rights, and this, too, is enshrined in the UNDHR, Article 26:

2. Education shall be directed to the full development of the human personality and to the strengthening of respect for human rights and fundamental freedoms. It shall promote understanding, tolerance and friendship among all nations, racial or religious groups, and further the activities of the United Nations for the maintenance of peace.

Recent work by McCowan on education as a human right highlights the non-conditional nature of rights, and the fact that from a rights-based perspective, the cost-benefit logic that underpins human capital and other economically-driven theories is not relevant.[32]

## Global security

The global security framework is concerned with the threat to human well-being and 'security' in the broad sense of the word (that is, beyond the military definition). It is a composite perspective which draws on three interrelated areas of knowledge:

- development, including such areas as economics, governance and human service provision
- environment, including environmental and ecological sciences and health
- violence, including international relations, conflict and mediation, terrorism, and criminology.[33]

Survival is an issue at individual, community, and global levels. The relationship between the threat to human survival and security and education is a two-way one. Research might focus on how education can contribute to redressing global security threats, for example through environmental and peace education, and through modelling good governance and conflict mediation practices. From the other direction, another focus for the global security lens is how these threats might impact on education: how education is affected in conflict zones, for example, or how environmental threats such as poor nutrition can impair learning potential.

Increasing concerns over all the parameters of this framework – development, the environment, and conflict – ensure that even when they are not brought together, they will receive ongoing attention individually. However, this perspective specifically demands that they be operationalized in unison. Williams argues that the global security perspective is a vital new direction for the field, '... which can situate the eclectic interests of International Education within a simple framework that builds on previous education endeavour and is more compatible with contemporary international analysis in other fields'.[34]

## Research questions

Researchers from within each of the perspectives above tend to choose research areas relevant to their own ways of viewing the developing world. They generate research questions and research designs that are in sympathy with their own perspectives. To illustrate the effect of these different lenses focusing on one area of research, let us use the example of the broad research area of the implementation of Education for All in developing country 'X'. Some research questions that might arise from each of the perspectives above will be suggested, along with the sorts of methods likely to be employed in the research.

An economic rationalist perspective on EFA in X might concern itself with some of the following questions: At what financial cost could EFA be achieved? How could these costs be met? What are the economic barriers to access, such as opportunity costs to parents? Through increased enrolment in basic education, based on comparative evidence, what are the returns to the country likely to be, particularly in the form of economic growth, and what evidence exists that these expected benefits are being felt? What is the minimum government investment required to ensure these returns, and how much can households be expected to bear? The studies are most likely to be quantitative in nature, and based on statistical analysis of such facts as government budgets from the tax base and from overseas development assistance, enrolment ratios, and household spending patterns.

A Marxist perspective would focus on the impact of class inequalities within the country, and the dependencies that exist between X and countries of the metropole. So, for example, some questions might arise related to inequalities of access: which groups of children in X are most disadvantaged in terms of their opportunities to attend school? Why do these disadvantages exist, and do more advantaged groups actually help to create them, and benefit from them? To what extent does the education on offer generate equality of opportunity, or do children from the lower socio-economic groups learn simply to be productive for the benefit of those in higher groups? On a global scale, who benefits more if country X achieves EFA: citizens of X, or citizens of the metropolitan nations? A range of methods might be applied, as well as theoretical frameworks such as dependency and world systems.

An anthropologist's perspective on EFA might be concerned with deep understanding of the local and national cultural factors that impact on the implementation of EFA. So, for example, exploration of parental views of schooling could be key to understanding barriers to participation. How do parents value education? How well does the schooling on offer reflect local priorities and belief systems? Ethnography is likely to be an approach employed by these researchers, who would insist that long enculturation in the context is a necessary part of accessing local understandings.

Post-colonial perspectives would be most concerned with how the colonial legacy is embedded in the implementation of EFA. There would be concern, for example, for the identity formation of children attending schools, and the researchers would wish to understand and expose the inequalities and hegemonies that are inherent in the policy. Questions might include: To what extent does the curriculum value the indigenous culture, and to what extent is it driven by conceptions of learning that are derived in more powerful countries? What is the relative importance placed on 'world' languages and the mother tongues of learners, and how does this shape how learners see themselves? How was the policy on EFA derived, and what global hegemonies and pressures exist as a legacy of a colonial past and a fossilized neo-colonial present? Under these conditions, is an EFA policy appropriate at all?

An obvious starting point for researchers focusing on gender issues would be the disparities between girls' and boys' participation and achievement in basic schooling, and the reasons behind these. Quantitative data might be primary here. However, beyond access and achievement, questions might also be asked which demand qualitative methodology. How do pedagogies affect girls' and boys' experiences of schooling? How does the curriculum help to construct or interrogate notions of femininity and masculinity? How does gender difference as understood culturally affect the need for, and implementation of, EFA?

A human rights framework for studies of EFA would focus the lens on the declared universal human right to education. The government of X and the international community would have the responsibility to provide education for all of the citizens of the country. Research might evaluate the extent to which this responsibility is being met, and what impediments exist. Rights within education are equally important, regardless of the imperatives of access, and a researcher might ask questions such as: Are children protected from violence in the classroom? If not, why not? Who is violating the rights, and how? How can the right to safety and health be ensured? A human rights perspective might also be concerned with the education of learners in their rights and responsibilities: Does the curriculum include this knowledge, and develop attitudes in learners that encourage them to defend their own rights and the rights of others?

From a global security perspective, the researcher might ask: What contribution to human security will this EFA policy make for individuals and communities in X, and globally? For example, how does the curriculum contribute to enhancing survival, in areas such as drugs and AIDS education; and the understanding of risk? Or does it focus on the traditional areas of literacy and numeracy to the exclusion of these? How does the teaching of conflict and portrayals in textbooks construct 'others', and hence contribute either to national security, or conversely, to tension? Does the policy for EFA sufficiently reach those who are socially excluded and particularly at risk? From the other side of the perspective, research questions might include: What is the effect of local, regional, and international conflict on the prospects for EFA in X? The eclectic nature of this framework calls for eclectic methods of research.

# Practical and ethical issues in researching in less developed areas

Cook makes the following blunt observation, based on his experience in Egypt:

> Researchers, when doing educational research in developing countries, face certain inevitable hazards. It just goes with the territory.[35]

He raises the issues of access, data quality, and reliability, being an outsider, and language. These experiences were highlighted for him as a researcher from an industrialized nation through a comparison with his experiences at 'home', and through his heightened sense of difference. None of these issues is unique to developing country contexts, and a researcher from a developing country is likely to face them working in the north. Additionally, as we continue to emphasize, the developing world is not homogeneous, and conducting research in any given situation is likely to bring ungeneralizable experiences. However, the reality of the world's imbalances in power and resources means that there are far more researchers from the north generating knowledge about education in the south than the other way around:

> In this there is disequilibrium. It is unlikely for novice transient researchers from one rich country to do applied research that will affect the internal policy of another, but this is expected of transient, even student researchers from rich countries working in those that are poor. It is very rare for even senior academics from poorer parts of the world to take part in such transient activities in rich countries, although this is where most have at some time been trained.[36]

Additionally, the post-colonial nature and contexts of stringency of the developing world may exacerbate some factors in the research context and relationships. It is therefore not unreasonable to discuss these as a constellation of issues that might be part of the process. These arise not so much from a static reality in the host country, but as a consequence of the interaction of the researcher's culture and expectations with those encountered in the research process. The following description serves to highlight a number of noteworthy points around resource implications and local perceptions, which are likely to impinge on the researcher's experience in a less developed area:

> The question of access, arrangement, and arrival sets the tone for the entire interview, an area underplayed by texts on interviewing that focus simply on 'getting permission'. In Botswana, I arrived at the boarding school principal's house hot, sweaty and anxious, having been put off the bus what looked like miles from anywhere and trudging blindly across the bush in what I hoped was the right direction. The principal gave me a glass of water and serenely continued breastfeeding her sixth child. In no way did I represent a threat, and indeed I was the one who had to be reassured and calmed down. The teachers were delighted, for they had been told to expect 'a doctor' and the dust-covered spectacle they encountered did not fit their apprehensions of a formidable researcher. I think I was able to gain confidence and trust reasonably quickly, as it was appreciated that I had made such efforts to come to that school.[37]

To Cook's notion of the outsider, we might add a variety of cultural values that affect research relationships, such as gendered expectations and the formalities of hospitality traditions, and understandings of friendship and reciprocity.[38] Finally, the political realities of instability and corruption are factors that researchers may encounter in any context, but given the prevalence of conflict in developing counties,[39] and given the correlation between underdevelopment and a high score on corruption indices,[40] they are more likely to be issues in poorer areas.

Considering this constellation of troublesome issues, how best to maintain high standards of rigour and ethics? Arguably, the root of many of these issues lies in the ethnocentric perspective of the outsider researcher, and the mediating solutions lie in wider deployment of local researchers as primary and collaborating researchers. This often requires capacity building in terms of research skills, where the human resource has not had opportunities to develop them. Participatory development approaches have been influential in promoting greater equality in the relationships between donors and recipients, and development workers and local communities.[41] The same values underpinning these can be used to challenge traditional 'outsider' and 'top-down' research. The 'three pillars' underlying this ethical approach are based on:

- the behaviour and attitudes of outsiders, who facilitate, not dominate
- the methods, which shift the normal balance from closed to open, from individual to group, from verbal to visual and from measuring to comparing
- partnership and sharing of information and experience between insiders and outsiders and between organizations.[42]

What might be considered appropriate in terms of research ethics in a given context depends, however, on local cultural norms, further complicating the question of how outsiders can best ensure that they are behaving ethically in their research practice:

> Taking a cross-cultural perspective on research ethics is thus not just about comparing one value system with another, but as much about understanding the cultural context in which ethical codes have been developed [...] The question arises as to how far ideas about ethics are ethnocentric. Are there universal values that researchers should hold (as PRA [Participatory Rural Approval] suggests – 'be humble', 'be sensitive'[43]) and just different ways of going about ensuring these values inform research (such as written contracts in place of oral interaction)? How far are the key concepts underpinning ethical codes of conduct – such as 'secrecy' or even 'democracy' – culturally embedded? For example, Warwick[44] identifies the 'wide cross-cultural differences in the value and meaning of privacy'. If privacy is not a strongly held value in a certain cultural context, should protection of data and individual identity be a key issue to address with regard to research ethics?[45]

Such issues are of particular relevance to outside researchers, or insiders whose work has to adhere to standards of more than one context (such as an international student based overseas but studying their own country, or a local researcher employed by an international NGO). The ongoing interest in insider and outsider perspectives – and the increasingly blurred boundaries between them – reflects broader concern for the ethics of international research and the importance of authentic voice and the agency that it can bring, as well as the opportunities and challenges that new technologies, new transnational and hybrid identities, and new modes of partnership offer. A current thematic forum within the British Association for International and Comparative Education[46] is testament to the importance of these issues.

# Conclusion

In this chapter we have explored issues in the process of researching education and development. We have seen how different perspectives inform and shape the aims, processes, and outcomes of research. The sample of perspectives here serves to illustrate the diversity of worldviews from which research emerges; in order to understand the starting point of researchers, it is helpful to be able to place their studies within one of these, or other, categories. We have also considered some of the realities and ethics of conducting research in less developed contexts, starting to unravel some of the complexities of ethnocentrism and asking questions about how it can be avoided.

As a concluding note, this chapter taken together with Chapter 5 could leave the reader with the impression that education is at the centre of development debates. Given the MDGs, the prominence of Human Capital as a guiding theory and of Human Rights as a perspective within development, this does in many ways seem to be the case. However, there is concern in many quarters for the impact of research in this area, in a context of demand for quick-fix solutions to development. This is mirrored in a rather poor degree of understanding of educational issues reflected in key contemporary development texts.[47] As the richness of theories, perspectives and empirical evidence on the links between education and development continues to grow, it is also important that it is mainstreamed in the discourses of both development and educational studies, and the lack of consensus and easy solutions does not interrupt this.

# Notes

1.  Mitchell, Joni, 'Both Sides Now', from the Album *Clouds.*
2.  For a more detailed discussion of development discourse, see Robinson-Pant, 'Development as discourse'.
3.  Broadfoot, Foreword, p. xii.
4.  Stirrat, 'Economics and Culture', p. 34.
5.  Diebolt, 'Towards a comparative economics of education', p. 3.
6.  Schultz, quoted in Colclough and Lewin, 1993, p. 27.
7.  Colclough, 'Education Poverty and Development'.
8.  For a discussion of critiques of human capital theory, see Little, 'Motivating Learning'.
9.  Tembon, 'Educational Finance Strategies', p. 207.
10. Diebolt and Fontvieille, 'Dynamic Forces in Educational Development', p. 301.
11. Marx, *Das Kapital.*
12. Harber, 'Education and theories of development', pp. 54–5.
13. Carnoy, 'Education as Cultural Imperialism'.
14. Bowles and Gintis, *Schooling in Capitalist America.*
15. Fife, 'The importance of fieldwork'.
16. Robinson-Pant, Why Eat Green Cucumbers at the Time of Dying?
17. Maddox, 'What can ethnographic approaches teach us?'

18.  Street, 'Meanings of culture in development'.
19.  Crossley and Tikly, 'Post-colonial perspectives', p. 147.
20.  Hickling-Hudson et al., *Disrupting Preconceptions*.
21.  Crossley and Tikly, 'Post-colonial perspectives', p. 148, drawing on Ashcroft et al., *The Post-colonial Studies Reader*.
22.  Crossley and Tikly, *Comparative Education*, Vol. 40, No. 2 and Hickling-Hudson et al., *Disrupting Preconceptions*.
23.  Hickling-Hudson and Ahlquist, 'The Challenge to Deculturation'.
24.  Bean, 'The role of multicultural literature'.
25.  Singh, 'Offshore Australian higher education'.
26.  Crowley, 'Perverse Hybridisations'.
27.  Rassool, 'Sustaining linguistic diversity'.
28.  UNESCO, *Gender and Education for All*, p. 21.
29.  Colclough, *Education Outcomes and Poverty*.
30.  Brock and Cammish, *Gender, Education and Development*.
31.  Leach et al., *An Investigative Study of the Abuse of Girls*.
32.  McCowan, *Education as a Human Right*.
33.  Williams, 'Education and human survival'.
34.  Ibid., p. 199.
35.  Cook, 'Doing educational research in a developing country', p. 92.
36.  Preston, 'Integrating paradigms in educational research', p. 56.
37.  Davies, 'Interviews and the study of school management', p. 138.
38.  See, for example, Shaw and Ormton, 'Values and vodka', and Schweisfurth, 'Coming in from the cold'.
39.  Davies, *Education and Conflict*.
40.  Corruption Perception Index, at Transparency International.
41.  Robinson-Pant, *Cross-cultural Perspectives on Educational Research*.
42.  Chambers, *Whose Reality Counts?*, pp. 105–6.
43.  Kumar, 'ABC of PRA'.
44.  Warwick, 'The politics and ethics of field research', p. 327.
45.  Robinson-Pant, *Cross-cultural Perspectives on Educational Research*, p. 99.
46.  http://baice.ac.uk/2012/revisiting-insideroutsider-perspectives-in-international-and-comparative-education-a-baice-thematic-forum/
47.  McGrath, 'The role of education in development'.

# 8

# Comparative Education Research: Survey Outcomes and Their Uses

It is highly unlikely that a national ministry of education will allow an international test to dictate its national curriculum.

*Postlethwaite*[1]

There is no such thing as facts, only interpretation.

*Nietzsche*

## Large-scale studies of pupil attainment

It is inevitable that those responsible for a nation's educational provision will wish to know how their children of school age are performing in comparison with children from other countries. In addition, they will want to have a sense of how their education system – as a whole and in individual aspects of its operation – stands in international comparison. Much of the early work comparing education systems was, as we have seen, of a descriptive kind. And an early (1902) study of comparative education concluded that it was impossible to go beyond an understanding of the individuality of an education system and to evaluate it in terms of its performance *vis-à-vis* other systems; this was 'an old truth':

Each system of education can only be understood when seen in its own setting. Each is an expression of its nation's genius; it is characteristic of its people. In so far as it is thriving it is truly popular, and only so far as it is popular and peculiar is it national. The *habitat* of each system is fixed, it is an indigenous product; consequently it is not only unscientific, but it is impossible to measure comprehensively any system of national education in terms of another. These systems cannot be arranged in order of merit. The finer elements, the more ethical and spiritual factors in national culture, defy the balance of the analyst and the scalpel of the anatomist; they are susceptible to no quantitative tests.[2]

Now sophisticated methods of analysis have facilitated more scientific and reliable ways to compare performance in various contexts within and between countries and to address the fundamental question posed by Reynolds and Farrell: 'How does one measure the influence of the educational system and its responsibility for variation in educational achievements?'[3]

In this first part we shall be concerned with the following questions:

- Why are international studies of pupil achievement necessary/ desirable?
- What is their purpose?
- What subjects should/can be covered?
- How can comparability between samples be achieved?
- What are the data collection problems?
- How can the data be analysed?
- What use can/should be made of the data?

Though there had been some previous studies of this kind, it was in 1958 that the work of what was to become the International Association for the Evaluation of Educational Achievement (IEA) began and thus marked the start of a hugely influential series of international investigations. A survey of the educational achievements of 13-year-old children in 12 countries was undertaken by Foshay and others during the period 1959–61 and its results were published in a report from the UNESCO Institute for Education in 1962. In a foreword to the report Saul Robinsohn, describing it as possibly 'an unusual addition to the literature of education', saw considerable potential in investigations of this kind:

> The results [...] suggest that both empirical educational research and comparative education can gain new dimensions, the one by extending its range over various educational systems, the other by including empirical methods among its instruments.[4]

There followed a series of investigations by the IEA – more than 30 so far

– of an increasingly sophisticated and wide-ranging kind, among them an early project on home and school factors affecting achievement in mathematics (1962–6), surveys on science, reading comprehension, literacy, first foreign languages (French and English) and civic education (1966–75), and further large-scale studies of mathematics, reading, computer literacy, teacher education and science; arguably the most influential among these is the Third International Mathematics and Science Survey (TIMSS). IEA states the purpose and significance of its studies as aiming to:

- provide international benchmarks to assist policy-makers in identifying the relative strengths and weaknesses of their education systems
- provide high-quality data to increase policy-makers' understanding of key school- and non-school-based factors that influence teaching and learning
- provide high-quality data that will serve as a resource for identifying areas of concern and action, and for preparing and evaluating educational reforms
- develop and improve the capacity of education systems to engage in national strategies for educational monitoring and improvement
- contribute to the development of a worldwide community of researchers in educational evaluation.[5]

While the work of IEA continues, other organizations have also become involved in surveys of attainment on a huge scale, most notably the Organisation for Economic Cooperation and Development (OECD) whose PISA (Programme for International Student Assessment) project – the first results of which appeared in 2001[6] – has had considerable impact on the governments of the countries participating.[7]

Why are such studies undertaken? They are, of course, intrinsically interesting; but beyond their fundamental scientific value and that of the methodological challenges they pose to investigators, they serve to identify strengths and weaknesses and therefore to inform policy debates in education with evidence which is calculated to be as objective as possible, and they establish benchmarks for future surveys and so enable comparisons to be made over time. They can be instrumental in identifying good practice, though any authoritative views in this regard would depend on convincing evidence of causation. Agreement to participate in them constitutes for the most part a laudably responsible act of governments – which take part partly because it is difficult for them not to do so, but also because they like to be seen as wishing to learn from a disinterested outside investigation of attainment within their education systems. That said, however, these studies clearly serve political purposes insofar as a government might use the results to vindicate its current and future policies or to criticize the policies of its predecessors, or – as Gita Steiner-Khamsi puts it – to 'glorify' or to 'scandalize' depending on the political agenda. Countries which have done well become the subject of considerable scrutiny by those seeking to improve their performance, and the lessons drawn from these transfer-oriented studies are inevitably selective to fit the overarching policy agenda of the country seeking to improve. The discourse and arguably the role of the OECD have shifted over time, towards a greater emphasis on the question of why some countries have been successful and the use of these lessons as policy drivers, and their website points immediately to the policy potential of lessons from the results. As the editors of one recent volume claim:

> ...PISA seems well on its way to being institutionalized as the main engine in the global accountability juggernaut, which measures, clarifies and ranks students, educators and school systems from diverse cultures and countries using the same standardized benchmarks. The OECD, in turn, begins assuming a new institutional role as arbiter of global education governance, simultaneously acting as diagnostician, judge and policy advisor to the world's school systems.[8]

The authors link this to wider shifts in public management linked to globalization, competition, and the pressing quest for economic growth (Grek has used the term 'governing by numbers' to describe the confluence of PISA with these[9]). They also note a series of 'puzzles and paradoxes' which make causation difficult to establish and transfer of policy lessons problematic (which will come as no surprise, based on this book's ongoing cautions in these regards). Finland is held up as a consistent success, yet its approach to education is defiantly different from the OECD's 'standard reform package'.[10]

As well as raw test scores, however, a range of data is collected which permits additional significant analyses beyond league tables of achievement. For example, information is gathered including students' gender, proxies for their socio-economic status, and the kind of school they attend, which has permitted sophisticated within and between country studies to investigate questions of gender and class equity, aspiration, and types of schooling. It is possible to use the extensive databanks of the OECD to ask questions not only about the overall performance of pupils of the same age in different countries, but about whether this correlates with their personal and schooling circumstances. What is interesting about the results of some of the top-performing countries – Finland included – is that success has been quite well distributed among the population, while in other countries it is more dependent on socio-economic status and the type of school attended.

Which subjects are covered in these large-scale surveys? Mathematics has figured prominently, since – so it is argued – it is one of the three basic and common subjects of the school curriculum (alongside mother tongue and science), and it is possible to devise tests that are relatively culture-free and so usable in classrooms throughout the world. That is to say, a task in mathematics is not so dependent on factors extraneous to the subject being tested (as would be the case with, say, history, or literature). Mathematicians do not necessarily accept this argument, and they point to the problems involved with a focus on abstraction in school mathematics to the extent that socio-cultural context is removed.[11] But it is nevertheless probably more straightforward to devise a test in mathematics that is appropriate for pupils from a wide range of different countries than it is to devise such a test in other subjects of the curriculum. What is more, since there is a commonly held view that mathematical ability – or at the very least basic numeracy – plays an important part in occupations that are seen to contribute to a country's economic success and international competitiveness, it is understandable that there should be a focus on mathematics in IEA and other surveys.[12]

But of course, as we have seen, other subjects are also commonly included, chief among them pupils' first language and science. The OECD's PISA studies cover these on a rotational basis, and have shifted the focus to what is termed reading, mathematical and scientific 'literacy', i.e. to a concept of attainment which is defined as 'much broader than the historical notion of the ability to read and write':

> Literacy is measured on a continuum, not as something that an individual does or does not have. It may be necessary or desirable for some purposes to define a point on a literacy continuum below which levels of competence are considered inadequate, but the underlying variability is important. A literate person has a range of competencies. There is no precise dividing line between a person who is fully literate and one who is not.[13]

Knowledge, in PISA's terms, is assessed with regard to *content/structure*, and *processes* that pupils need to be able to perform, and *contexts* in which skills are applied. The focus here is more on application than the testing of learnt subject knowledge; in their own words:

PISA is unique because it develops tests which are not directly linked to the school curriculum and provides context through the background question-naires which can help analysts interpret the results. The tests are designed to assess to what extent students at the end of compulsory education, can apply their knowledge to real-life situations and be equipped for full participation in society.[14]

But whatever the focus of these large-scale international studies, there are a number of problems associated with data collection and analysis.

First, there is the important question of sampling, both within and between countries. There should not be any incomparability of sampling in terms of overall percentages, types of school represented, or pupils excluded. Nor, of course, should there be variations in the age of the pupils involved (to the extent, for example, of pupils who are repeating a year being included as if they were of the same chronological age of pupils in the same grade). Though those responsible for large-scale international surveys will set rules about the latitude allowable in individual country samples, there is not always absolute control over what is ultimately managed. If the rules are not followed, country samples which fall short of the requirements should be excluded from the analysis. These problems are addressed by the OECD in its PISA surveys:

> In order to ensure the comparability of the results across countries, PISA needs to assess comparable target populations. Differences between countries in the nature and extent of pre-primary education and care, in the age of entry to formal schooling, and in the structure of the education system do not allow school grades to be defined so that they are internationally compa-rable. Valid international comparisons of educational performance must, therefore, define their populations with reference to a target age. PISA covers students who are aged between 15 years 3 months and 16 years 2 months at the time of the assessment, regardless of the grade or type of institution in which they are enrolled and of whether they are in full-time or part-time education. The use of this age in PISA, across countries and over time, allows the performance of students shortly before they complete compulsory education to be compared in a consistent way.[15]

Variations in response rate resulted in some exclusions from the 2003 PISA survey. That for the UK, for example, did not satisfy the response rate standards set, and so comparability *over time* (with the results of PISA 2000) was not possible and is specifically warned against by the OECD.

Clearly, too, the test items should be designed in such a way as to test pupils' knowledge, skills, and abilities in a realistic fashion. Survey teams will examine curricula and syllabuses in great detail and reach conclusions about what pupils in a range of countries might reasonably be expected to achieve. Others, and PISA is the best example of this to date, will be less concerned with testable knowledge and will focus on the applicability of skills.

Translations should be managed in such a way as to ensure maximum comparability, a frequently used technique being that of 'back translation', which, as we have seen, involves an initial translation that is then separately re-translated into the original language. If significant variations emerge, there will be questions about the adequacy of the original translation.

Data collection problems are potentially huge. With very large samples in many different countries there has to be considerable reliability on the efficiency of local arrangements for the administration of tests and also for the collection of background data which can help in the contextualization and eventual interpretation of results. Manuals should be produced with detailed guidance for test administrators. Training sessions should be arranged. Certain individuals should be excluded from involvement in testing (PISA suggests excluding anyone teaching the pupils being tested, and, if possible, all those teaching in schools participating in tests). As far as possible, tests should be administered under similar conditions (although this is hugely problematic, given the differing attitudes to testing in particular and to international testing among both staff and students).

Analysis of the data should of course be statistically rigorous. Much of the scientific discussion which ensues when results are published centres on complex questions of statistical analysis, and sometimes data have to be corrected as a result. Surveys like PISA produce huge amounts of data which allow for sophisticated analysis not just in terms of international comparison but also of within-country differences. In the case of PISA 2000, for example, it was possible to analyse variations in performance between the various *Länder* of Germany.

The use made of the data raises several questions, chief among them the desirability of the creation of 'league tables'. Harvey Goldstein describes the main criticism:

> One of the more misleading presentations of results of comparative studies is the emphasis given to aggregate scores of 'mathematics' or 'science'. Such scale scores typically are formed by averaging the responses for all the items in a subject area. This has two principal drawbacks. The first is that much of the real interest lies in individual topic areas and the second is that this reflects the weightings of topic items chosen by the test constructors.[16]

Tests might pay more attention to particular 'topic areas' (aspects of, say, mathematics) that are given more weight in the curriculum of country X than country Y – to the obvious detriment of the results achieved by country Y. Equally, one needs to ask whether what is being measured is actually the performance of the education system, or something else. For example, in countries where there is a prominent 'shadow' education system, and where most young learners attend intensive additional tuition classes, this is likely to have a substantial impact on results, and therefore lessons drawn from schooling practices are not the only or main relevant ones. In the same contexts, cultural attitudes to learning are likely to be an underlying factor not easily replicated in countries keen to achieve similar test results.[17]

There is usually a flurry of reporting when results are published. Since these studies produce rankings the results can be depicted in overall performance tables which allow the press to say which countries' children are achieving the most and the least from their education. It is left to specialists to analyse the results more closely and to debate sometimes highly technical issues relating, for example, to sampling or to statistical analysis.[18] But for the general reader of reports in the popular press these subtleties will not be apparent, and what will remain fixed in the mind is that country X is 'better' than country Y, even though in terms of aggregated scores they might only be decimal points apart.

The task for the comparativist is to monitor both the way in which international surveys of attainment are conducted and the reporting of results. This might require to some degree detailed specialist knowledge (on the statistical approaches used, for example) but there are also useful checklists of questions that need to be asked of any such surveys, of the kind produced by Neville Postlethwaite, who was one of the leading world experts in the field,[19] and those concerned with using survey results should be familiar with such questions. Here, for example, are the basic questions Postlethwaite suggested should be applied to data analysis:

> In reporting test scores (either total scores or subscores), were sufficient items used to create the score? [...]
>
> Were the appropriate variables taken into account when examining relationships between variables?
>
> Have the standard errors of sampling been reported for every estimate in the report?[20]

But perhaps the most important question to be asked of any international survey of attainment is whether it compares like with like. The best studies will bear this constantly in mind. Some – especially small-scale surveys without the resources of IEA or the OECD – might fall far short of this fundamental requirement. Caroline St John Brooks reminded us of the basic problems:

> Different countries have widely varying aims for their education systems, different curricula, and may organize their school systems in a variety of ways. The length of the school day may differ, or the number of days in the school year. Children may start school at five, or six, or seven; they may be taught in large or small classes, they may be separated according to their ability – in different schools or in different streams or 'sets' within schools.[21]

This checklist of factors affecting comparability applies not only to the design of surveys but also to ways in which the results can be analysed and interpreted. In attempting to identify causation, analysts will look closely at some of the variables identified here, especially perhaps at grouping by ability within or between schools. This factor has been seen as significant in terms of explaining Germany's poor performance in the PISA studies. (Germany still has for the most part a tripartite system of secondary education, though patterns differ among the 16 *Länder* which make up the Federal Republic.)

The governments which agree to take part in surveys such as those run by IEA or the OECD face the task of explaining the results and acting upon them. As we have seen, they might wish to use the results to 'glorify' policies, or to 'scandalize' the efforts of a previous administration – or even their own if they wish to make a case for reform. The parliaments of the German *Länder* were much occupied with soul-searching analysis and with proposals for reform after the results of PISA 2000, termed in Germany the 'PISA-Schock'. But caution is needed. One set of test results might be skewed for all kinds of reasons, including not only failings in the design but also particular circumstances affecting the cohort being tested (the influence of a widely used textbook with a new approach to teaching mathematics, for example). Rankings might disguise closeness rather than distance between countries. Some tests might not on close analysis be testing what the education system is aiming to achieve: the PISA tests are concerned with 'literacy' in the three subject areas, while the emphasis in some curricula might quite legitimately be on knowledge acquisition, with the application of knowledge given less attention. There is the danger that policy-makers might too readily legislate to abandon established practices on the basis of evidence that might eventually turn out to be idiosyncratic.

Despite all the caveats, however, large-scale surveys of pupil attainment continue to be of interest and considerable value. They have become ever more sophisticated in their design. They command attention. They cause people to think about what education systems are trying to achieve and about ways in which they might be falling short of their aims. They are the culmination of what the early comparativists were hoping might one day be possible – the systematic collection of comparable data which would form the basis for progress in education.

# Achievement studies in less developed areas

The imperative to compare like with like extends beyond sample size and makeup, and beyond the particular aims of a given education system. Given the resource and other challenges facing education in poorer parts of the world, their inclusion in the sorts of studies of achievement discussed so far in this chapter is highly problematic. When lower-middle income or developing countries have been included in such studies, the results tend to put them at the tail end of the achievement curve (for example, South Africa and Ghana in TIMSS, where most students did not reach the lowest benchmarks of attainment[22]). Despite this general observation, the relationship between development and achievement of the kind measured by the TIMSS and PISA studies is imperfect at best. From the most-recently published 2009 results, for example, the biggest success story across all subjects in PISA was China (a middle-income country, but it is important to note that only Shanghai participated, which is very different from poorer and rural parts of the country). Learners in other countries, such as Korea and Estonia, fared better than their counterparts in wealthier countries such as the USA and UK.[23] However, in the most deprived contexts, there are a number of factors which make it impossible to include them fairly in such international rankings of achievement. These include, for example: shortage of classroom teaching and learning aids; very large classroom sizes; underqualified or unqualified teachers; poor health among learners; and a prevalence of illiteracy among parents. Even the logistics of conducting a rigorous data collection in contexts with poor infrastructures would contribute to undermining the reliability and comparability of such a survey.

Concerns about cognitive achievement are not diminished by these realities, and the stakes are high in poorer countries for children to perform well. The contribution to personal success for individuals, and to national development for the benefit of all have already been discussed. Examination scores are widely used as a proxy indicator by parents and policy-makers alike for the quality of individual schools. Where examinations are common across a number of countries, such as is the case with the West African Examination Council (WAEC) and Caribbean Examination Council (CXC) tests at the end of secondary school, they are also sometimes used as a comparative indicator of the performance of a national system. The same sorts of pitfalls exist with these comparisons as with those between richer nations. One of the present authors has observed the use of relatively low national CXC results as evidence of the need for major educational reform in one small Caribbean state. In reality, the comparison was invalid on at least two fronts. Firstly, in the country under scrutiny, all learners finishing school sat the examinations, while in the higher achieving example, only those likely to perform well were entered. Inevitably, the inclusion of the less able or less interested brought the overall results down, with no reflection on educational quality. Secondly, when the results were disaggregated by gender, a massive discrepancy between girls and boys was revealed, with girls' results being overall much higher. If there was a problem with the education system, it was specifically with the schooling of boys. In developing countries, it is also likely that the differences between schools will be greater owing to the urban–rural gap, among other factors. Aggregation of examination results to the system level will disguise this.

Outside of the surveys described above which are dominated in terms of participation and achievement by developed countries, data collection to compare educational attainment in developing countries does go on, with a more convincing record of comparing like with like. In Southern and Eastern Africa, for example, the organization conducting these surveys and collating and analyzing the results and contextualizing them in policy and wider realities is the Southern and Eastern Africa Consortium for Monitoring Educational Quality (SACMEQ). Fifteen countries in the region participate. Its mission is stated as:

> To undertake integrated research and training activities that will expand opportunities for educational planners and researchers to: (a) receive training in the technical skills required to monitor, evaluate, and compare the general conditions of schooling and the quality of basic education; and (b) generate information that can be used by decision-makers to plan the quality of education.[24]

It is noteworthy that training and other goals are placed before the information itself, reflecting an ethos of capacity building. As well as monitoring achievement, such locally relevant data as the numbers of schools with running water and libraries and teacher characteristics are collected. As with other cross-national tests of achievement, some of the results are surprising, and again, the correlation between national levels of development and achievement is imperfect at best.

As we have seen from the discussion of EFA in previous chapters, in most developing nations, the first educational challenge is to reach full enrolment by improving access to schooling, take-up of available places, retention once children are enrolled, and provision of minimum standards of quality. Commissioned by UNESCO on behalf of the international community, comparative national progress towards Education for All is studied and reported by the EFA Global Monitoring Team, which annually publishes a themed report.[25]

These reports use an Education for All Development Index (EDI) to compare 'achievement' in this regard. Given that EFA consists of a number of goals, the EDI is not just a question of the proportion of children in school. The EDI uses four different indicators as proxy measures for four of the EFA goals: universal primary education (UPE), adult literacy, gender parity, and the quality of education. Each of these is problematic to measure and compare. UPE is represented by the net enrolment ratio, which reflects the percentage of children of school age who are enrolled in school. If this ratio is 100 per cent, then all eligible children are enrolled. A major source of difficulty here is that countries are self-reporting in terms of school enrolment, and so accuracy of data is variable and often dependent on schools and districts' own reports additionally, enrolment does not necessarily reflect attendance. The second constituent of EDI, adult literacy, is the literacy rate of those over age 15. The 2003–4 report noted some of the problems with the measure and use of this indicator:

> … the existing data on literacy are not entirely satisfactory. Efforts to provide a new data series will, however, take some years to materialize, and the literacy estimates used are presently the best available on an international basis. As regards relevance, it should be noted that the indicator for adult literacy is a statement about the stock of human capital. As such it is slow to change, and it could be argued that it is not a good 'leading indicator' of progress towards improvement in literacy levels on a year-by-year basis.[26]

The third constituent of EFA included in EDI, quality of education, is measured using data on the number of learners remaining in school until the fifth year. As in all international comparative studies of achievement, quality is a particularly difficult concept to understand and measure, and the appendix to the 2003–4 report is worth quoting at length:

> Several proxies are generally used to measure quality and they are all far from satisfactory. They include the pupil/teacher ratio – although its impact on students' performance is ambiguous, and its distribution is as important as the national average value; the repetition rate, which can be a reasonable proxy of quality but policies of automatic promotion undermine its value as an indicator in a number of countries; the percentage of trained teachers, which is problematic because national definitions vary considerably and data availability is limited; public current expenditure variables, which also suffer from limited data coverage and provide only a rough proxy of quality; learning outcome measures, which would constitute the most appropriate proxy of the quality of education, but again the lack of comparable data across countries makes their inclusion impossible at present. [...] There is a strong link between survival within the primary cycle and educational achievement. The survival rate to Grade 5 – often taken as the threshold for acquisition of literacy – also captures aspects of grade repetition, promotion policy and early drop-out.[27]

The final EDI component uses a composite index to measure gender equity and create a gender-related EFA index (GEI). Two sub-goals figure in the equation: gender parity (equal participation of boys and girls in schooling, according to disaggregated enrolment rates) and gender equality. The second is a particularly challenging aspect of the index, and the monitoring team admits that 'the second aspect of the EFA gender goal is not fully reflected in the GEI'.[28]

The extent to which data are complete has been improving over time; however, in 2010, only 120 out of 205 countries submitted sufficient data on all four indicators needed to calculate the EDI.[29] Given these difficulties in selecting indicators and measuring progress towards goals, the EFA 'league tables' while extremely useful cannot be considered a particularly robust way to compare countries' achievement of EFA in relation to each other. Despite this, they are widely used in determining national and donor aid policy. Apart from comparing EFA in different contexts in order to illustrate the progress and relative performance of each country, however, the large-scale analysis of these data helps to provide a global picture of progress towards EFA, and begins to answer the question: Is the world on track?[30] Given the global commitment to EFA goals, these answers are of importance. Additionally, the analysis aims to draw out lessons that all countries can learn from. For example, the association of EDI with other variables has been analysed in order to suggest factors which may contribute to the achievement of EFA. Among the findings of this analysis are the following patterns of performance:[31]

- Economic growth does not correlate strongly with EDI but is mediated by other factors, especially how well the institutions of the country function. This indicates the importance of well-managed growth.
- Per capita value of total aid flows has a positive impact if institutional structures are strong and the environment is democratic.
- Where living standards are high, the correlation is strong between legal guarantees of free education and EDI.
- School fees have a negative effect on EDI.

It is noteworthy that many of these factors work together towards (or against) EDI in a given context, and are conditional upon each other in complex ways: economic growth, institutional development, higher living standards, and greater democracy. Such lessons, while difficult to act upon, are among the most significant contributions of the monitoring exercise, but they rely of course on the potentially problematic comparisons of how far countries have come in the quest for EFA.

# Notes

1. Postlethwaite, *Monitoring Educational Achievement*, p. 79.
2. Hughes, *The Making of Citizens*, p. 387.
3. Reynolds and Farrell, *Worlds Apart?*, p. 8.
4. Foshay et al., *Educational Achievements of Thirteen-Year-Olds*, p. 5.
5. IEA Mission Statement, …accessed April 2013.
6. OECD, *Knowledge and Skills for Life*.
7. For more on the work of the OECD with regard to PISA, see their website at http://www.oecd.org/pisa/, which includes background information and a useful animation.
8. Meyer and Benavot, 'PISA and the globalization of education governance', pp. 7–8.
9. Grek, 'Governing by numbers'.
10. Simola et al., 'Finland's PISA results'.
11. Cf. Phillips and Jaworski, 'Looking abroad', pp. 11–13.
12. Baumert and Lehmann argue in their analysis of TIMSS that even if

there is scepticism about the 'all too direct' association of mathematical and scientific skills with innovation and competitiveness this does not diminish the importance of good performance in those subjects in terms of a modern general education (*Allgemeinbildung*). *TIMSS – Mathematisch-naturwissenschaftlicher Unterricht im internationalen Vergleich*, p. 17.

13. OECD, *Knowledge and Skills for Life*, pp. 18–19.
14. http://www.oecd.org/pisa/
15. OECD, *Learning For Tomorrow's World*, p. 27.
16. Goldstein, *Interpreting International Comparisons*, p. 20.
17. Bray, 'Private supplementary tutoring'.
18. Cf. the exchange of views on the PISA results between Prais and Adams in the *Oxford Review of Education*, Vol. 29, Nos. 2 and 3, and Vol. 30, No. 4.
19. See, for example, his *International Studies of Educational Achievement* (1999) or *Monitoring Educational Achievement* (2004).
20. Postlethwaite, *Monitoring Educational Achievement*, p. 104.
21. Brooks, 'How can international comparisons help us to improve education in English schools?', p. 63.
22. http://timss.bc.edu/PDF/t03_download/T03_M_Chap2.pdf for descriptions of benchmarks and countries achieving them
23. See full results and discussion in documents at http://www.oecd.org/pisa/pisaproducts/pisa2009/pisa2009keyfindings.htm
24. http://www.sacmeq.org/about.htm#mission
25. The past and current reports are available at www.unesco.org/education/efa/index.shtml. The themes were listed in Chapter 5 as an indication of thematic priorities in developing countries.
26. UNESCO 2004 *EFA Global Monitoring Report*, p. 284.
27. Ibid., pp. 284–5.
28. Ibid., p. 285.
29. UNESCO *2012 EFA Global Monitoring Report*.
30. UNESCO 2002 *EFA Global Monitoring Report*.
31. All of these patterns are found in the UNESCO 2004 *EFA Global Monitoring Report*, pp. 192–3.

# 9

# Outcomes of Comparative Education: Selected Themes

What if we insist that some of the comparative education written in universities should aspire to make truth statements (or at least temporarily 'warranted assertions') of a theoretical kind?

*Robert Cowen*[1]

In this chapter we shall exemplify some of the issues discussed so far in terms of research in comparative and international education in relation to various areas of inquiry. We also attempt to illustrate what has been learnt by examining these issues from a comparative perspective. These areas are: processes of transition in post-communist countries; education in post-conflict situations; education in small states; pedagogy; and education for citizenship. Any number of possible themes might have been chosen, but we have selected these partly for their significance and long-term interest as topics of study in the field, but primarily because we have been personally involved in research in these areas. These themes also represent a cross-section that covers a range of levels of education systems, from the nation-state to the classroom. While these are by no means exhaustive literature reviews, it is useful to look at research in these areas which has led in some cases to models and theories, and in others to useful distinctions between the generalizable and the context-specific, which have been able to inform policy. Single-country studies also contribute to these comparative research bases, and can help to test the validity of any theories or assertions generated.

# Transition

An important focus for comparative research in education emerged following the events of 1989 in Eastern Europe and the subsequent collapse of the Soviet Union. Once the German Democratic Republic, Hungary, Poland, Czechoslovakia, and Romania had undergone relatively peaceful revolutions, overthrowing regimes that had seemed until then to be so impregnable, it was possible to anticipate periods of change and development towards new conditions for educational provision at all levels. The countries concerned were said to be 'in transition'.

There is a terminological problem here (as is the case with a descriptor like 'policy borrowing'). 'Transition' suggests a progression from one set of conditions (a starting point) to another set of conditions (an end point). In order for anything to be said to be in a 'state of transition' the end point, the 'destination', must be clear. But if we consider the situation in the former eastern bloc countries in the early 1990s, 'end points' were not at all clear, except perhaps in the eyes of western observers who imagined that the end point for all the countries concerned was some version of their own types of liberal democracy.

In the immediate aftermath of the political upheaval experienced in all the countries concerned, optimism soon gave way to despair at lack of progress towards some kind of hoped-for betterment of educational provision for everyone and at all levels. That despair often manifested itself – not surprisingly – in nostalgia for the security of the replaced system. The goal of a free, equitable, democratic, properly managed, and financed system seemed to be elusive.

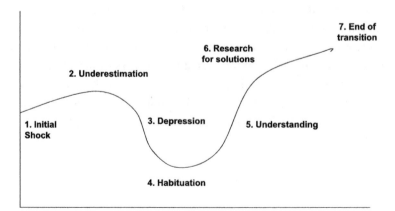

**Figure 13** Bîrzea's description of transition processes

In a much-cited graphic representation of processes of transition, based on an earlier model by Hopson,[2] César Bîrzea posits seven stages, ranging from 'initial shock' to the 'end of transition' (see Figure 13).

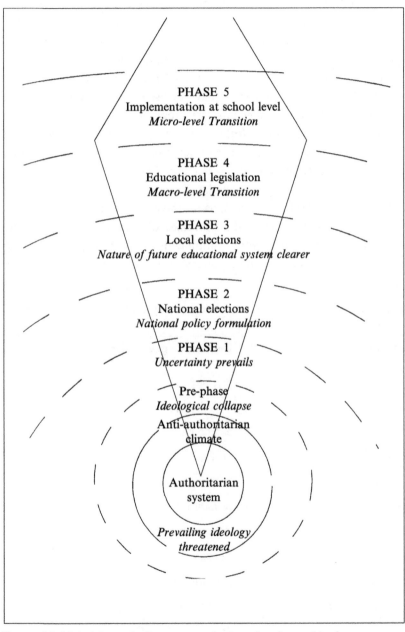

**Figure 14** McLeish et al.: Processes of educational transition[3]

This model includes the phenomenon of 'depression', or 'anomie', to describe the hopelessness felt by many in post-socialist systems (including the former German Democratic Republic, with its relative advantage of being absorbed into the rich and powerful West Germany) as they struggled towards solutions to the immense problems created by a sudden abandoning of systems that were at least secure and reliable in what they offered. Often recourse would be had to the *opposite* of what had gone before on the grounds that complete change had to be a good thing. And so there was – and still is – much faith, for example, in privatization and the force of markets.

McLeish and others in Oxford have devised another way of looking at transition, which associates political progress with educational development, showing movement from a 'closed' system, through ideological collapse and uncertainty, to the micro-level changes once the laws governing education have been promulgated (see Figure 14).

The lozenge shape imposed on the diagram indicates the growth and relative decline of feelings of nostalgia for the former status quo.

These ways of looking at the processes of transition can assist the comparativist seeking to identify commonalities and divergences. As with the models describing educational policy borrowing (see Chapter 5), they

**Figure 15** Characteristics of autocratic and democratic styles of provision in education[5]

| Authoritarianism | Democratic government |
| --- | --- |
| uniformity | diversity |
| conformity | individuality |
| control | autonomy |
| rigidity | flexibility |
| predictability | uncertainty |
| dogma | pluralism |
| centralization | decentralization |
| censorship | freedom |
| nationalization | privatization |
| didactic teaching | inductive learning |
| etc. | etc. |

still need to be developed in the light of detailed investigation of individual contexts. The model of McLeish et al., for example, was tested with respect to developments in South Africa post-Apartheid. As a further exemplar, a recent set of studies[4] tests Fullan's 'Triple I' model of educational change against events in five central/eastern European countries, resulting in a version of the original model revised in the light of the specifics of these contexts. A process of re-examination and revision will produce heuristic devices such as these with increasingly convincing explanatory power. With these and other models an attempt is made to achieve what Noah, as we have seen in Chapter 1, has described as one of the tasks of comparative education, namely to replace the names of countries with the names of variables and thus to arrive at theoretical understanding of significant phenomena in education.

**1.  Reconstruction**

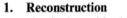

physical     ideological     psychological          demographic

aid                 're-education'          training/redeployment

**2.  Transition**
From what to what?
How can the stages of transition be defined?
How can we know when transition has ended?

**3.  Educational Change**

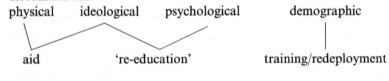

centralization     decentralization     privatization

control                 autonomy             competition

power to effect        diversity            the market
   change

**4.  Context**

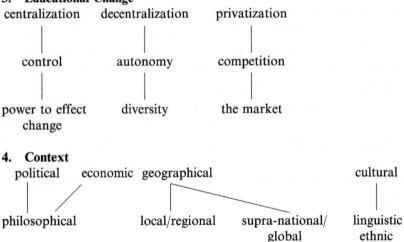

political    economic  geographical                    cultural

philosophical           local/regional    supra-national/    linguistic
                                               global         ethnic
                                                              religious

**Figure 16** Issues in the analysis of education in transitional countries

Bîrzea[6] lists the characteristics of open and totalitarian societies. In an earlier Oxford study attempts were made to list the descriptors applicable to western democratic styles of education and those to be found in the eastern bloc, but the result was an unsatisfactory list of opposites (see Figure 15).

Lists of opposites – descriptive as they may be of general characteristics – convey nothing of the individuality of contexts. The former eastern bloc countries have long individual cultural traditions, and they represent a wide range of languages, ethnic groups, and religious persuasions. They differed in the way they approached the Soviet Union and its interpretation of Marxism-Leninism as applied to education. Hungary, for example, allowed the use of (uncensored) western textbooks for the teaching of English and – through its important 1985 Education Act – sanctioned certain forms of decentralization, while the German Democratic Republic was more conformist in terms of Soviet-style educational provision.

And yet there is a tendency to group these diverse nations together as if they were a homogeneous entity. Even more precise groupings like 'the Baltic States' or 'the Central Asian Republics' deny the richness of the individual cultures of the countries concerned. The commonalities came through their adherence to forms of communist ideology and survive now mainly insofar as they have all entered a post-communist era. (We are aware, of course, that the term 'post-communist' is problematic, since the countries concerned did not describe themselves as 'communist' countries: the term is a western construct, but one that was widely used.)

How might we determine the features of educational provision in the countries 'in transition'? Building on the work of Arnhold and others,[7] we can suggest a checklist of areas of investigation to aid the analysis of transition processes (see Figure 16). This 'mapping' of the areas to be investigated reveals the complexities which have to be tackled before any comparative analysis can be undertaken.

An important question for comparativists to ask would be 'What was worth preserving in the former systems of the eastern bloc countries?' In an important study of 1969, Nigel Grant attempted a composite picture of the typical education system in eastern bloc countries (see Figure 17). What is striking to a western observer in this typical pattern are the following features:

- developed pre-school education
- a common system of primary and lower secondary schools
- selection allowed post-14 or post-16

- differentiated pathways at selection stage, including academic-type secondary schools
- mixed ability teaching as the norm
- absence of any type of competition from a privatized sector.

The systems seemed to:

- be based on egalitarian principles
- allow children's strengths to be built upon at the selection stage

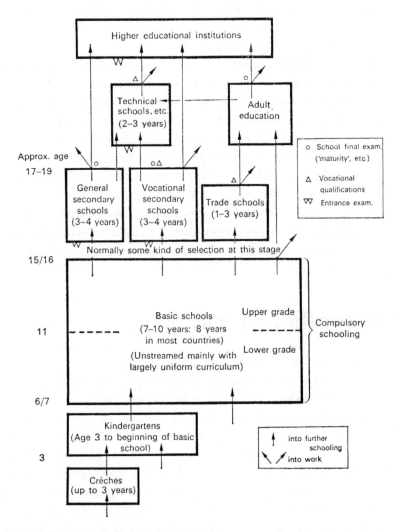

**Figure 17** Grant: Patterns of schooling in eastern Europe; the typical system[8]

- have good pre-school provision to help working mothers
- have strict uniformity of provision so that everyone knew what to expect from a particular system.

There appear then to have been some intrinsically good features in the eastern bloc systems which were at risk as the processes of post-communist transition began. And so the abandonment of any of these features becomes an interesting focus for analysis in the post-communist dispensation. What has replaced the former provision? What have been the external influences that have encouraged change? How effective is it? Does it 'work' in the particular context? Is the workforce trained to cope with it? Has the situation improved or worsened as a result?

'Transition' in education provides a rich area of inquiry for the comparativist which has to do with some of the very fundamentals of education. It is argued that political transition is relatively swift, that economic transition takes much longer, and that cultural transition might take a generation to achieve. As the post-communist countries continue to evolve comparativists will be concerned to report on the efficacy of change and the influences that have shaped it, as in recent work by Iveta Silova.[9] Equally, it will be of interest to see whether some of the generalizations that have emerged from these comparative studies of transition apply to countries undergoing political changes of other kinds, with different drivers, such as the countries experiencing the so-called 'Arab Spring' of democratization in the period from 2011.

# Post-conflict education

Again at the interface of politics and education, another field of inquiry that has received renewed attention in recent years is the relationship between education and conflict. The role of education in preventing or fuelling conflict, the provision of education in zones of ongoing conflict, and education in areas emerging from conflict are all of concern to comparativists; we will focus here on some of what has been learnt about post-conflict situations. Much early work in this area concentrated on educational reconstruction following the Second World War, especially in Germany and Japan. This research continues, exemplified by a fine comparative study by Shibata[10] of the role of the USA in educational reform in both Germany and Japan after the war.

Post-war Germany, with its four zones of occupation, offers rich sources for comparative historical investigation of the problems in education following large-scale conflict. Educational reconstruction in such circumstances involves the physical, ideological, psychological, and demographic domains we have described above in connection with processes of transition in the post-communist countries. In their study of 1998, Arnhold et al. listed the imperatives for the western Allies in Germany after the war and argued that they mirror those of present-day post-conflict situations:

- the need to plan adequately for the human and physical resources that would be required
- the need to purge the teaching force of people whose political involvement would make them unsuitable for any role in the reconstruction process
- the need to encourage democratic processes while not appearing to impose such processes
- the need to create a climate in which longer-term reform might be possible.[11]

Studies of contemporary post-conflict situations have adopted different perspectives on educational issues. For a start, recent comparative evidence highlights the problems of defining when a country is emerging from conflict; ceasefires and peace accords may only be temporary markers of transition.[12] Themes from some of these studies include the impact of conflict on human as well as physical resources, and the undermining of social cohesion by conflict, and the implications of these for schooling.[13] Smith has distinguished between reconstruction and reconciliation: the first being about rebuilding physically, psychologically and socially, and the second being about the process of healing and securing peace. In the first case, reconstructing education is itself part of the process, while in the second, the role of education is paramount in the process itself:

It is a clear challenge for education to provide a framework for teaching and learning about reconciliation that may help children and survivors of conflict avoid transmitting the conflict from generation to generation.[14]

Davies has used complexity theory as a framework for an international analysis of the role of education in conflict and post-conflict societies.[15] She cites examples from a wide range of contexts, including Northern Ireland, Kosovo, Afghanistan, Bosnia, Cyprus, Palestine, Sri Lanka, Serbia, Rwanda, and South Africa. In line with other recent studies,[16] her analysis starts from the perspective that schools can be and usually are part of the problem as well as the solution to conflict, and that therefore, in post-conflict situations, it is desirable not to (more or less) reconstruct what existed before as 'normality', but radically to transform schooling. This requires reflection on an appropriate 'trajectory of change', based on the nature of the conflict, its cause, and the future envisaged. Different stakeholders may envisage different futures. Davies cites the example of officials in Kosovo in 2001 who, after many chaotic years, desired 'a fresh organizational reality which was economically sound and rationally structured [...] integration and peace were not high on the agenda'.[17] So, the question of who plans and decides on reconstruction is crucial. The example of Palestine poses difficult questions in this regard, given that:

> ... schools in the Gaza strip follow an Egyptian curriculum and those in the West Bank a Jordanian curriculum. The Palestinian National Authority is creating its own Palestinian curriculum.[18]

The next question is: What is to be reconstructed? Davies distinguishes five areas: relationships; the culture of learning; language usages; curriculum and textbooks; and governance.

As a case study, Rwanda, a little more than a decade after the genocide which saw a million people killed in a hundred days, constitutes a salutary example of some of these issues. Slightly different interpretations of what educational reconstruction should entail exist among various stakeholders, and regional and international forces have been influential in shaping policy. For example, should the first priority be to get all children back into school, or should it be to reconstruct teacher education and the curriculum so that what is learnt there is more likely to interrupt than rekindle conflict?[19]

One area where these theories, assertions, and questions have proved useful is in the practical literature on education in emergencies, produced mainly by agencies active in the field. For example, the UN through UNESCO, UNICEF, and UNHCR plays various roles, from the promotion of the right to education in post-conflict zones, to providing 'education kits' for use during periods of reconstruction, to the education of refugees. The theming of the 2011 EFA Global Monitoring Report on *The Hidden Crisis: armed conflict and education* signals the growing recognition of conflict as a major force impacting on all aspects of education, from access, through quality and experience of provision, to outcomes. NGOs such as Save the Children have also produced relevant materials, both for use in the field and as case studies to illustrate good practice.[20] And consolidating much work across donors, NGOs, and other interested parties, the International Network of Education in Emergencies (INEE) offers a widely used set of minimum standards for the provision of education in and after emergencies, with conflict inevitably as an important focus, given its global prevalence. These are described as 'global best practice' and are based on research evidence and wide consultation.[21]

# Education in small states

Another area of interest for comparativists has been education in small states, nominally defined as states with populations of below 1.5 million.[22] This particular domain of comparative inquiry has helped to identify shared characteristics of these countries, in order to inform policy within individual countries and in the wider regional and international networks which support them, such as the Commonwealth.

Small states are not unusual, particularly among former colonies: of the Commonwealth's 54 members, 32 have populations of below 1.5 million.[23] Among the shared general characteristics of these states, Brock has described three major categories that have important implications for education: scale, isolation, and dependence.[24] Among the 'warranted assertions' in terms of the educational ramifications of these factors are the following:

Smallness of scale creates:
- Difficulties in mapping education provision to manpower needs. For example, a very small state may need only two doctors – how many should be trained so that this need is consistently met? What kind of curriculum can meet both general educational needs and specific labour requirements?
- Diseconomies of scale leading to higher unit costs. One manifestation of this is in the area of curriculum publications; producing national textbooks for a small number of learners is very expensive.
- A tendency to work through interpersonal networks (since many citizens know each other), which may affect educational management styles and career prospects, both negatively and positively.
- The need for versatility among education personnel. Teachers may need to cover several subjects, in multigrade teaching contexts. Ministry personnel need to be specialists in everything from curriculum to economics.

- On the positive side, the potential for more efficient educational reform as the scale of the system allows a quicker response.

Isolation creates:
- For remote small island states in particular, transportation challenges that can lead to prohibitive costs in importing educational goods.
- A strong local culture but tension between this and regional and global foci in curriculum and labour planning.

Dependency creates:
- A 'brain drain' to larger metropolitan centres.
- The establishment of cooperative regional networks and organizations among clusters of smaller states in an otherwise isolated region like the South Pacific, such as the Caribbean Examinations Council and the University of the South Pacific.

In terms of the repercussions for policy and practice, a number of widely applicable solutions to the educational disadvantages of small states have been proposed, which also draw on their strengths. Networking has particular potential. One way that this has been used is to share resources in terms of tertiary education, which would be too expensive and difficult for single small states to provide: examples include the University of the South Pacific and the University of the West Indies. The proliferation of transnational campuses and the promises that technology-assisted distance learning offer have also shaped the possibilities for tertiary education in small states.[25] Similarly, regional examinations take the burden of administering examinations away from individual states and create a regional standard which helps to make qualifications more marketable. The Caribbean Examinations Council is one example. In addition to these regional links, there are more international networks. As the prevalence of small scale is so high among former British colonies, the Commonwealth Secretariat has played a substantial role in facilitating comparative research and the sharing of common problems and policy solutions. For example, a meeting held in Mauritius in 1985 – the Pan Commonwealth Experts Meeting on Educational Development: The Small States of the Commonwealth – was the impetus for influential earlier publications on education in small states,[26] and meetings continue to be held, such as that in the Seychelles in 2000[27] and one specifically on School Evaluation Best Practices in Small States in Malta in 2003.[28] As Phillips and Ochs note, such meetings have important roles to play in facilitating the cross-national attraction, decision-making, implementation and internalization stages of the policy borrowing process.[29] Significant policy solutions include a focus on the specifics of manpower planning, and much attention has been paid to the capacity building of polyvalent personnel able to fill a range of roles.

Of course, while they share some characteristics, small states are not all alike. A population of 1.5 million is a random point at which to draw the line. Within this there are microstates with populations of less than 100,000, such as one country of 15,000 people studied by one of the present authors, where she was able easily to visit every primary school in the archipelago in the space of a week.[30] In contrast, for some of the countries nearer the top limit in population, scale, isolation and dependence are lesser issues. Some of the poorest countries in the world are small, but so are some of the richest, such as Monaco; these can tap into their financial resources to solve problems for which poorer states need to find alternative solutions. Some small states are essentially city-states with a very dense population; others are spatially much larger and have internal remoteness to contend with as well as distance in relation to other states.

Much comparative research on small states has helped to generate this catalogue of the educational advantages and disadvantages of smallness of scale, and the policy solutions mentioned above. Additionally, small developing countries arguably have a particular relationship with development and research partners, and this has become another cluster of interest to comparativists interested in participatory research and development paradigms and post-colonial perspectives:

> Education systems in such contexts are particularly vulnerable to the influence of international agendas and to the transfer of external research paradigms, methodologies and priorities. This is partly due to the dependence of their economies on world markets and partly due to the limited human and material resources available to analyse interrelations between local, regional and global contexts. There are also influential historical factors relating to the colonial period. Many small states became independent relatively recently and retain strong links with former colonial powers.[31]

Because of these preconditions, Crossley and Holmes argue that in small states, particular care should be taken to avoid the pitfalls of uncritical policy transfer, and that the development of research capacity and attention to the distinctive 'social ecology' of these nations are needed. These can be facilitated through genuine north–south partnerships, and critical engagement with international developments.

# Pedagogy

Let us move now from the nation-state to the classroom, where the comparative study of pedagogy presents particular challenges, and as a consequence is an under-researched area:

> The neglect of pedagogy is fairly easy to explain. It is not, by and large, the intellectual field from which comparativists have traditionally emerged. It encapsulates all that is most difficult and problematic about cross-cultural and cross-national investigation, being time-consuming, labour intensive, methodologically fraught and acutely vulnerable to charges of cultural naïveté and ethnocentrism.[32]

Some of the methodological complications emerge from the multifaceted nature of pedagogy and its close relationship to natural culture and values. These are enacted in classroom relationships, constructions of knowledge and therefore of teachers' roles and teaching methods, and in the many handed-down rituals that govern classroom life. However, there are good reasons to examine pedagogy from a comparative perspective. Alexander cites three categories of justification: the *political* imperative to take internal national debates beyond well-worn rhetorical stances; the *conceptual* imperative of informing theoretical views of education; and in terms of *methodology*, the need to address perennial research problems of classroom research methods by studying their application across different contexts. What are some of the lessons that have been learnt through the work of comparativists on this complex endeavour?

One early and influential study is Edmund King's *Other Schools and Ours: Comparative Studies for Today*, the first of five editions appearing in 1958. King's analysis of schooling in Denmark, France, the UK, the USA, the Soviet Union, and Japan explored the importance of context, concepts, institutions, and operations. While his book was not specifically or exclusively about pedagogy, King complemented systems-level analysis with descriptions of classroom life, such as the following excerpt from an account of typical Danish classrooms:

> When little children first go to school, they pass from one kind of parental atmosphere to another. The teacher is generally greatly respected. Even in kindergarten, little girls may curtsey to the teacher and the little boys bow and shake hands [.... T]he somewhat austere lessons begin again.[33]

He also saw the potential of his comparative study to inform policy, for example by identifying growth-points for innovation.

King's findings are not easily summarized, and their impact is not readily measured. He was careful to draw parallels between pedagogy and culture, linking classroom rituals and preferred teaching methods to national character. The national case studies were intended to help readers to look at the 'ecology' of education in their own countries in a new light:

> They are not a kind of academic tourism to be simply enjoyed or passively reflected on. They show that great educational problems which concern us (perhaps everyone) arise in other contexts in forms which challenge our identification of them. Those alien constellations of interest and the local recognition-patterns in those contexts make us acknowledge our own partiality. We are partial in the sense of being biased, as we know. We may also be partial in the sense of being incomplete – a much more serious matter.[34]

The anthropological approach used by Tobin, Wu, and Davidson in their 1989 work *Preschool in Three Cultures* developed these themes of the interface of culture and pedagogy through a close study of the ecology of pre-school classrooms in Japan, China and the USA. The researchers videotaped a pre-school in each context, and showed the recordings to staff, parents, and child development experts in all three countries, triangulating the insiders' and outsiders' explanations for what they saw, a methodology which they termed 'visual anthropology and multivocal ethnography'. Their book uses thick descriptions to bring these classrooms to life, such as in these excerpts of accounts of two consecutive episodes in a Chinese pre-school:

> With Ms Wang playing an up-tempo song on a small organ, Ms Xiang leads the children in callisthenics. All of them participate with enthusiasm and surprising grace. Dancing and singing follow callisthenics. Ms Wang announces, 'Let's do the "Little Train Friendship Song".' The children smile and clap, a few jumping in anticipation. Ms Wang, inside the circle of children, begins to dance and sing: 'I'm a little train, looking for some friends. Who will come and ride on me?'
>
> [...]
>
> The children begin to work in silence. Those who are working in a nonorderly way are corrected: a child whose box is placed askew on her desk has it placed squarely in the desk's upper right-hand corner by Ms Xiang.[35]

The comparative perspective generated across these three contexts through the insider and outsider perspectives pointed to a number of key themes and concepts which were equally important but which manifested themselves slightly differently in the three settings. These were: language, pre-school as school, 'spoiling', parental investment in children, the narrowing world of the child in modern life and the need to widen this, the development of 'group feeling', working mothers, gender issues in relation to teaching, the socio-economics of pre-school, and, ultimately, the question of whether pre-schools are conserving or transforming social values. All of these relate profoundly to cultural norms, but also to contemporary concerns about how social change is impacting on the socialization of children in these countries.

These themes were picked up in earnest by Robin Alexander in his comparative study of pedagogy in France, Russia, India, the USA, and England. This acclaimed study, like the Tobin, Wu, and Davidson research, uses videotapes of a small number of lessons in each country, complemented by interviews, whole-school observations, and data from the policy level. Again, the visual material and transcriptions generate thick description of pedagogical practice, such as this fragment of a Russian mathematics lesson:

> Teacher tells class to open rough exercise books and to participate in a 'control check' on the standards they have achieved in calculations undertaken previously (in their rough exercise books the pupils must show the calculation as well as the solution). She invites those who achieved a score of five (the highest) to stand up. None do. Teacher invites those who achieved a four to stand. Several do. Teacher then announces that they will check together the working out of one of these problems, step by step. Pupils respond to her questions.[36]

Out of these data Alexander develops a range of analytical tools for comparing practice across countries, and for placing these practices within

|  | Rules and reminders | Work-in-progress | Showcase |
|---|---|---|---|
| England |  | ************************ |  |
| France | ************************** |  |  |
| India | *********** |  |  |
| Russia | ***************** |  |  |
| USA | ********************************** |  |  |

**Figure 18** Cross-cultural continuum of wall-mounted teaching materials

their cultural, policy, and structural contexts. Among these tools, he has constructed a set of 'cross-cultural continua', which allow practices to be placed somewhere along a line between extremes. So, for example, 'wall-mounted teaching materials' are a component of pedagogy which may be used for diverse purposes, from rules and reminders, to the display of work-in-progress, to showcasing. He places observed practice from the five countries as shown in Figure 18.[37]

As with other studies of pedagogy, Alexander's overall findings are too complex and varied to summarize, but his overall verdict on the relationship between culture and pedagogy might be summed up thus:

> ... this is not a one-way trip in which one level presumed to determine the character of the next. Schools and classrooms are microcultures in their own right. They mediate messages and requirements coming from above and add some of their own. And each level is its own kind of window on the larger culture.[38]

These approaches and findings are in distinct contrast to the comparative treatment of pedagogy in some of the school effectiveness literature of the same period. The focus here was on finding the 'best' teaching methods to achieve educational goals. A widely publicized example of this genre is the work of David Reynolds and his colleagues.[39] The earlier of these has been widely criticized for its tendency to create causes out of correlations, for example by causally linking high examination performance and national economic growth with a pedagogical preference for whole-class teaching. It has also been accused of 'cherry picking' findings in line with government policy plans, so that the findings fit the political agenda.[40] The findings of the later nine-country International School Effectiveness Research Project have suggested that the emphasis on cultural factors in classroom practice as found in other studies may be overstated, but still rather complex:

> We cannot stress this too highly: *many factors that make for good schools are conceptually quite similar in countries that have widely different cultural, social and economic contexts. The factors hold true at school level, but the detail of how school level concepts play out within countries is different between countries. At the classroom level, the powerful elements of expectation, management, clarity and instructional quality transcend culture.* (Emphasis in original.)[41]

The researchers go on to note the policy implications of this combination of similarity and difference, with particular reference to the universals in pedagogical effectiveness:

... policymakers' ability to use studies such as ours with the confidence that the same school-level concepts discriminate between good and less good practice internationally should not be confused with the simple borrowing of the *detail* of these concepts and school practices. As an example, although the principal appears as a key factor in determining what are effective schools virtually across the globe, the precise way in which a principal is more effective in a Taiwanese context (by being rather vertical in leadership orientation) and in a Norwegian context (by often being quite horizontal or lateral) are somewhat different.

In the classroom, teaching and instructional area, by contrast, it seems that not only do the same *concepts* explain which classrooms and schools 'work', but that the precise *detail* of the effective factors themselves often look identical in different country settings. As an example, questioning techniques, giving opportunities to review and practice [...] are micro-level behaviours which appear to be identical in the classrooms of effective schools in all countries.[42]

In another set of studies starting in the late 1980s, beginning with comparative work between England and France and later including Denmark, the relationship between culture and pedagogy is further elaborated by incorporating concepts of teacher identity and learners' experiences of school. The earlier studies showed how 'teachers'' classroom practice is a reflection of both these nationally distinctive professional values and associated understandings about the choice of pedagogic approaches to pursue these',[43] while the more recent emphasis has been on how constructions of 'child' and 'youth' interact with the structures, organization, and ethos of schools.[44] Single-country studies have complemented these different kinds of comparative findings by going into discursive depth to show how pedagogy relates to other contextual factors in classrooms in a given country. Hufton and Elliott, for example, have analysed how a 'pedagogical nexus' in Russian schools, related to widely held social values and expectations, contributes to high levels of pupil motivation and achievement.[45] In the less developed context of Malawi, Croft has observed how teachers use the limited resources available to them to teach the basics, while using rituals of song and chanting that are part of local culture for both cognitive and affective purposes.[46] The extensive interest in learner-centred pedagogy as a particular approach to teaching and learning has made it a travelling policy and the subject of considerable research interest. The *International Journal of Educational Development*, for example, published at least 72 articles on this theme up to 2011.[47] As a policy and practice, it has origins that extend back to Socrates, but it came into prominence in the US and Western Europe during various stages of the progressive and child-centred movements. As an import into developing countries, it has been fuelled by a combination of 'top-down pressures and bottom-up desires'[48] with various policy, advocacy and research narratives pointing to its potential for learning effectiveness, personal and political emancipation, and preparation for knowledge economies of the future. However, as the policy borrowing and policy sociology literature might predict, what takes place in class-rooms in contexts of policy changes in this direction is very different from policy-level prescriptions, with a wide range of studies pointing to 'tissue rejection'[49] and failure of teachers to make the 'paradigm shift'.[50] A host of reasons account for this, including classroom resources, cultural 'fit', teacher preparation, examination backwash effects, and policy processes. However, nuanced studies of classroom practices in such contexts reveal problems with the teacher-centred vs learner-centred dichotomy, and subtle ways in which teachers and learners mediate policy directives concerning LCE in order to adapt it to fit their own cultural and resource contexts.[51] They also demonstrate the centrality of language of instruction as an issue for teachers: when they are teaching in a language not their mother tongue, teachers do not feel comfortable with more open forms of pedagogy and are much more likely to want a lesson to be tightly framed and driven by what they know.[52]

Perhaps the main take-home message from these comparative studies of pedagogy concerns the nature of the relationship between culture and pedagogy. Is it entirely symbiotic, or are there universals that can directly inform the policy process? Alexander's continua bridge the universal and the culture-specific, and provide a framework for contemplating this question. The lessons from the work of many of these comparativists mainly concern how context shapes pedagogy, and they therefore provide a cautionary tale against the 'cherry picking' of pedagogical approaches from other countries by policy makers in the quest for effective classrooms. However, school effectiveness literature appears to defy these socio-cultural observations by pointing to pedagogical universals across contexts in seeking the 'holy grail' of effective teaching and learning. These studies provide a rich set of concepts and understandings through which we can analyse our own classroom contexts, whether this means our own pedagogical practice as teachers, our own expectations of education as parents, or our own experi-ences of schooling as learners.

# Citizenship education in comparative perspective

Through civics education students learn to become citizens of their own country and of the world. Given such a role, it is a subject of great importance to national governments and is likely to reflect national needs and national culture in particular ways that mathematics, for example, is less likely to do. It can, for instance, be used conservatively to perpetuate the status quo, or its more radical forms can facilitate the development of critical civic engagement and a questioning attitude to the state. In some contexts it is a discrete subject area; in others it is delivered across the curriculum or through other social science subjects.[53] A range of comparative studies has been conducted on how citizenship (or civics) education is provided in different national contexts. The largest-scale study is the 1999 IEA Civic Education Study, which compared provision and learning across 28 developed or middle-income democratic countries.[54] The first phase explored the contexts, meaning, and provision of civics; the second phase tested the knowledge, skills, and attitudes of a representative sample of 14-year-olds in each country. While there are also detailed variations, among the broad findings are indications that:

- Students in most countries have some understanding of democracy in terms of values and institutions, but that the understanding is rather superficial.
- Schools that are democratic, in that they model democratic practice and have a democratic ethos in, for example, facilitating open discussion and involving students actively in shaping school life, are also most effective in promoting civic knowledge and engagement. However, such democratic schools are not the norm internationally.
- Students are sceptical about politics beyond mere voting, and four out of five overall show no interest in such activities as joining a political party or writing letters on political issues to newspapers. However, they are much more likely to be willing to be engaged in other civic activities such as raising money for charity or participating in non-violent protest.
- Students have faith in youth organizations, and their potential to create positive change and be a positive influence on young people.

- Television (rather than print, or what they learn in school) is the main source of news for students.
- Trust in government institutions varies widely between countries.
- Although civic education has low status in many of these countries, teachers recognize its importance. Although teachers generally favour a vision of civics which emphasizes critical thinking, in reality most teaching is instructional and knowledge-based.
- Patterns of civic knowledge, and attitudes toward democracy, do not conform to any pattern based on whether the country is a new or established democracy.[55]

A number of smaller-scale and more theoretically oriented studies complement this large-scale survey, and add to our understanding of purposes, processes, and outcomes of citizenship education in different contexts. In terms of purposes of citizenship education, for example, we might quote the following comparative or single-country studies as examples, using different theoretical frameworks for citizenship:

- a framework analysis of how education has been used for state formation in Europe and Asia[56]
- a study of textbooks for citizenship education in Australia, Canada, and England, in terms of the forms of citizenship education they embrace and the orthodox agendas embedded in them[57]
- a set of continua which may be used to characterize citizenship education as to whether it is more oriented to socialization or to critical education[58]
- a comparison of policy texts in England and France in relation to the promotion of critical citizenship.[59]

The following actual or posited studies shed light on the processes of citizenship education in different contexts, and across different subject areas:

- a study of how music education is used as part of the civics agenda in two different Chinese communities, Hong Kong and Taiwan[60]
- analyses of how national values impact on citizenship education in different countries of the Asian Pacific Rim[61]
- a study of teachers' and learners' experiences of global citizenship education in schools in England[62]
- a study across Denmark, England, Germany, The Netherlands, and the USA to explore classroom climate, in terms of democratic inquiry

and discourse, as a dimension of the learning of values and attitudes relevant to citizenship.[63]

And in terms of the outcomes of the process, the following studies are among those that inform our understanding. However, in the analysis of the outcomes of citizenship education, it is inevitable that other factors in the context will affect learners' knowledge, skills, and attitudes:

- a comparison of English and Chinese students on initial teacher education programmes, in terms of their knowledge, attitudes and activities[64]
- a four-country study, including Botswana, India, Northern Ireland, and Zimbabwe, on how human rights are understood by students, in relation to how these concepts figure in the curriculum.[65]

What begins to emerge from a cumulative perspective of these studies is a picture of how the national political and cultural contexts shape the provision of citizenship education in different countries, and learners' understandings of themselves as citizens. The comparative picture hints at considerable faith among teachers and learners in the importance of democratic citizenship as a concept and a curriculum subject, but also at limitations in how schooling delivers on this front.

# Conclusion

A brief overview of international research on these various themes begins to reveal the sorts of understandings that emerge from individual comparative studies, and from a cumulative overview of these areas. While this is a small, select list of themes, they are important, and they serve to illustrate the diversity of the comparative endeavour, ranging as they do from analyses of education at the nation-state level in particular categories of country (transitional, post-conflict, or small in scale), through an examination of the interplay of culture with that most complex of educational phenomena, pedagogy, to a consideration of how one curricular area is conceived, taught and learnt. There is interplay between these themes as well. For example, small states share a particular set of concerns with regard to citizenship education, and a Commonwealth Secretariat network has been established to research this and facilitate the sharing of experiences and resources. One of us has researched how pedagogy has been expected to change, and the realities of these changes, in the transitional countries of Russia and South Africa.[66] The forms of citizenship education appropriate in post-conflict countries has been another important topic of research,[67] and learner-centred classroom practice is set as one of the minimum standards for education in crisis situations by the INEE.[68]

Having explored examples of what we can learn from international comparison through a small sample of studies on a small sample of themes, we can now revisit some of the main points in relation to theory, method, and outcomes of comparative and international education and attempt an overview of how these fit together.

# Notes

1. Cowen, *Comparing Futures* or *Comparing Pasts?* p. 336.
2. Bîrzea, *Educational Policies of the Countries in Transition;* Hopson, 'Transition'.
3. McLeish and Phillips, *Processes of Transition.*
4. Polyzoi, Fullan and Anchan 2003, *Change Forces in Post-Communist Eastern Europe.*
5. McLeish and Phillips, p. 7.
6. Bîrzea, *Educational Policies of the Countries in Transition*, pp. 11–12.
7. Arnhold et al., *Education for Reconstruction.*
8. Silova, *Globalisation on the Margins* and Silova, *Post-socialism is Not Dead*
9. Grant, *Society, schools and progress in Eastern Europe.*
10. Shibata, *Japan and Germany under the US Occupation.*
11. Arnhold et al., *Education for Reconstruction*, pp. 11–12.
12. Smith et al., *Education, Conflict and International Development.*
13. Coletta and Cullen, *Violent Conflict and the Transformation of Social Capital.*
14. Smith et al., *Education, Conflict and International Development*, p. 50.
15. Davies, *Education and Conflict.*
16. E.g. Harber, *Schooling as Violence;* Leach et al., *An Investigative Study of the Abuse of Girls in African Schools.*
17. Davies, *Education and Conflict*, p. 167.
18. Ibid., p. 169.
19. Obura, *Never Again*, and Schweisfurth, 'Global and cross-national influences on education in post-genocide Rwanda'.
20. Smith et al., *Education, Conflict and International Development.*
21. http://www.ineesite.org/en/
22. Crossley and Holmes, 'Challenges for educational research'.

23. Bray and Steward, *Examination Systems in Small States*.
24. Brock, 'The Educational Context'.
25. Martin and Bray, *Tertiary Education in Small States*.
26. Bacchus and Brock, *The Challenge of Scale*.
27. Crossley, 'Education in small states'.
28. Degazon-Johnson, 'School improvement in small states'.
29. Phillips and Ochs, 'Educational policy borrowing: some questions for small states'.
30. Schweisfurth, *Educational Quantity and Quality in the Turks and Caicos Islands*.
31. Crossley and Holmes, 'Challenges for Educational Research', pp. 402–3.
32. Alexander, *Comparing Classrooms and Schools*, p. 109.
33. King, *Other Schools and Ours*.
34. Ibid.
35. Tobin, Wu, and Davidson, *Preschool in Three Cultures*, pp. 76–7.
36. Alexander, *Culture and Pedagogy*, p. 287.
37. Ibid., p. 333.
38. Ibid., p. 531.
39. Reynolds and Farrell, *Worlds Apart?*; Reynolds et al., *World Class Schools*.
40. For example, Alexander, *Other Primary Schools and Ours*.
41. Reynolds et al., *World Class Schools*, p. 279.
42. Ibid., pp. 279–80.
43. Osborn et al., *A World of Difference?*, p. 12.
44. Ibid.
45. Hufton and Elliott, 'Motivation to learn'.
46. Croft, 'Singing under a tree'.
47. Schweisfurth, 'Learner-centred education in developing countries'.
48. Chisholm and Leyendecker, 'Curriculum reform in post-1990s sub-Saharan Africa', p. 691.
49. Harley et al., 'The real and the ideal'.
50. Tabulawa, 'Education reform in Botswana'.
51. Schweisfurth, 'Learner-centred education in international perspective'. See also Sriprikash, 'Child-centred education and the promise of democratic learning' (on India); Barrett, 'Beyond the polarization of pedagogy' (on Tanzania), and Vavrus, 'The cultural politics of constructivist pedagogies' (on Tanzania).
52. Brock-Utne and Holmarsdottir, 'Language policies and practices'.
53. Schweisfurth, 'Citizenship education and Commonwealth values'.
54. IEA, *Citizenship and Education in Twenty-Eight Countries*, and IEA, *Civic Education across Countries: Twenty-four national case studies from the IEA Civic Education Project*.
55. Ibid.

56. Green, 'Education and state formation in Europe and Asia'.

57. Davies and Issitt, 'Reflections on citizenship education in Australia, Canada and England'.

58. Schweisfurth, 'Citizenship education and Commonwealth values'.

59. Johnson and Morris, 'Critical citizenship in England and France'.

60. Ho, 'Democracy, citizenship and extra-musical learning in two Chinese communities'.

61. Thomas, 'Values and citizenship: cross-cultural challenges' and Grossman et al. *Citizenship Curriculum in Asia and the Pacific*; Kennedy et al. *Citizenship Pedagogies in Asia and the Pacific*.

62. Yamashita, 'Global citizenship and war'.

63. Hahn, *Becoming Political*.

64. Hudson and Meifang, 'An Anglo-Sino study of young people's knowledge'.

65. Bourne et al., 'School-based understanding of human rights in four countries'.

66. Schweisfurth, *Teachers, Democratisation and Educational Reform*.

67. Rutayasire et al., 'Re-defining Rwanda's future'.

68. http://www.ineesite.org/en/

# Conclusions

The way ahead is not internecine warfare between paradigms, methodologies or disciplines. Rather it is a passion to explore the constituents and
significance of culture as the driving force of experience using the unique
potential of the comparative way of life.

*Patricia Broadfoot*[1]

In this book we have attempted to introduce key theories and concepts in
the field of comparative and international education. We have also sought to
convince of the importance of comparative and international inquiry, and
to map some of the main approaches used in educational research which is
explicitly or implicitly comparative.

'We are all comparativists now' – and internationalists. We would argue
that it is not possible to be one without being the other, however we might
define international education. When international education is policy
oriented or development focused, it should be informed by comparative
research. Many people in the field of comparative and international education
straddle both, and are what Wilson describes as 'academic-practitioners':

> The academic-practitioner, whom I characterized as unique to our twin
> fields, is one who alternates between academic *milieux*, where comparative
> studies reside, and field-based practitioner involvement, where the 'fruits'
> of comparative studies are applied internationally to ameliorate national
> education systems.[2]

Beyond purposeful application in education policy and practice, if academic
research is implicitly comparative by virtue of the situation of the researcher,
and therefore international in that sense, the comparison should be made
reflexively explicit. On the other hand, the basis of any comparison is an
understanding of the discrete contexts under study. Thus area studies are
the foundation of comparative research. We need both terms to describe
the field adequately. Comparative education without the 'international'

qualifier might be comparing anything: two learners in one classroom; three textbooks in one subject. International education without comparison denies its intellectual foundations.

We can see this symbiotic relationship in action in a number of examples discussed in earlier chapters. Human capital theory, so influential in national and aid policy in both richer and poorer parts of the world, has been both derived and tested by comparing development in different countries with differing education inputs and economic outcomes. Conversely, the IEA studies of citizenship education discussed in Chapter 9 are contextualized initially in single-country policy analyses which inform the comparison.

In the main, we have purposely avoided using illustrative examples from particular national contexts, as these are inevitably fixed in a particular time and can date quickly. Between the first proposal for this book in 2003 and the time of putting together this revised second edition in 2013 the world has seen events with vast implications for education: the Iraq War; the Asian tsunami; referendum voting against ratification of the EU constitution; the continuing exponential growth of the Chinese economy, transformed by open trade, and an attendant opening outwards to the world; the 'Arab spring' violence and democratization movements and their aftermaths; the global economic crisis from 2007 onwards. Global trends over the same period make a snapshot picture equally problematic. Sadly, we know that the Millennium Development Goals will not be reached, but we do not know the extent of the shortfall or what the implications will be, and we cannot know who will be at the top (and bottom) of the next major international study of achievement in mathematics or reading. University internationalization in its twin (but not always shared) concerns for profit-making and intercultural understanding continues to fuel global mobility but the patterns are shifting for a range of political and economic reasons. Some of these reflect a general tilting of the world's axis figuratively eastwards.

As Goethe famously puts it in *Torquato Tasso*: 'Compare yourself! Discover what you are!'[3] We have argued that comparative inquiry is both a fundamental part of the mental processes by which we reach decisions and judgements, and an essential aspect of investigation in education generally. We are all comparativists now. But we have made no great claims for the subject as a discipline; we see it rather as having discipline-like features while depending on the established approaches of other disciplines for its methodological strength. Those who have made significant contributions to the development of the field have come from a wide variety of disciplinary backgrounds and have brought with them multiple perspectives from which comparative inquiry has benefited. When comparativists meet there is not a uni-disciplinary focus to their interaction but an engagement with educational issues that is informed by a large variety of intellectual approaches brought together in a common pursuit – that of comparing. In Rolland Paulston's terms, the field is 'synthetic', rather than 'generic'.[4]

Epstein and Carroll have warned against what they call 'abusing ancestors'.[5] The early comparativists, among them significant nineteenth-century scholars of the calibre of Matthew Arnold, still have much to teach us about the nature of comparative investigation in education. Much of what they and their twentieth-century successors had to say specifically on comparison, and much of what is evident in their work, still applies: it has not been simply replaced by subsequent thinking but added to. Serious present-day comparativists will benefit from reading Sadler, Bereday, King, and Holmes, and be familiar with Kandel, Hans, and Lauwerys, as well as others of later generations who have explored the complexities of comparison in education and its uses. Contemporary theorizations, in line with intellectual developments in other fields, reflect the convergence that seems inevitable in an increasingly interconnected world where policies travel, influences become imperatives, and norms of what constitutes good education are underpinned by global agreements. However, an equally compelling trend is a focus on how at the micro level difference and divergence remain and even grow. Sadler identified many of the problems which still occupy us a hundred and more years later – in particular the central importance of context for the proper understanding of educational phenomena 'elsewhere', and this is no less true in a context of apparently inexorable globalization.[6]

Definitions remain problematic. The term 'international education' is especially difficult, since it can be interpreted in so many ways (not least, as we have seen, as relating to the education of children in various types of international school[7]). But of one thing we are fully convinced, and that is that 'comparative' and 'international' education (broadly conceived) are not separate but essentially interdependent areas of scholarship and research. Their actual separation in university courses, where this has happened, has led to a regrettable tendency to regard them as explicitly separate and this has created confusion and – in our view – damage, since the separation implies that each can do without the other. We see their symbiosis as an aspect of what Crossley and Watson have advocated: the 'bridging of cultures and traditions'[8] as part of a reconceptualization of comparative and international education.

For international and comparative researchers in education, especially those relatively new to the field, we hope that this book has contributed to an understanding which will facilitate the placement of their own work in the context of established theories, methods, and practices. This has been our prime goal. From our analyses of the development of comparative and international education and of a number of issues relating to research and its outcomes and uses, we also see a number of challenges for the future. Among them are these:

- To continue to explore what we have seen as one of the central purposes of inquiry in comparative and international education, namely to improve provision 'at home' by identifying successful provision 'elsewhere'. This does not mean resorting to the 'quick fix' approach exemplified in publications like the US Department of Education's *What Works*.[9] It means rather using the expertise available in the field to analyse and understand what is happening outside of a particular national context and to make recommendations which are sensitive to both contexts: outside and inside.

- To maintain a critical commentary on educational policy decisions which purport either to import ideas which have not been successful in other contexts, or to use the foreign example to criticize ('scandalize', as Gita Steiner-Khamsi puts it) provision in the home context. All too often politicians and administrators and commentators of various persuasions will pronounce on subjects about which there is ample research evidence and/or practical experience of which they are completely unaware. It is for the comparativist to act as a check to over-hasty decision-making based on ignorance of the wider scene.

- To promote positive developments in the ethics of working with and researching 'the other', and to advance intercultural understanding and social justice in and through education. This will require researchers to be attuned to social science perspectives that respect diversity in all its local and global manifestations. It also demands practical ways of working that reflect equitable relationships, and in many cases, an engagement with power politics, through lobbying, for example. International and comparative education can and should have a moral purpose as well as an academic or practical one.

- To keep monitoring the work of international agencies, including those primarily concerned with development assistance, in order to assess the impact of strategies and interventions and to offer advice and warnings where necessary.

- To develop methods for comparative inquiry which build on the strengths of a range of other disciplines. Harold Noah relates how he took on board the notion of replacing the names of systems (countries) with the names of concepts (variables) from work in political science.[10] As an essentially multi- and interdisciplinary field, comparative education can and must use the successful methods of other disciplines, especially those in other social sciences. Engagement with other multidisciplinary fields, such as development studies, should be part of this.

- To continue exploration of what has been termed the global/local nexus in education. The tensions between the theories associated with globalization and convergence on the one hand and local and cultural imperatives on the other has the potential to be a fruitful one and increasingly sophisticated theorization will be needed to capture this dialectic and how it plays out in educational arenas.[11]

- To facilitate cooperation with specialists outside of education. There are possibilities for teams of researchers to collaborate in comparative inquiry, with the non-educationists – who might be economists, social scientists, psychologists, management specialists, or academics with expertise in international law – contributing valuable innovative insights into the processes of comparison. Good examples are afforded by research conducted by the OECD, or by smaller organizations like the (non-aligned) National Institute of Economic and Social Research in London.[12]

- To celebrate the impact of comparative and international research outside of academic worlds, whether it is impact on national policy, the operations of international organizations, or local practice. Documenting these fruitful interactions will attest to the health and importance of the field.

These and other challenges form the basis for a lively and significant future for comparative and international education. The study of education without a comparative dimension is the poorer for it; thinking and engaging internationally is a prerequisite for all serious scholarship and research. Combining both is the task of everyone involved in a field which it is becoming increasingly important to sustain and develop in our globalized world.

# Notes

1. Broadfoot, 'Not So Much a Context', p. 30.
2. Wilson, 'The future of comparative and international education', p. 18.
3. Goethe, 'Vergleiche dich! Erkenne was du bist!', Antonio to Tasso in Act V, scene v of *Torquato Tasso* (1790).
4. Interview in Steiner-Khamsi, *Comparatively Speaking*.
5. Epstein and Carroll, 'Abusing ancestors: Historical functionalism and the postmodern deviation in comparative education'.
6. See Phillips, 'Michael Sadler and comparative education'. See also Schriewer, *Re-conceptualising the Local/Global Nexus*.
7. See the detailed coverage of this important area in the *Journal of Research in International Education* (Sage), founded in 2002.
8. Crossley and Watson, *Comparative and International Research in Education*, p. xi.
9. United States Department of Education, *What Works. Research About Teaching and Learning*, 1986.
10. Interview in Steiner-Khamsi, *Comparatively Speaking*. Noah cites the work of Przeworski and Teune (1970).
11. See, for example, the four editions of the text *Comparative Education: the dialectic of the global and the local* (Arnove and Torres).
12. Cf. in particular the work of S. J. Prais in the National Institute. Prais is an economist who has made a valuable contribution to the discussion of educational issues.

# References

ActionAid: www.actionaid.org.uk

Adams, John Quincy (1804): *Letters on Silesia, Written During a Tour Through that Country in the Years 1800, 1801*, London (J. Budd).

Adams, Raymond J. (2003): 'Response to "Cautions on OECD's recent educational survey (PISA)"', *Oxford Review of Education*, Vol. 29, No. 3, pp. 377–89.

Alexander, Robin (1999): 'Comparing Classrooms and Schools', in Alexander, Robin, Broadfoot, Patricia and Phillips, David (eds), *Learning from Comparing: New Directions in Comparative Educational Research*, Vol. 1: *Contexts, Classrooms and Outcomes*, Wallingford (Symposium Books).

—(2000): *Culture and Pedagogy: International Comparisons in Primary Education*, Oxford (Blackwell).

Alexander, Robin, Broadfoot, Patricia and Phillips, David (eds) (1999): *Learning from Comparing: New Directions in Comparative Educational Research*, Vol. 1: *Contexts, Classrooms and Outcomes*, Wallingford (Symposium Books).

Alred, G. (2003): 'Becoming a "Better Stranger": A Therapeutic Perspective on Intercultural Experience and/as Education', in Alred, G., Byram, M. and Fleming, M. (eds), *Intercultural Experience and Education*, Clevedon (Multilingual Matters).

Alred, G., Byram, M. and Fleming, M. (eds) (2003): *Intercultural Experience and Education*, Clevedon (Multilingual Matters).

Altbach, Philip J. and Kelly, Gail P. (eds) (1985): *New Approaches to Comparative Education*, Chicago and London (University of Chicago Press).

Arnhold, Nina, Bekker, Julia, Kersh, Natasha, McLeish, Elizabeth and Phillips, David (1998): *Education for Reconstruction: The Regeneration of Educational Capacity Following National Upheaval*, Wallingford (Symposium).

Arnold, Matthew (1868): *Schools and Universities on the Continent*, London (Macmillan and Co.).

Arnove, Robert F. (2009): 'World-Systems Analysis and Comparative Education in the Age of Globalization', in Cowen, Robert and Kazamias, Andreas M. (eds), *International Handbook of Comparative Education*, Dordrecht, etc. (Springer), Vol. 1, pp. 101–19.

Arnove, Robert F. and Torres, Carlos Alberto (eds) (2013): *Comparative Education: The Dialectic of the Global and the Local* (4th edition), Lanham (Rowman and Littlefield).

Ashcroft, A., Griffiths, G. and Tiffin, H. (eds) (1995): *The Post-colonial Studies Reader*, London (Routledge).

Ashton, D. and Green, F. (1996): *Education, Training and the Global Economy*, Cheltenham (Edward Elgar).

Avert.org: www.avert.org

Bacchus, Kazim and Brock, Colin (eds) (1987): *The Challenge of Scale: Educational Development in the Small States of the Commonwealth*, London (Commonwealth Secretariat).

Baker, David and LeTendre, Gerald (2005): *National Differences, Global Similarities: World Culture and the Future of Schooling*, Stanford, CA (Stanford University Press).

Bangay, Colin and Latham, Michael (2013): 'Are we asking the right questions? Moving beyond the state vs non-state providers debate: Reflections and a case study from India'. *International Journal of Educational Development*, Vol. 33, No. 3, pp. 244–52.

Barker, Ernest (1927): *National Character and the Factors in its Formation*, London (Methuen).

Barr, Pat (1967): *The Coming of the Barbarians. A Story of Western Settlement in Japan, 1853–1870*, London (Macmillan).

Barrett, Angeline (2007): 'Beyond the polarization of pedagogy: models of classroom practice in Tanzanian primary school', *Comparative Education*, Vol. 43, No. 2, pp. 273–94.

Baumert, Jürgen and Lehmann, Rainer (1997): *TIMSS – Mathematisch-naturwissenschaftlicher Unterricht im internationalen Vergleich. Deskriptive Befunde*, Opladen (Leske and Budrich).

Bean, T. (2004): 'The Role of Multicultural Literature as a Counter-force to the Literary Canon', in Hickling-Hudson, Ann, Matthews, J. and Woods, A. (eds), *Disrupting Preconceptions: Postcolonialism and Education*, Flaxton (Post Pressed), pp. 57–76.

Bebbington, David (1979): *Patterns in History*, Leicester (Inter-Varsity Press).

Bennell, P. (1996): 'Using and abusing rates of return: A critique of the world bank's 1995 education sector review', *International Journal of Educational Development*, Vol. 16, No. 3, pp. 235–48.

Bereday, George Z. (1964): *Comparative Method in Education*, New York, etc. (Holt, Rinehart and Winston, Inc.).

—(1969): 'Reflections on Comparative Methodology in Education, 1964–1966', in Eckstein, Max A. and Noah, Harold J. (eds), *Scientific Investigations in Comparative Education*, London (Macmillan), pp. 3–24.

Bîrzea, C. (1994): *Educational Policies of the Countries in Transition*, Strasbourg (Council of Europe Press).

Blishen, Edward (ed.) (1969): *Blond's Encyclopaedia of Education*, London (Blond Educational).

Bourne, R., Gundara, J., Dev, A., Rasoma, N., Rukanda, M., Smith, A. and Birthistle, U. (1997): *School-based Understanding of Human Rights in Four Countries: A Commonwealth Study*, Education Research Series 22, London (Department for International Development).

Bowles, Samuel and Gintis, Herbert (1976): *Schooling in Capitalist America*, London (Routledge).

Boyle, S., Brock, A., Mace, J. and Sibbons, M. (2002): *Reaching the Poor: The 'Costs' of Sending Children to School. A Six-Country Comparative Study*, London (DFID).

Bray, Mark (2003): *Comparative Education: Continuing Traditions, New Challenges, and New Paradigms*, London (Kluwer).

—(2006): 'Private supplementary tutoring: comparative perspectives on patterns and implications'. *Compare*, Vol. 36, No. 4, pp. 515–30.

Bray, Mark and Murray, Thomas, R. (1995): 'Levels of comparison in educational studies: Different insights from different literatures and the value of multilevel analyses', *Harvard Educational Review*, Vol. 65, No. 3, pp. 472–90.

Bray, Mark and Steward, Lucy (eds) (1998): *Examination Systems in Small States: Comparative Perspectives on Policies, Models and Operations*, London (Commonwealth Secretariat).

Brereton, Cloudesley (1913): *Studies in Foreign Education*, London (Harrap).

Brewer, Walter Vance (1971): *Victor Cousin as a Comparative Educator*, New York (Teachers College Press).

Broadfoot, [Pa]Tricia (1977): 'The comparative contribution – a research perspective', *Comparative Education*, Vol. 13, No. 2, pp. 133–7.

—(1997): 'Foreword', in Crossley, M. and Vulliamy, G. (eds), *Qualitative Educational Research in Developing Countries: Current Perspectives*, London (Garland), pp. xi–xiii.

Broadfoot, Patricia (1999): 'Not So Much a Context, More a Way of Life? Comparative Induction in the 1990s', in Alexander, Rosin, Broadfoot, Patricia, and Phillips, David, *Learning from Comparing: New Directions in Comparative Educational Research*, Vol. I: *Contexts, Classrooms and Outcomes*, pp. 21–31.

Broadfoot, Patricia and Osborn, Marilyn (1993): *Perceptions of Teaching. Primary School Teachers in England and France*, London (Cassell).

Brock, Colin (1987): 'The Educational Context', in Bacchus, Kazim and Brock, Colin (eds), *The Challenge of Scale*, London (Commonwealth Secretariat), pp. 11–25.

Brock, Colin and Cammish, Nadine (1999): *Gender, Education and Development: A Partially Annotated and Selective Bibliography*, London (DFID).

Brock-Utne, Birgit and Holmarsdottir, Halla (2004): 'Language policies and practices in Tanzania and South Africa: Problems and challenges', *International Journal of Educational Development*, Vol. 24, pp. 67–83.

Brooks, Caroline St John (2000): 'How Can International Comparisons Help us to Improve Education in English schools?', in Prais, Sig, Brooks, Caroline St John et al., *Comparing Standards*, The Report of the Politeia Education Commission, pp. 63–71.

Brown, R. (2002): 'Cultural dimensions of national and international educational assessment', in Hayden, Mary, Thompson, Jeff and Walker, G., *International Education in Practice: Dimensions for National and International Schools*, pp. 66–79.

Buchert, L. (1998): *Education Reform in the South in the 1990s*, Paris (UNESCO).

Byram, M. (2003): 'On Being "Bicultural" and "Intercultural"', in Alred, G., Byram, M. and Fleming, M. (eds), *Intercultural Experience and Education*, Clevedon (Multilingual Matters).

Cardoso, Fernando Henrique and Faletto, Erizo (1979): *Dependency and Development in Latin America*, Los Angeles (University of California Press).

Carney, Stephen; Rappleye, Jeremy; and Silova, Iveta (2012): 'Between faith and science: World culture theory and comparative education', *Comparative Education Review*, Vol. 56, No. 3, pp. 366–93.

Carnoy, Martin (1974): *Education as Cultural Imperialism*, New York (David McKay).

Castle, E. B. (1965): *Ancient Education and Today*, Harmondsworth (Penguin Books).

Chambers, Robert (1997): *Whose Reality Counts? Putting the First Last*, London (Intermediate Technology).

Chisholm, L. and Leyendecker, R. (2009): 'Curriculum Reform in Sub-Saharan Africa: When Global Meets Local', in Cowen, Robert and Kazamias, Andreas M. (eds), *International Handbook of Comparative Education*, Dordrecht, etc. (Springer).

Choksi, Archana and Dyer, Caroline (1997): 'North-South Collaboration in Educational Research: Reflections on Indian experience', in Crossley, M. and Vulliamy, G. (eds), *Qualitative Educational Research in Developing Countries*, London (Garland), pp. 265–94.

Chronic Poverty Research Centre (2008): *The Chronic Poverty Report 2008–2009: Escaping Poverty Traps*, Manchester (Chronic Poverty Research Centre).

Colclough, Christopher (2012): 'Education, poverty and development: mapping their interconnections', *Comparative Education*, Vol. 48, No. 2, pp. 135–48.

—(ed.) (2012): *Education Outcomes and Poverty*, Special Issue of *Comparative Education*, Vol. 48, No. 2.

Colclough, Christopher and Lewin, Keith (1993): *Educating all the Children: Strategies for Primary Schooling in the South*, Oxford (Clarendon Press).

Collins, K. T., Downes, L. W., Griffiths, S. R. and Shaw, K. E. (1973): *Key Words in Education*, London (Longman).

Coltta, N. J. and Cullen, M. J. (2000): *Violent Conflict and the Transformation of Social Capital: Lessons from Cambodia, Rwanda, Guatemala and Somalia*, Washington DC (World Bank).

Conrad, Clifton F. and Serlin, Ronald C. (eds) (2006): *The Sage Handbook for Research in Education. Engaging Ideas and Enriching Inquiry*, Thousand Oaks (Sage).

Cook, B. (1998): 'Doing education research in a developing country: Reflections on Egypt', *Compare*, Vol. 28, No. 1, pp. 93–103.

Coulby, David and Jones, Crispin (1996): 'Post-modernity, education and European identities', *Comparative Education*, Vol. 32, No. 2, pp. 171–84.

Cousin, Victor (1834): *Report on the State of Public Instruction in Prussia*, London (Effingham Wilson).

Cowen, Robert (1996): 'Last past the post: Comparative education, modernity and perhaps post-modernity', *Comparative Education*, Vol. 32, No. 2, pp. 151–70.

—(2000): 'Comparing futures or comparing pasts?', *Comparative Education*, Vol. 36, No. 3, pp. 333–42.

—(2009): 'The transfer, translation and transformation of educational processes: and their shape-shifting?', *Comparative Education*, Vol. 45, No. 3, pp. 315–27.

—(2009): 'Editorial Introduction: The National, The International, The Global', in Robert Cowen and Andreas Kazamias (eds), *International Handbook of Comparative Education*, Dordrecht, etc. (Springer) pp. 337–40.

Cowen, Robert and Kazamias, Andreas M. (eds) (2009): *International Handbook of Comparative Education* (2 Vols), Dordrecht, etc. (Springer).

Croft, Alison (2002): 'Singing under a tree: Does oral culture help primary teachers be learner-centred?', *International Journal of Educational Development*, Vol. 22, Issue 3–4, pp. 321–37.

Cross Report (1888): *Final Report of the Commissioners Appointed to Enquire into the Elementary Education Acts, England and Wales*, C.-5485, London (HMSO).

Crossley, Michael (2000): 'Bridging cultures and traditions in the reconceptualisation of comparative and international education', *Comparative Education*, Vol. 36, No. 3, pp. 319–32.

—(2004): 'Education in small states: Priorities and prospects', in Matlin, Stephen (ed.), *Commonwealth Education Partnerships*, London (Commonwealth Secretariat/The Stationery Office), pp. 122–5.

Crossley, Michael and Holmes, Keith (2001): 'Challenges for educational research: International development, partnership and capacity building in small states', *Oxford Review of Education*, Vol. 27, No. 2, pp. 395–410.

Crossley, Michael and Tikly, Leon (2004): 'Postcolonial perspectives and comparative and international research in education: A critical introduction', *Comparative Education*, Vol. 40, No. 2, pp. 147–56.

Crossley, Michael and Vulliamy, Graham (eds) (1997): *Qualitative Educational Research in Developing Countries: Current Perspectives*, London (Garland).

Crossley, Michael and Watson, Keith (2003): *Comparative and International Research in Education*, London (RoutledgeFalmer).

Crowley, V. (2004): 'Perverse Hybridisations, Queering Postcolonial Pedagogies', in Hickling-Hudson, A., Matthews, J. and Woods, A. (eds), *Disrupting Preconceptions: Postcolonialism and Education*, Flaxton (Post Pressed), pp. 175–92.

Cunningham, J. W. (1818): *Cautions to Continental Travellers*, London (Ellerton and Henderson).

Davies, Ian and Issitt, John (2005): 'Reflections on citizenship education in Australia, Canada and England', *Comparative Education*, Vol. 41, No. 4, pp. 389–410.

Davies, Lynn (1997): 'Interviews and the Study of School Management: An International Perspective', in Crossley, M. and Vulliamy, G. (eds), *Qualitative Educational Research in Developing Countries*, London (Garland), pp. 133–59.

—(2004): *Education and Conflict: Chaos and Complexity*, London (RoutledgeFalmer).

—(2006): 'Global citizenship: Abstraction or framework for action?', *Educational Review*, Vol. 58, No. 1, pp. 5–26.

Debeauvais, Michel (1985): 'Documentation in Comparative Education', in Husén, Torsten and Postlethwaite, T. Neville (eds), *The International Encyclopedia of Education*, second edition, Oxford (Pergamon), pp. 859–65.

Degazon-Johnson, Roli (2004): 'School Improvement in Small States: The Role of the Commonwealth', in Matlin, Stephen (ed.), *Commonwealth Education Partnerships*, London (Commonwealth Secretariat/The Stationery Office), pp. 126–30.

Development Education Association: www.dea.org.uk

DfEE (2000): *Developing a Global Dimension in the School Curriculum*, London (DfEE).

DFID (2000): *Eliminating World Poverty: Making Globalization Work for the Poor. White Paper on International Development*, London (DFID/HMSO).

Diebolt, C. (2001): 'Towards a comparative economics of education', *Compare*, Vol. 31, No. 3, pp. 3–13.

Diebolt, C. and Fontvieille, L. (2001): 'Dynamic forces in educational development: A long-run comparative view of France and Germany in the 19th and 20th centuries', *Compare*, Vol. 31, No. 3, pp. 295–310.

Dore, R. (1976/1997): *The Diploma Disease: Education, Qualification and Development*, London (Allen and Unwin/Institute of Education).

Durkheim, Emile (1982) [1901]: *The Rules of Sociological Method and Selected Texts on Sociology and its Method*, Steven Lukes (ed.), London (Macmillan).

Dyer, Caroline (2013): 'Educating the Poorest and Ideas of Poverty', *International Journal of Educational Development*, Vol. 33, No. 3, pp. 221–24.

Eckstein, Max A. (1985): 'The comparative mind', in Altbach, Philip G. and Kelly, Gail P. (eds), *New Approaches to Comparative Education*, Chicago and London (University of Chicago Press), pp. 167–78.

—(1988): 'Concepts and Theories in Comparative Education', in Postlethwaite, T. Neville (ed.), *The Encyclopedia of Comparative Education and National Systems of Education*, Oxford (Pergamon Press), pp. 7–10.

Eckstein, Max A. and Noah, Harold J. (eds) (1969): *Scientific Investigations in Comparative Education*, London (Macmillan).

Epskamp, K. (2000): *Education in the South: Modalities of International Support Revisited*, Amsterdam (Nuffic).

Epstein, E. H. (1994): 'Comparative and International Education: Overview and Historical Development', in Husén, Torsten and Postlethwaite, T. Neville (eds), *The International Encyclopedia of Education*, 2nd edition, Oxford (Pergamon), pp. 918–23.

Epstein, Erwin H. and Carroll, Katherine T. (2005): 'Abusing ancestors: Historical functionalism and the postmodern deviation in comparative education', *Comparative Education Review*, Vol. 49, No. 1, pp. 62–88.

European Commission (2002): 'EURYDICE, the Information Network on Education in Europe', Brussels (EURYDICE European Unit).

Fägerlind, Ingemar and Saha, Lawrence (1983): *Education and National Development: A Comparative Perspective*, Oxford (Pergamon).

Farrell, Michael, Kerry, Trevor and Kerry, Carolle (1995): *The Blackwell Handbook of Education*, Oxford (Blackwell).

Fife, W. (1997): 'The Importance of Fieldwork: Anthropology and Education in Papua New Guinea', in Crossley, M. and Vulliamy, G. (eds), *Qualitative Educational Research in Developing Countries*, London (Garland), pp. 86–111.

Foshay, A. W., Thorndike, R. L., Hotyat, F., Pidgeon, D. A. and Walker, D. A. (1962): *Educational Achievements of Thirteen-Year-Olds in Twelve Countries*, Hamburg (UNESCO Institute for Education).

Fraser, Stewart (1964): *Jullien's Plan for Comparative Education, 1816—1817*, New York (Teachers College).

Fraser, Stewart E. and Brickman, William W. (1968): *A History of International and Comparative Education*, Glenview, IL (Scott, Foresman and Company).

Freeman, Kenneth J. (1907): *Schools of Hellas: An Essay on the Practice and Theory of Ancient Greek Education from 600 to 300 BC*, London (Macmillan).

Freire, Paolo (1972): *Pedagogy of the Oppressed*, London (Penguin Books).

Fullan, Michael (2003): 'The Emergence of a Conceptual Framework', in Polyzoi, E., Fullan, M. and Anchan, J., *Change Forces in Post-Communist Eastern Europe*, London (RoutledgeFalmer).

Gardiner, Patrick (1961): *The Nature of Historical Explanation*, Oxford (Oxford University Press).

Garton, B. (2002): 'International Schools and Their Wider Community: The Location Factor', in Hayden, M. and Thompson, J. (eds), *International Education in Practice: Dimensions for National and International Schools*, London (Kogan Page).

Ginnis, Paul (2002): *The Teacher's Toolkit*, Carmarthen (Crown House Publishing).

*Globalisation, Societies and Education*, Oxford (Taylor & Francis).

Goldstein, Harvey (1995): *Interpreting International Comparisons of Student Achievement*, Paris (UNESCO).

—(2004): 'Education for all: The globalization of learning targets', *Comparative Education*, Vol. 40, No. 1, pp. 7–14.

Goodman, Joyce (2002): 'A historiography of founding fathers? Sarah Austin (1793–1867) and English comparative education', *History of Education*, Vol. 31, No. 5, pp. 425–35.

Gordon, Peter (ed.) (1996): *A Guide to Educational Research*, London and Portland (Woburn Press).

Gottlieb, Esther E. (2000): 'Are we Post-Modern yet? Historical and Theoretical Explorations in Comparative Education', in Moon, Bob, Ben-Peretz, Miriam and Brown, Sally (eds), *Routledge International Companion to Education*, London and New York (Routledge).

Graham-Brown, Sarah (1991): *Education in the Developing World: Conflict and Crisis*, London (Longman).

Grant, Nigel (1969): *Society, Schools and Progress in Eastern Europe*, Oxford (Pergamon Press).

Green, Andy (1997): 'Education and State Formation in Europe and Asia', in Kennedy, Kerry (ed.), *Citizenship Education and the Modern State*, London (Farmer), pp. 9–26.

Grek, Sotiria (2009): Governing by Numbers: the PISA effect in Europe, *Journal of Education Policy, 24(1)*, pp. 23–37.

Grossman, David L., Lee, Wing On and Kennedy, Kerry J. (eds) (2008): *Citizenship Curriculum in Asia and the Pacific,* Hong Kong (CERC).

Hahn, Carole (1998): *Becoming Political: Comparative Perspectives on Citizenship Education,* New York (State University of New York Press).

Hallak, Jacques (1990): *Investing in the Future: Setting Educational Priorities in the Developing World,* Paris (IIEP/UNESCO).

Halls, W. D. (1973): 'Culture and Education: The Culturalist Approach to Comparative Studies', in Evans, Reginald, Holmes, Brian and Van de Graaff, John (eds), *Relevant Methods in Comparative Education,* Hamburg (UNESCO Institute for Education), pp. 119–35.

—(ed.) (1990): *Comparative Education: Contemporary Issues and Trends,* London (Jessica Kingsley/UNESCO).

Hans, Nicholas (1949): *Comparative Education. A Study of Educational Factors and Traditions,* London (Routledge & Kegan Paul).

Haq, M. (1995): *Reflections on Human Development,* New York (Oxford University Press).

Harber, Clive (1999): 'Education and Theories of Development', in Lemmer, Eleanor (ed.), *Contemporary Education: Global Issues and Trends,* Sandton, South Africa (Heinemann).

—(2004): *Schooling as Violence: An International Study of how Schools Harm Pupils and Societies,* London (RoutledgeFalmer).

Harber, Clive and Davies, Lynn (1997): *School Management and Effectiveness in Developing Countries,* London (Cassell).

Harley, K., Barasa, F., Bertram, C., Mattson, E. and Pillay, S. (2000): ' "The real and the ideal": teacher roles and competences in South African policy and practice', *International Journal of Educational Development,* Vol. 20, pp. 287–304.

Hayden, Mary and Thompson, Jeff (1995): 'International schools and international education: A relationship reviewed', *Oxford Review of Education,* Vol. 21, No. 3, pp. 327–45.

Hayden, Mary, Thompson, Jeff and Walker, G. (2002): *International Education in Practice: Dimensions for National and International Schools,* London (Kogan Page).

Hegedüs, Adam de (1937): *Hungarian Background,* London (Hamish Hamilton).

Hegel, G.W.F. (1944) [1830]: *The Philosophy of History,* New York (Willey).

Herodotus (1959): *The Histories,* (tr.) de Sélincourt, Aubrey, Harmondsworth (Penguin Books).

Hickling-Hudson, A. and Ahlquist, R. (2004): 'The Challenge to Deculturalisation: Discourses of Ethnicity in the Schooling of Indigenous

Children in Australia and the USA', in Hickling-Hudson, A., Matthews, J. and Woods, A. (eds), *Disrupting Preconceptions: Postcolonialism and Education*, Flaxton (Post Pressed), pp. 39–56.

Hickling-Hudson, A., Matthews, J. and Woods, A. (eds) (2004): *Disrupting Preconceptions: Postcolonialism and Education*, Flaxton (Post Pressed).

Higginson, J. H. (ed.) (1979): *Selections from Michael Sadler*, Liverpool (Dejall and Meyorre).

Hill, D. (2002): 'The History of International Education', in *International Education in Practice: Dimensions for National and International Schools*, London (Kogan Page).

Hills, P. J. (1984): *A Dictionary of Education*, London (Routledge & Kegan Paul).

Hinsdale, B.A. (1913): *Horace Mann and the Common School Revival in the United States*, New York (Scribner's Sons).

Ho, Wai-Chung (2002): 'Democracy, Citizenship and Extra-Musical Learning in Two Chinese Communities in Taiwan and Hong Kong', in Schweisfurth, Michele, Davies, Lynn and Harber, Clive (eds), *Learning Democracy and Citizenship: International Experiences*, Wallingford (Symposium), pp. 195–210.

Holmes, Brian (1971): 'Comparative Education: Some Considerations of Method', in Deighton, Lee C. (ed.), *The Encyclopedia of Education*, New York (The Macmillan Company), pp. 357–63.

Hopson, B. (1984): 'Transition: Understanding and Managing Personal Change', in Cooper, C. L. and Makin, P., *Psychology for Managers*, London (Macmillan), pp. 133–56.

Hudson, George and Meifang, Wang (2002): 'An Anglo-Sino Study of Young People's Knowledge, Attitudes and Activities as they Relate to Citizenship', in Schweisfurth, Michele, Davies, Lynn and Harber, Clive (eds), *Learning Democracy and Citizenship: International Experiences*, Wallingford (Symposium), pp. 95–108.

Hufton, Neil and Elliott, Julian (2000): 'Motivation to learn: The pedagogical nexus in the Russian school: Some implications for transnational research and policy borrowing', *Educational Studies*, Vol. 26, No. 1, pp. 115–36.

Hughes, R. E. (1901): *Schools at Home and Abroad*, London (Swan Sonnenschein).

—(n.d. [1902]): *The Making of Citizens. A Study in Comparative Education*, London and Felling-on-Tyne (Walter Scott Publishing Co.).

Husén, Torsten and Postlethwaite, T. Neville (eds), *The International Encyclopedia of Education*, second edition, Oxford (Pergamon), pp. 859–65.

Inkeles, Alex and Smith, David Horton (1976): *Becoming Modern: Individual Change in Six Developing Countries*, Harvard (Harvard University Press).

*International Journal of Educational Development*, Kidlington (Elsevier).

International Society for the Study of Behavioural Development (1998): 'TIMSS: Mathematics and science achievement in international comparison: Goals, design and research questions' www.issbd.org/newsletter_l98.pdf

Jackson, Raymond (1984): 'Comparative education', in Hills, P. J., *A Dictionary of Education*, London (Routledge & Kegan Paul), pp. 17–21.

Jaworski, Barbara and Phillips, David (eds) (1999): *Comparing Standards Internationally; Research and Practice in Mathematics and Beyond*, Wallingford (Symposium).

Johnson, Laura and Morris, Paul (2012): Critical citizenship education in England and France: a comparative analysis, *Comparative Education*, Vol. 48, No. 3, pp. 283–302.

Jones, Phillip E. (1971): *Comparative Education: Purpose and Method*, St Lucia, Queensland (University of Queensland Press).

Jones, Thomas Jesse (n.d.): *Education in East Africa*, London (Edinburgh House Press).

Jullien, M[arc]-A[ntoine] (n.d.): *Esquisse d'un Ouvrage sur l'Éducation Comparée*, Ann Arbor/London (University Microfilms, Inc.).

Kandel, I. L. (1933): *Studies in Comparative Education*, London (Harrap).

Kay, William (1985): 'National Character – Concept, Scope and Uses', in Watson, Keith and Wilson, Raymond (eds), *Contemporary Issues in Comparative Education*, London (Croom Helm).

Keene, Donald (1969): *The Japanese Discovery of Europe, 1720–1830*, Stanford (Stanford University Press).

Kelly, Gail P. and Slaughter, Sheila (eds) (1991): *Women's Higher Education in Comparative Perspective*, The Netherlands (Kluewer).

Kennedy, Kerry (ed.) (1997): *Citizenship and the Modern State*, London (Farmer Press).

Kennedy, Kerry; Lee, Wing On and Grossman, David L. (eds) (2010): *Citizenship Pedagogies in Asia and the Pacific*, Hong Kong (CERC).

Kerr, C. (1990): 'The internationalisation of learning and nationalization of the purposes of higher education: Two "laws of motion" in conflict?', *European Journal of Education*, Vol. 25, Issue 1, pp. 5–22.

King, Edmund J. (1968): *Comparative Studies and Educational Decision*, Indianapolis and New York (Bobbs-Merrill).

King, Kenneth (1999): 'Introduction: New Challenges to International Development Co-operation in Education', in King, Kenneth and Buchert, Lene (eds), *Changing International Aid to Education: Global Patterns and National Contexts*, Paris (UNESCO).

King, Kenneth and Buchert, Lene (1999): *Changing International Aid to Education: Global Patterns and National Contexts*, Paris (UNESCO).

Kumar, Somesh (1996): 'ABC of PRA: Attitude and behaviour change', *PLA Notes*, Vol. 27.

Kunitake, Kume (2002): *The Iwakura Embassy, 1871–73. A True Account of the Ambassador Extraordinary & Plenipotentiary's Journey of Observation Through the United States of America and Europe*, compiled by Kume Kunitake. Editors-in-Chief: Graham Healey and Chushichi Tsuzuki (The Japan Documents).

Laczik, Andrea (2005): School Choice from the Perspectives of the Parents: Case studies in Hungary and Russia, unpublished D.Phil. thesis, Oxford.

Lauwerys, Joseph A. (1969): 'Comparative Education', in Blishen, Edward (ed.), *Blond's Encyclopaedia of Education, London* (Blond Educational), pp. 152–5.

Lawler, Sheila (2000): *Comparing Standards: The Report of the Politeia Education Commission*, London (Politeia).

Leach, F., Fiscian, V., Kadzamira, E., Lemani, E. and Machakanja, P. (2003): *An Investigative Study of the Abuse of Girls in African Schools*, London (DFID).

Leach, Fiona and Little, Angela (eds), *Education, Cultures and Economics: Dilemmas for Development*, London (Falmer Press).

Lewin, Keith (1993): *Education and Development: The Issues and the Evidence*, London (DFID).

Lewin, Keith and Akyeampong, Kwame (2009): Education in sub-Saharan Africa: researching access, transitions and equity, *Comparative Education*, Vol. 45, No. 2, pp. 143–50.

Little, Angela (2003): 'Motivating learning and the development of human and social capital', *Compare*, Vol. 23, No. 4, pp. 435–52.

Little, Angela, Hoppers, Wim and Gardner, Roy (eds) (1994): *Beyond Jomtien: Implementing Education for All*, London (MacMillan).

Lulat, Y. (1988): 'Education and national development: The continuing problems of misdiagnosis and irrelevant prescriptions', *International Journal of Educational Development*, Vol. 8, No. 4, pp. 315–28.

Maddox, B. (2007): 'What can ethnographic approaches teach us about adult literacy?', *Comparative Education,* Vol. 43, No. 2, pp. 253–71.

Magee, Bryan (1998): *Confessions of a Philosopher*, London (Phoenix).

Mallinson, Vernon (1957): *An Introduction to the Study of Comparative Education*, London (Heinemann).

Mann, Horace (1846): *Report on an Educational Tour in Germany, and Parts of Great Britain and Ireland*, London (Simpkin, Marshall and Company).

Manzon, Maria (2011): *Comparative Education: The Construction of a Field*, Hong Kong (Springer).

Matlin, Stephen (ed.) (2004): *Commonwealth Education Partnerships*, London (Commonwealth Secretariat/The Stationery Office).

McCowan, Tristan. (2013), *Education as a Human Right: Principles for a Universal Entitlement to Learning.* London (Bloomsbury).

McGrath, Simon (2010): 'The role of education in development: an educationalist's response to some recent work in development economics', *Comparative Education*, Vol. 46, No. 2, pp. 237–53.

McLean, Martin (1992): *The Promise and Perils of Educational Comparison*, London (Tufnell Press).

McLeish, Elizabeth A. and Phillips, David (eds): *Processes of Transition in Education Systems*, Wallingford (Symposium).

McLelland, David C. (1961): *The Achieving Society*, Princeton, NJ (Van Nostrand).

Meighan, Roland (1994): *The Freethinkers Guide to the Educational Universe*, Nottingham (Educational Heretics Press).

Messerli, Jonathan (1971): *Horace Mann. A Biography*, New York (Alfred A. Knopf).

Meyer, Heinz-Dieter and Benavot, Aaron (2013): 'PISA and the Globalization of Education Governance: Some Puzzles and Problems', in Heinz-Dieter Meyer and Benavot, Aaron (eds), *PISA, Power and Policy: The Emergence of Global Educational Governance*, Didcot (Symposium), pp. 7–20.

—(eds) (2013): *PISA, Power, and Policy. The Emergence of Global Educational Governance*, Didcot (Symposium).

Moon, Bob, Ben-Peretz, Miriam and Brown, Sally (eds) (2000): *Routledge International Companion to Education*, London and New York (Routledge).

Moritz, Carl Philip[p] (1983) [1783]: *Journeys of a German in England*, London (Eland Books).

Morris, Paul (1998): 'Comparative education and educational reform: Beware of prophets returning from the Far East', *Education 3 to 13*, Vol. 26, No. 2, pp. 3–7.

Murray, G. and Tagore, R. (1935): *East and West: An International Series of Open Letters*, Paris (International Institute of Intellectual Cooperation).

Murray, Nicholas (1996): *A Life of Matthew Arnold*, London (Sceptre).

New Internationalist (2002): *The World Guide: An Alternative Reference to the Countries of our Planet*, Oxford (New Internationalist Publications).

Newcastle Report (1861): *Report of the Commissioners Appointed to Inquire into the State of Popular Education in England*, London (HMSO).

Nish, Ian (ed.) (1998): *The Iwakura Mission in America and Europe. A New Assessment*, Richmond, Surrey (Curzon Press).

Noah, Harold J. (1973): 'Defining Comparative Education: Conceptions', in Edwards, Reginald, Holmes, Brian and Van de Graaff, John (eds), *Relevant Methods in Comparative Education*, Hamburg (UNESCO Institute for Education), pp. 109–17.

—(1983): *The Use and Abuse of Comparative Education*, New York (Teachers College).

—(1985): 'Comparative Education: Methods', in Husén, Torsten and Postlethwaite, T. Neville (eds), *The International Encyclopedia of Education*, second edition, Oxford (Pergamon), pp. 869–72.

Noah, Harold J. and Eckstein, Max A. (1969): *Toward a Science of Comparative Education*, London (Macmillan).

Nóvoa, António (1998): *Histoire and Comparaison (Essais sur l'Éducation)*, Lisbon (Educa).

Nowak, Stefan (1977): 'The Strategy of Cross-National Survey Research for the Development of Social Theory', in Szlai, A. and Petralla, R. (eds), *Cross-National Comparative Survey Research: Theory and Practice*, Oxford (Pergamon Press), pp. 3–47.

Nussbaum, Martha (2000): *Women and Human Development*, New York (Cambridge University Press).

Nyerere, Julius (1978): 'Development is For Man, By Man, and Of Man', quoted in Hall, Budd and Kidd, J. Roby (eds): *Adult Education: A Design for Action*, Oxford (Pergamon).

Obura, Anna (2001): *Never Again: Educational Reconstruction in Rwanda*, Paris (IIEP).

Ochs, Kimberly and Phillips, David (2005): 'Processes of Educational Borrowing in Historical Context', in Phillips, David and Ochs, Kimberly (eds), *Educational Policy Borrowing: Historical Perspectives*, Wallingford (Symposium Books), pp. 7–23.

OECD (1997): *Internationalisation of Higher Education*, Paris (OECD).

—(2001): *Knowledge and Skills for Life. First Results from the OECD Programme for International Student Assessment (PISA) 2000*, Paris (OECD).

—(2004): *Learning for Tomorrow's World: First Results from PISA 2003*, Paris (OECD).

—(2004): *Education at a Glance, OECD Indicators 2004*, Paris (OECD).

—(2011): How many students study abroad?, in *Education at a Glance 2011: Highlights*. Paris (OECD).

—(2012): *Connecting with Emigrants: A Global Profile of Diaspora*, Paris (OECD).

Office for Standards in Education (Ofsted) (1993): *Reading Recovery in New Zealand. A Report from the Office of Her Majesty's Inspector of Schools*, London (HMSO).

Oxfam: www.oxfam.org

Ozga, Jenny and Lingard, Bob (2007): Globalisation, Education Policy and Politics, in B.Lingard and J.Ozga (eds), *The RoutledgeFalmer Reader in Education Policy and Politics*, Chapter 5, pp. 65–82, Oxon (Routledge).

Pattison, Mark (1860): 'Report of Assistant Commissioner the Rev. Mark Pattison, B. D., Fellow of Lincoln College, Oxford, on the state of elementary education in Germany, *Newcastle Report*, Vol. IV, pp. 161–266.

Phillips, David (1999): 'On Comparing', in Alexander, Robin, Broadfoot, Patricia and Phillips, David (eds), *Learning from Comparing: New Directions in Comparative Educational Research*, Vol. 1: *Contexts, Classrooms and Outcomes*, Wallingford (Symposium Books), pp. 15–20.

—(2000): 'Learning from elsewhere in education: Some perennial problems revisited with reference to British interest in Germany', *Comparative Education*, Vol. 36, No. 3, pp. 297–307.

—(2002): *Reflections on British Interest in Education in Germany in the Nineteenth Century*, Lisbon (Educa).

—(2006): 'Comparative Education: An Approach to Educational Inquiry', in Conrad, Clifton F. and Serlin, Ronald C. (eds), *The Sage Handbook for Research in Education. Engaging Ideas and Enriching Inquiry*, Thousand Oaks (Sage), pp. 279–94.

—(2006): 'Michael Sadler and comparative education', *Oxford Review of Education*, Vol. 32, No. 1, pp. 39–54

—(2010): 'International Comparisons of Educational Attainment: Purposes, Processes, and Problems', in Walford, Geoffrey, Tucker, Eric, and Viswanathan, Madhu (eds), *The Sage Handbook of Measurement*, Los Angeles etc. (Sage).

—(2011): *The German Example. English Interest in Educational Provision in Germany Since 1800*, London (Continuum).

Phillips, David and Jaworski, Barbara (1999): 'Looking Abroad: International Comparisons and the Teaching of Mathematics in Britain', *Comparing Standards Internationally: Research and Practice in Mathematics and Beyond*, Phillips, David and Jaworski, Barbara (eds), Wallingford (Symposium Books), pp. 7–22.

Phillips, David and Ochs, Kimberly (2004): 'Education Policy Borrowing: Some Questions for Small States', in Matlin, Stephen (ed.), *Commonwealth Education Partnerships*, London (Commonwealth Secretariat/The Stationery Office), pp. 131–6.

—(2004): 'Researching policy borrowing: Some methodological challenges in comparative education', *British Educational Research Journal*, Vol. 30, No. 6, pp. 773–84.

Pike, G. (2001): 'Re-evaluating global education: Opinions from the field', *Issues in Global Education*, Issue 168.

Pike, G. and Selby, D. (1991): *Global Teacher, Global Learner*, Kent (Hodder & Stoughton).

Polyzoi, E. and Cerna, M. (2003): 'Educational Change in the Czech Republic', in Polyzoi, E., Fullan, M. and Anchan, J., *Change Forces in Post-Communist Eastern Europe*, London (RoutledgeFalmer).

Polyzoi, E., Fullan, M. and Anchan, J., *Change Forces in Post-Communist Eastern Europe*, London (RoutledgeFalmer).

Popper, Karl R. (1991) [1957]: *The Poverty of Historicism*, London and New York (Routledge).

—(1992) [1959]: *The Logic of Scientific Discovery*, London and New York (Routledge).

Postlethwaite, T. Neville (1988): 'Preface', in Postlethwaite, T. Neville (ed.), *The Encyclopedia of Comparative Education and National Systems of Education*, Oxford (Pergamon Press), pp. xvii–xxvii.

—(1999): *International Studies of Educational Achievement: Methodological Issues*, Hong Kong (University of Hong Kong Comparative Education Research Centre).

—(2004): *Monitoring Educational Achievement*, Paris (IIEP).

Prais, S. J. (2003): 'Cautions on OECD's recent educational survey (PISA)', *Oxford Review of Education*, Vol. 29, No. 2, pp. 135–63.

—(2004): 'Cautions on OECD's recent educational survey (PISA): Rejoinder to OECD's response', *Oxford Review of Education*, Vol. 30, No. 4, pp. 569–73.

Prais, S. J. and Wagner, Karin (1985): 'Schooling standards in England and Germany: Some summary comparisons bearing on economic performance', *National Institute Economic Review*, No. 112, May, pp. 53–76.

Pratt, Samuel Jackson (1797): *Gleanings Through Wales, Holland, and Westphalia*, London (N. Longman), 3 Vols.

Preece, Julia (2002): 'The Learning of Citizenship and Governance: A Gender Perspective', in Schweisfurth, Michele, Davies, Lynn and Harber, Clive (eds), *Learning Democracy and Citizenship: International Experiences*, Wallingford (Symposium Books), pp. 81–94.

Preston, Rosemary (1997): 'Integrating Paradigms in Educational Research: Issues of Quantity and Quality in Poor Countries', in Crossley, M. and Vulliamy, G. (eds), *Qualitative Educational Research in Developing Countries*, London (Garland), pp. 31–64.

Przeworski, A. and Teune, H. (1970): *The Logic of Comparative Social Inquiry*, New York (Wiley).

Psacharopoulos, George (1985): 'Returns to education: A further international update and implications', *Journal of Human Resources*, Vol. 20, No. 4, pp. 583–604.

Psacharopoulos, George and Patrinos, Harry (2004): 'Returns to investment in education: a further update', *Education Economics*, Vol. 20, No. 4, pp. 583–97.

Pyke, Nicholas (2002): 'Poor children, poor results', *Times Educational Supplement*, 11 October.

Rassool, N. (2004): 'Sustaining linguistic diversity within the global cultural economy: Issues of language rights and linguistic possibilities', *Comparative Education*, Vol. 40, No. 2, pp. 199–214.

Reynolds, D. and Farrell, S. (1996): *Worlds Apart? A Review of International Surveys of Educational Achievement Including England*, London (HMSO).

Reynolds, David, Creemers, Bert, Stringfield, Sam, Teddlie, Charles and Schaffer, Gene (2002): *World Class Schools: International Perspectives on School Effectiveness*, London (RoutledgeFalmer).

Riggs, F. (1964): *Administration in Developing Countries: The Theory of Prismatic Society*, Boston (Houghton Mifflin).

Robinson-Pant, Anna (2001): 'Development as discourse: What relevance to education?', *Compare*, Vol. 31, No. 3, pp. 311–28.

—(2005): *Cross-Cultural Perspectives in Educational Research*, Oxford (Oxford University Press).

—(2000): *Why Eat Green Cucumbers at the Time of Dying? Women's Literacy and Development in Nepal*, Hamburg (UNESCO).

Robertson, Susan L.; Bonal, Xavier and Dale, Roger (2002): 'GATS and the education service industry: The politics of scale and global Reterritorialization'. *Comparative Education Review*, Vol. 46, No. 4 (November 2002), pp. 472–95.

Rust, Val D., Soumaré, Aminata, Pescador, Octavio and Shibuya, Megumi (1999): 'Research strategies in comparative education', *Comparative Education Review*, Vol. 43, No. 1, pp. 86–109.

Rutayisire, John (2004): 'Redefining Rwanda's Future: The Role of Curriculum in Social Reconstruction', in Tawil, Sobhi and Harley, Alexandra (eds), *Conflict and Social Cohesion*, Paris (IIEP), pp. 315–73.

Sahlberg, Pasi (2011): *Finnish Lessons. What can the World Learn from Educational Change in Finland?*, New York and London (Teachers College Press).

Samoff, Joel (2003): 'Institutionalising international influence', *Safundi: The Journal of South African and American Studies*, Vol. 4, No. 1, pp. 1–35.

—(ed.) (1994): *Coping with Crisis: Austerity, Adjustment and Human Resources*, London (Cassell).

Schneider, Friedrich (1947): *Triebkräfte der Pädagogik der Völker. Eine Einführung in die Vergleichende Erziehungswissenschaft*, Salzburg (Otto Müller Verlag).

—(1964): 'Vergleichende erziehungswissenschaft', in *Lexikon der Pädagogik*, Freiburg, etc. (Herder), Vol. 5, pp. 768–71.

Schriewer, Jürgen (ed.) (2012): *Re-conceptualising the Global/Local Nexus: Meaning Constellations in the World Society*, special issue of *Comparative Education*, Vol. 48, No. 4.

Schultz, T. (1961): 'Investment in human capital', *American Economic Review*, Vol. 51, March, pp. 1–17.

Schweisfurth, Michele (1999): 'Coming in From the Cold: A Reflexive Account of an Outsider Researching Education in Russia', in Sayer, John (ed.), *Preparing Teachers to Meeting Special Educational Needs in Russia*, Leuven (Garant), pp. 41–54.

—(2002): *Teachers, Democratisation and Educational Reform in Russia and South Africa*, Oxford (Symposium Books).

—(2004): 'Citizenship Education and Commonwealth Values', in Matlin, Stephen (ed.), *Commonwealth Education Partnerships*, London (Commonwealth Secretariat/The Stationery Office), pp. 179–82.

—(2006): 'Education for global citizenship: Teacher agency and curricular structure in Ontario schools', *Educational Review*, Vol. 58, No. 1, pp. 41–50.

— (2006), 'Global and cross-national influences on education in post-genocide Rwanda', *Oxford Review of Education*, Vol. 32, No. 5.

—(2011): Learner-centred education in developing country contexts: from solution to problem? *International Journal of Educational Development*, Vol. 31, pp. 425–32.

—(2013): *Learner-centred Education in International Perspective: Whose Pedagogy for Whose Development?*, Abingdon (Routledge).

Schweisfurth, Michele, Davies, Lynn and Harber, Clive (eds) (2002): *Learning Democracy and Citizenship: International Experiences*, Wallingford (Symposium).

Scottish Executive (2004): *Think Global, Act Local: International Education in Communities*, Edinburgh (Scottish Executive).

Selby-Bigge, Sir Lewis Amherst (1927): *The Board of Education*, London and New York (G. P. Putnam's Sons).

Sen, Armartya (1999): *Development as Freedom*, Oxford (Oxford University Press).

Shaw, M. and Ormton, J. (2001): 'Values and vodka: Cross-cultural anatomy of an Anglo-Russian educational project', *International Journal of Educational Development*, Vol. 21, Issue 2, pp. 119–34.

Shibata, Masako (2005): *Japan and Germany under the US Occupation: A Comparative Analysis of the Post-war Education Reform*, Lanham (Lexington Books).

Silova, Iveta (2010): *Globalisation on the Margins: Education and Post-socialist Transformations in Central Asia*. Charlotte, NC (Information Age Publishing).

—(2010): *Post-socialism is Not Dead: (Re)Reading the Global in Comparative Education*. Cambridge (Emerald Publishing).

Simola, Hannu; Varjo, Janne and Rinne, Risto (2013): Finland's PISA results: an analysis of dynamics in education politics, in Heinz-Dieter Meyer and Benavot, Aaron (eds), *PISA, Power and Policy: The Emergence of Global Educational Governance*, Didcot (Symposium), pp. 51–76.

Singh, P. (2004): 'Offshore Australian higher education: A Case of Pedagogic Work in Indonesia', in Hickling-Hudson, A., Matthews, J. and Woods, A. (eds), *Disrupting Preconceptions: Postcolonialism and Education*, Flaxton (Post Pressed), pp. 211–34.

Skelton, M. (2002): 'Defining "International" in an International Curriculum', in Hayden, M. and Thompson, J. (eds), *International Education in Practice: Dimensions for National and International Schools*, London (Kogan Page), pp. 39–54.

Smith, Adam (1937) [1776]: *An Inquiry into the Nature and Causes of the Wealth of Nations*, New York (The Modern Library).

Smith, Alan and Vaux, Tony (2001): *Education, Conflict and International Development*, London (DFID).

Sriprakash, Arathi (2010): 'Child-centred education and the promise of democratic learning: pedagogic messages in rural Indian primary schools', *International Journal of Educational Development*, Vol. 30, pp. 297–304.

Steiner-Khamsi, Gita (ed.) (2004): *The Global Politics of Educational Borrowing and Lending*, New York and London (Teachers College, Columbia University).

—(2006): *Comparatively Speaking*, DVD of interviews, Comparative and International Society (CIES).

Steiner-Khamsi, Gita and Waldow, Florian (eds) (2012): *Policy Borrowing and Lending in Education*, London and New York (Routledge).

Stephens, David (1998): *Girls and Basic Education: A Cultural Enquiry*, London (DFID).

Stiglitz, Joseph (2002): *Globalisation and its Discontents*, London (Penguin).

Stirrat, R.L. (1999): 'Economics and Culture: Towards an Anthropology of Economics', in Leach, Fiona and Little, Angela (eds), *Education, Cultures and Economics: Dilemmas for Development*, London (Falmer Press), pp. 33–48.

Street, Brian (1999): 'Meanings of Culture in Development: A Case Study From Literacy', in Leach, Fiona and Little, Angela (eds), *Education, Cultures and Economics: Dilemmas for Development*, London (Falmer Press), pp. 49–68.

Stromquist, Nelly (2006): 'Gender, education and the possibilities of transformative knowledge', *Compare*, Vol. 36, No. 2, pp. 145–61.

Sylvester, B. (2002): 'The First International School', in Hayden, Mary, Thompson, Jeff and Walker, G. (eds), *International Education in Practice: Dimensions for National and International Schools*, London (Kogan Page), pp. 3–17.

Tabulawa, Richard (2009): 'Education reform in Botswana: reflections on policy contradictions and paradoxes', *Comparative Education*, Vol. 45, No. 1.

Taine, Hippolyte (1957): *Notes on England*, London (Thames and Hudson).

Taylor, J. Orville (1836): *A Digest of M. Victor Cousin's Report on the State of Public Instruction in Prussia* (etc.), Albany (Packard and Van Benthuysen).

Tembon, Mercy (1999): 'Educational Finance Strategies', in Leach, F. and Little, A. (eds), *Education, Culture and Economics*, London (Falmer).

Theisen, Gary and Adams, Don (1990): 'Comparative Education Research', in Thomas, R. Murray (ed.), *International Comparative Education*, Oxford (Pergamon Press), pp. 277–300.

Thomas, R. Murray (ed.) (1990): *International Comparative Education*, Oxford (Pergamon Press).

Thompson, Jeff (2002): 'International education: Towards a shared understanding', *Journal of Research in International Education*, Vol. 1, No. 1, pp. 5–8.

Tikly, L., Lowe, J., Crossley, M., Dachi, H., Garrett, R. and Mukabaranga, B. (2003): *Globalisation and Skills for Development in Rwanda and Tanzania*, London (DFID).

Tikly, Leon and Barrett, Angeline (2011): 'Social justice, capabilities and the quality of education in low income countries', *International Journal of Educational Development*, Vol. 31, No. 1, pp. 3–14.

Tobin, Joseph, Wu, David and Davidson, Dana (1989): *Preschool in Three Cultures: Japan, China and the United States*, New Haven (Yale University Press).

Torney-Purta, Judith, Lehmann, Rainer, Oswald, Hans and Schulz, Wolfram (2001): *Citizenship and Education in Twenty-eight Countries: Civic Knowledge and Engagement at Age Fourteen*, Amsterdam (IEA Secretariat).

Torney-Purta, Judith, Schwille, John and Amadeo, Jo-Ann (1999): *Civic Education Across Countries: Twenty-four National Case Studies from the IEA Civic Education Project*, Amsterdam (IEA Secretariat).

Transparency International (1995–2012); Global Corruption Report and Corruption Perception: www.transparency.org

Trollope, Mrs [Frances] (1834): *Belgium and Western Germany in 1833*, 2 Vols, London (John Murray).

Turner, David A. (2004): *Theory of Education*, London (Continuum).

Tye, K. (1991): *Global Education: From Thought to Action*, Virginia (Association for Supervision and Curriculum Development).

UNDP (1999, 2000, 2001, 2002, 2003, 2004, 2005, 2013): *Human Development Report*, New York (United Nations). http://hdr.undp.org/statistics/data/indicators

UNESCO (2000): *The Dakar Framework for Action, Education for All: Meeting our Collective Commitments*, Adopted by the World Education Forum, Dakar, Senegal: www.unesco.org

—(2002): *EFA Global Monitoring Report: Education for All – Is the World on Track?*, Paris (UNESCO).

—(2002): *World Education Report*, Paris (UNESCO).

—(2004): *EFA Global Monitoring Report: Gender and Education for All – The Leap to Equality*, Paris (UNESCO).

UNESCO: *Culture and Development:* www.unesco.org/culture_and_ development

United Nations (1948): *Universal Declaration of Human Rights:* www.un.org/ overview/rights.html

—(1989): *UN Convention on the Rights of the Child:* www.therightssite.org.uk

United States Department of Education (1986): *What Works. Research about Teaching and Learning,* Washington DC (US Department of Education).

Unterhalter, Elaine (2005): 'Global inequality, capabilities, social justice: the millennium development goal for gender equality in education', *International Journal of Educational Development,* Vol. 25, No. 2, pp. 111–22.

Van Daele, Henk (1993): *L'Éducation Comparée,* Paris (Presses Universitaires de France).

Van der Wende, M. (1997): 'Internationalising the Curriculum in Higher Education', in OECD, *The Internationalisation of Higher Education,* Paris (OECD).

Vavrus, Frances (2009): 'The cultural politics of constructivist pedagogies: teacher education reform in the United Republic of Tanzania', *International Journal of Educational Development,* Vol. 29, pp. 303–11.

Vexliard, Alexandre (1965): 'L'Education comparée et la notion de caractère national', *Revue de Psychologie des Peuples,* No. 2, pp. 179–203.

Walker, David M. (1980): *The Oxford Companion to Law,* Oxford (Clarendon Press).

Walker, George (2012): 'Postscript', *Journal of Research in International Education* (tenth anniversary special issue), Vol. 11 No. 3, pp. 275–79.

Warwick, D. P. (1983): 'The Politics and Ethics of Field Research', in Bulmer, M. and Warwick, D. P. (eds), *Social Research in Developing Countries: Surveys and Answers in the Third World,* Chichester (Wiley), pp. 315–30.

Watkins, Kevin (2000): *Education Now: Break the Cycle of Poverty,* Oxford (Oxfam).

Watson, Keith (1996): 'Comparative Education', in Gordon, Peter (ed.), *A Guide to Educational Research,* London and Portland (The Woburn Press), pp. 360–97.

Watson, Keith and Wilson, Raymond (eds) (1985): *Contemporary Issues in Comparative Education,* London (Croom Helm).

Wiley, Peter Booth (1991): *Yankees in the Land of the Gods. Commodore Perry and the Opening of Japan,* Harmondsworth (Penguin Books).

Williams, C. (2000): 'Education and human survival: The relevance of the global security framework to international education', *International Review of Education,* Vol. 46, Issues 3–4, pp. 183–203.

Wilson, D. (2003): 'The Future of Comparative and International Education in a Globalised World', in Bray, Mark (ed.), *Comparative Education:*

*Continuing Traditions, New Challenges, and New Paradigms*, London (Kluwer), pp. 15–33.

Winch, Christopher (1964): 'Understanding a primitive society', *American Philosophical Quarterly*, Vol. 1, No. 4, pp. 307–24.

Windham, D. (1997): 'Overview and Main Conclusions of the Seminar', in OECD, *Internationalisation of Higher Education*, Paris (OECD), pp. 7–33.

Woodhall, Maureen (1991): *Education and Training under Conditions of Economic Austerity and Restructuring*, Paris (UNESCO).

World Bank (2012): 'Pupil-teacher Ratio, Primary'. Downloaded from http://data.worldbank.org/indicator/SE.PRM.ENRL.TC.ZS, 10 April 2013.

Yamashita, Hiromi (2006): 'Global citizenship education and war: The needs of teachers and learners', *Educational Review*, Vol. 58, No. 1, pp. 27–39.

Yoneyama, Shoko (2004): 'Review of *Can the Japanese Change Their Education System?*', *Japanese Studies*, Vol. 24, No. 1, May, pp. 139–42.

Zajda, Joseph (ed.) (2005): *International Handbook on Globalisation, Education and Policy Research: Global Pedagogies and Policies*, Dordrecht (Springer).

Zajda, Joseph and Zajda, Rea (2002): 'Reinventing the Past to Create the Future: The Rewriting of School History Textbooks in Post-Communist Russia', in Schweisfurth, Michele, Davies, Lynn and Harber, Clive (eds), *Learning Democracy and Citizenship: International Experiences*, Wallingford (Symposium Books), pp. 211–24.

# Index

Page references in **bold** refer to figures/tables